CATASTROPHE

ABOUT THE AUTHOR

RICHARD BOURNE is Senior Research Fellow at the Institute of Commonwealth Studies, London University, and a former journalist. In 1998 he founded the Commonwealth Policy Studies Unit; before that, in 1990, was the first director of the non-governmental Commonwealth Human Rights Initiative. He has written and edited ten books and numerous reports, including a biography of President Lula of Brazil (2008) and a collection of essays in honour of the eightieth birthday of Shridath Ramphal (2008). As a journalist he was education correspondent of the *Guardian* and deputy editor of the *London Evening Standard*.

CATASTROPHE

WHAT WENT WRONG IN ZIMBABWE?

RICHARD BOURNE

Zed Books

LONDON | NEW YORK

For Panashe, Tadiwanashe and Summer,
and the next generation of Zimbabweans, who will have
many questions for their elders

Catastrophe: What Went Wrong in Zimbabwe? was first published
in 2011 by Zed Books Ltd, 7 Cynthia Street, London N1 9JF, UK
and Room 400, 175 Fifth Avenue, New York, NY 10010, USA

www.zedbooks.co.uk

Designed and typeset in Monotype Bulmer by illuminati, Grosmont
Index by John Barker
Cover designed by Rogue Four Design
Printed and bound in Great Britain by
CPI Antony Rowe, Chippenham and Eastbourne

Distributed in the USA exclusively by Palgrave Macmillan, a division
of St Martin's Press, LLC, 175 Fifth Avenue, New York, NY 10010, USA

A catalogue record for this book is available from the British Library
Library of Congress Cataloging in Publication Data available

ISBN 978 1 84813 520 8 hb
ISBN 978 1 84813 521 5 pb

CONTENTS

GLOSSARY

AFRICAN NATIONAL CONGRESS Principal liberation movement in South Africa, in government from 1994.

ANC African National Council, body headed by Bishop Abel Muzorewa which became the United African National Council.

BRITISH SOUTH AFRICA COMPANY Company formed by Cecil Rhodes, responsible for colonisation of Rhodesia.

CFU Commercial Farmers Union in Zimbabwe.

CIO Central Intelligence Organisation, Rhodesian intelligence agency, then indigenised as security service for ZANU–PF government after independence.

COMMONWEALTH International association supporting Lancaster House negotiations, 1979, oversight of elections leading to majority rule, 1980.

DABENGWA, DUMISO Born 1939, head of ZIPRA intelligence in civil war, charged with treason in 1982, minister of home affairs, 1992–2000, helps revive ZAPU after 2008 elections.

DETENTE Period of negotiation, 1974–5, promoted by Presidents Vorster of South Africa and Kaunda of Zambia, and US Secretary of State Kissinger.

DFID Department for International Development, set up by Blair's Labour government in 1997 to replace the Overseas Development Administration within the UK Foreign and Commonwealth Office.

DISSIDENTS Armed opponents of ZANU government in 1980s.

ECOWAS Economic Community of West African States.

FEDERATION The Rhodesia and Nyasaland Federation, also known as the Central African Federation, 1953–64.

FRELIMO Frente para o Libertação do Mocambique, liberation movement which formed Mozambique government after independence in 1975.

FROLIZI Front for the Liberation of Zimbabwe, short-lived 1970s grouping.

GUKHURAHUNDI   Repression spearheaded by Fifth Brigade in Matabeleland, in 1980s.

HUGGINS, GODFREY (1883–1971)   Prime minister of Southern Rhodesia and then Federation for twenty-three years, created Viscount Malvern.

IMF   International Monetary Fund.

LANCASTER HOUSE   London location for 1979 talks leading to end of civil war and majority rule in Zimbabwe, giving its name to independence constitution.

MAKONI, SIMBA   Born 1951, formerly SADC secretary general and minister of finance, and independent presidential candidate 2008.

MDC   Movement for Democratic Change, opposition party formed in 1999.

MDC-M   Smaller MDC faction, following 2006 split, led first by Arthur Mutambara, then by Welshman Ncube.

MDC-T   Larger MDC faction, following 2006 split, led by Morgan Tsvangirai.

MK   Umkohonto we Size, literally 'Spear of the Nation', the armed wing of the ANC during the liberation struggle.

MNR/RENAMO   Armed insurgents against FRELIMO government, which became an opposition Mozambican political party as RENAMO after end of civil war, 1992.

MUGABE, ROBERT   Born 1924; leader of ZANU and ZANU–PF; imprisoned 1964–74, prime minister of Zimbabwe, 1980–87, executive president from 1987.

MUTAMBARA, ARTHUR   Born 1966; leader of smaller faction of MDC known as MDC-M until ousted in 2011, deputy prime minister in inclusive government formed in 2009.

MUZOREWA, ABEL (1925–2010)   Methodist bishop who coordinated opposition to provisional agreement between British and Ian Smith in 1971, then was prime minister of 'Zimbabwe-Rhodesia' as result of internal settlement with Smith in 1979.

NATIONAL CONSTITUTIONAL ASSEMBLY   Coalition of civil society, union and church bodies which campaigned for a new constitution and a No vote in 2000 referendum.

NCUBE, WELSHMAN   Born 1961; one of founders of MDC; elected leader of Mutambara faction in 2011; minister of industry and commerce in unity government.

NDP   National Democratic Party: African nationalist party which succeeded the Southern Rhodesian African National Congress; banned in 1962.

NKOMO, JOSHUA (1917–1999)   Trade unionist who successively led Southern Rhodesian ANC, NDP and ZAPU; home affairs minister 1980–82, then vice president 1987–99.

OAU   Organisation of African Unity, superseded by African Union.

OPERATION MURAMBATSVINA   Government-promoted clearance of informal urban dwellers in 2005, leading to displacements and human rights abuse criticised in a UN report.

RHODES, CECIL (1853–1962) Businessman and prime minister of Cape Colony, responsible for white colonisation of Southern and Northern Rhodesia.

RHODESIAN FRONT Rhodesian settler party which won 1962 election, led successively by Winston Field and Ian Smith, responsible for UDI.

SADC Southern African Development Community.

SITHOLE, NDABANINGI (1920–2000) Formed ZANU with Robert Mugabe and others; imprisoned 1964–74; overthrown as ZANU leader and joined Bishop Muzorewa in 'internal settlement' in 1979.

SMITH, IAN (1919–2007) Prime minister of Rhodesia, 1964–79.

SOAMES, CHRISTOPHER (LORD) (1920–1987) Last governor of Rhodesia, who oversaw transition to majority rule in Zimbabwe in 1980.

SOUTHERN RHODESIAN AFRICAN NATIONAL CONGRESS Early nationalist movement, led by Joshua Nkomo before it was banned.

TODD, GARFIELD (1908–2002) Prime minister of Southern Rhodesia, 1953–58.

TONGOGARA, JOSIAH (1938–1979) ZANLA commander, popular with his troops, who died just after Lancaster House agreement.

TSVANGIRAI, MORGAN Born 1952; secretary general of Zimbabwe Confederation of Trade Unions, 1987–99; then founder of MDC and leader of larger faction (MDC-T) after 2006 split; prime minister of Zimbabwe in inclusive government from 2009.

UANC United African National Council, body led by Bishop Abel Muzorewa which coordinated 1971 opposition to deal between Ian Smith and British, then partnered Smith in 'Zimbabwe-Rhodesia' in 1979.

UDI Unilateral Declaration of Independence by Smith government in 1965.

UNDP United Nations Development Programme.

UNICEF United Nations Children's Fund.

WELENSKY, ROY Northern Rhodesian politician, prime minister of Federation of Rhodesia and Nyasaland, 1957–64.

WFP World Food Programme.

ZANLA Zimbabwe African National Liberation Army, guerrilla army linked to ZANU.

ZANU Zimbabwe African National Union, political party initially led by Ndabaningi Sithole, then Robert Mugabe.

ZANU-PF ZANU-Patriotic Front, title of ZANU-led party after 1987 Unity Accord in which it merged with ZAPU.

ZAPU Zimbabwe African People's Union, political party from which ZANU broke away, led by Joshua Nkomo.

ZIMBABWE HUMAN RIGHTS NGO FORUM Umbrella group of Zimbabwean human rights and women's groups.

ZIPA Zimbabwe People's Army, short-lived alliance of ZANLA and ZIPRA.

ZIPRA Zimbabwe People's Revolutionary Army, guerrilla army linked to ZAPU.

ZUM Zimbabwe Unity Movement.

TIMELINE

1870   Lobengula establishes himself as ruler of the Ndebele, with suzerainty over much of today's Zimbabwe.

1887   Cecil Rhodes registers the Consolidated Gold Fields of South Africa Ltd in London.

1888   Lobengula awards Rhodes's company rights to metals and minerals in his kingdom, the so-called Rudd Concession.

1889   Rhodes gains a royal charter for the British South Africa Company, with wide powers, to which the Rudd Concession is transferred.

1890   A pioneer column, organised by the British South Africa Company, occupies Mashonaland and the Union Jack is hoisted at Fort Salisbury.

1893   The Ndebele are conquered and Lobengula dies.

1895   The British Post Office recognises 'Rhodesia'; the Jameson Raid fails, and Boers arrest the raiders.

1896   Ndebele rebellion, followed by a Shona uprising also; Rhodes makes peace with the Ndebele but the Shona are not crushed until the following year.

1899–1902   Anglo-Boer War. Rhodes dies in 1902.

1903   Rhodesia's legislative council approves the Immorality Suppression Ordinance, making extramarital sex between a black man and a white woman illegal.

1907   Settlers get an elected majority in Southern Rhodesia's legislative council.

1910   Creation of the Union of South Africa, with the possibility of Rhodesia joining as a fifth province; all Africans in Southern Rhodesia must carry a registration certificate.

1912   Foundation of Southern Rhodesian African National Congress.

1914–18   First World War: 5,500 Southern Rhodesian whites serve in German South West and East Africa, and two Rhodesian Native Regiments fight under white officers in East Africa.

1921   Privy Council finds that the British South Africa Company should get £4.4 million for its work for the Crown, but 'unalienated land' should belong to the Crown not the company; the company loses control of Southern Rhodesia.

1922   Whites vote in favour of 'responsible government' rather than union with South Africa in a referendum on Southern Rhodesia's constitutional future; although Southern Rhodesia is still a Crown colony, the United Kingdom government agrees that it will never legislate except at the request of the settler-controlled government in Salisbury.

1929   British Commission under Sir Hilton Young, reviewing boundaries, recommends merger between Uganda, Kenya and Tanganyika but rejects merger between Southern and Northern Rhodesia and Nyasaland.

1931   Land Apportionment Act awards 49 million acres for Europeans, 7.4 million acres for African purchase, plus tribal trust lands; almost every urban area is reserved for Europeans; Europeans do not occupy all their allocated farmland.

1933   Godfrey Huggins becomes prime minister of Southern Rhodesia, remaining so until 1953; his first party, the Reform Party, calls for segregation and removal of black voters from the electoral roll.

1939   UK Parliament supports findings of Bledisloe Commission, which rejects merger between the Rhodesias and Nyasaland, because of incompatibility between settler-controlled Southern Rhodesia and the two Colonial Office territories of Northern Rhodesia and Nyasaland where the African interest has priority.

1939–45   Second World War: major military participation by whites; Compulsory Native Labour Act, 1942, bans strikes by Africans; Southern Rhodesia hosts Empire Air Training Scheme.

1945   Successful strike by African railway workers leads to upsurge in African trade unionism.

1948   General strike, started by municipal workers in Bulawayo, brings out 100,000 workers; National Party wins election in South Africa and institutes apartheid; Godfrey Huggins wins an election in Southern Rhodesia and Roy Welensky wins in Northern Rhodesia – both thereafter campaign for a Central African Federation.

1951   Officials from UK, Nyasaland and Northern and Southern Rhodesia meet to plan federation.

1953   Rhodesia and Nyasaland Federation Act gets royal assent in London; 17 out of 35 seats in federal parliament allocated to Southern Rhodesia, with small likelihood of parliament having an African majority; strong opposition from Africans in Northern Rhodesia and Nyasaland.

1953   Garfield Todd, relatively liberal, becomes prime minister of Southern Rhodesia and stays in post until overthrown by racial conservatives in 1958.

1960   Following increased rejection of Federation by Africans in all three territories, Sir Edgar Whitehead, Southern Rhodesian prime minister, passes draconian Law and Order Maintenance Act and Emergency Powers Act.

1961   Whitehead wins referendum among overwhelmingly white electorate in Southern Rhodesia, which allows for A and B roll voting, and declaration of African rights, pointing to white-led independence; apartheid South Africa leaves the Commonwealth.

1962   More anti-African white party, Rhodesian Front, wins Southern Rhodesian election, seeking independence on basis of continuing white control.

1963   Federation collapses and the following year Nyasaland becomes independent as Malawi, and Northern Rhodesia as Zambia.

1964   Ian Smith replaces Winston Field as prime minister of (Southern) Rhodesia; Rhodesians repress African political organisations; Robert Mugabe is one of four who try to overthrow Joshua Nkomo, leader of Zimbabwe African Peoples Union (ZAPU) in Tanzania; Nkomo expels them; the four set up the Zimbabwe African National Union (ZANU); Smith bans both ZAPU and ZANU; Labour Party under Harold Wilson wins British election.

1965   Smith wins Rhodesian election overwhelmingly; Wilson rejects Commonwealth demands for military intervention and makes final visit to Salisbury; Smith declares unilateral declaration of independence (UDI).

1966–7   Nationalists commence military action against Smith regime, with armed wings attached to both ZAPU (ZIPRA) and ZANU (ZANLA); ZAPU/ZIPRA get training and assistance from Soviet bloc, ZANU/ZANLA from China.

1966   Failed British talks with Smith on HMS *Tiger*.

1968   Failed British talks with Smith on HMS *Fearless*.

1970   Conservatives under Edward Heath win British general election.

1971   British sign provisional agreement with Smith, to be tested by African opinion.

1972   Test of opinion by Lord Pearce shows Africans reject agreement; opposition is coordinated by Bishop Abel Muzorewa.

1974   Lusaka Accord, promoted by Dr Kissinger of United States, involves detente between President Kaunda of Zambia and President Vorster of South Africa in context of the collapse of the Portuguese Empire; Front Line, independent African states, withdraw recognition from

ZAPU and ZANU and recognise Bishop Muzorewa's United African National Council as nationalist representatives.

1975   Herbert Chitepo, external ZANU leader, assassinated; Josiah Tongogara, ZANLA commander, survives coup but is arrested by Zambia; Victoria Falls conference fails on Smith's obduracy, ending detente phase.

1976   Peace conference in Geneva fails, but demonstrates Robert Mugabe's leadership of ZANU and diplomatic skills.

1977   Cyrus Vance for United States and David Owen for United Kingdom develop new peace proposals, including a UN peacekeeping force and Zimbabwe Development Fund with up to $1,500 million.

1978   With growing war and white emigration, Smith makes deal with Muzorewa to create 'Zimbabwe-Rhodesia'.

1979   Commonwealth conference in Lusaka opens door to meaningful negotiations under British auspices, with Commonwealth support, at Lancaster House, London. Agreement for ceasefire and elections reached in December; Christopher Soames becomes governor of Rhodesia.

1980   Mugabe and ZANU win overall majority in elections, with ZAPU as junior coalition partner and Mugabe as prime minister; internationally recognised independence and departure of Governor Soames.

1982   Mugabe claims arms caches found on ZAPU-owned farm; ZAPU ministers fired.

1983–4   *Gukhurahundi* crackdown on 'dissidents' in Matabeleland, led by ruthless Fifth Brigade, with some 20,000 deaths and severe abuse.

1987   Unity accord between ZANU and ZAPU creates ZANU–PF, and almost a one-party state; departure from Lancaster House constitution (supposed to last for a decade) as Mugabe becomes executive president and protected white seats disappear in parliament.

1988   Morgan Tsvangirai elected secretary general of Zimbabwe Confederation of Trade Unions.

1990   ZANU–PF easily wins presidential and parliamentary elections; Edgar Tekere's Zimbabwe Unity Movement, with 18 per cent of votes, elects two MPs.

1991   Zimbabwe adopts Economic Structural Adjustment Policy; Commonwealth leaders meet in Harare and agree to promote democratisation and human rights; President Kaunda voted from office in Zambia after a switch to multiparty democracy.

1992   End of civil war in Mozambique; death of Sally Mugabe; Land Acquisition Act permits expropriation of commercial farms in place of 'willing-seller, willing-buyer' principle.

1994   Democratic elections in South Africa bring government of national unity, led by African National Congress and President Mandela; Mugabe makes state visit to United Kingdom.

1995   Margaret Dongo elected as independent MP in Harare, after exposing theft from war veterans' compensation fund.

1996   Mugabe marries second wife, Grace Marufu; nurses strike, leading to wider strike by civil servants.

1997   Award of Z\$50,000 (around US\$2,500) to war veterans; proposal to seize 800 white-owned farms; Blair and 'new' Labour win British election and Mugabe thinks Blair snubs him; Zimbabwe dollar crashes.

1998   Food riots in Zimbabwe lead to repression, and founding of Zimbabwe Human Rights NGO Forum; National Constitutional Assembly brings together civil society and unions to campaign for a new constitution; Zimbabwe joins war in Democratic Republic of Congo; UNDP organises donor conference on land, proposing \$2,000 million fund for resettlement.

1999   Government sets up Constitutional Commission; Movement for Democratic Change, opposition party with Morgan Tsvangirai elected president, founded with support from unions, civil society and commercial farmers.

2000   ZANU–PF defeated in February referendum on a new constitution; government starts intimidatory campaign to occupy white-owned commercial farms, and win parliamentary elections; MDC claims it can only campaign safely in 25 constituencies and in 49 it could not campaign at all; ZANU–PF wins 62 seats with 48 per cent of vote, MDC wins 57 seats with 47 per cent; National Association of Non-Governmental Organisations estimates that 1.2 million Zimbabweans will die of HIV/AIDS within five years.

2001   Inflation by June running at 64 per cent, year on year; Citizenship Amendment Act strips 30,000 farm workers and most whites of dual citizenship; police break up anti-government street demonstrations; United States passes Zimbabwe Democracy and Economic Recovery Act, making it hard for multilateral agencies to lend to Zimbabwe government.

2002   Mugabe defeats Tsvangirai in presidential elections by 1.685 million votes to 1.258 million following peak in ruling party violence with 54 reported murders, 945 reported cases of torture, and 70,000 displaced from their homes; treason charge against Tsvangirai; government passes Public Order and Security Act and Access to Information and Protection of Privacy Act; Commonwealth Ministerial Action Group suspends Zimbabwe.

2003   MDC jobs boycott and 'final push' on the streets fails to move the government.

2004   Tsholotsho Declaration promoted by Jonathan Moyo indicates divisions in ZANU-PF, with demands for ethnic balance in leadership and more party democracy; Mugabe reasserts his authority; inflation over 622 per cent and exports a third of 1977.

2005   ZANU-PF wins 78 seats to MDC's 42 in parliamentary elections; Operation Murambatsvina, drastic slum clearance programme in urban areas, destroys up to 700,000 homes and livelihoods, criticised by UN report; Tsvangirai loses majority on MDC executive, leading to party split, with most supporters backing Tsvangirai; South Africa deports 150,000 Zimbabweans.

2006   Maize output half of national requirement, increasing dependence on international food aid.

2007   Tsvangirai and others severely beaten up after Save Zimbabwe prayer march, leading to criticism by presidents of Zambia, Tanzania and UN secretary general; Thabo Mbeki, SADC mediator, intensifies efforts in Zimbabwe, though losing his presidency of ANC party in South Africa; ZANU-PF party congress nominates Mugabe, now 83, to be presidential candidate in harmonised elections of 2008.

2008   March elections see ZANU-PF lose in results for presidency, parliament and local government; after slow release by Election Commission it declares Tsvangirai with 47.9 per cent of vote to be short of majority, requiring rerun; Mugabe decides not to resign and terror is unleashed, especially in Shona rural areas which had defected from ZANU-PF; Tsvangirai withdraws from run-off; Mbeki negotiates 'global political agreement' to create government of national unity; Mbeki forced to resign as South African president.

2009   Zimbabwe dollar abandoned, replaced by US dollar and South African rand; inclusive government formed in February, with ZANU-PF retaining security, mining and local government portfolios and MDC factions gaining economic and social ministries; serious car crash injures Tsvangirai and kills his wife; with minimal payments to teachers and civil servants the inclusive government starts to restore social services; inflation killed at considerable cost; ZANU-PF develops new source of income from diamond fields; continuous friction between ZANU-PF and majority Tsvangirai MDC.

2010   Inflation down to 3.6 per cent, modest rise in economic activity; FAO/WFP estimates maize harvest at 1.14 million tonnes in 2009–10, over double 2008–9, but still a shortfall of 677,000 tonnes; law requires 51 per cent indigenisation of firms' ownership; Zimbabwe government wins Kimberley Process approval for diamond exports; Mugabe renominated as presidential candidate, begins agitation for 2011 elections; Zuma promotes roadmap with new constitution, followed by a referendum and clean elections.

PREFACE

The decline and fall of Zimbabwe is a modern morality tale. The hopes of 1980 turned to despair in scarcely two decades. In 1940, early in the Second World War, a famous best-seller was published in the United Kingdom, titled *Guilty Men*. Michael Foot and his fellow authors excoriated the group of British politicians responsible for the appeasement of Germany, and the Munich agreement of 1938 which surrendered Czechoslovakia to the Nazis. They had a single target. But an attempt to explain what went wrong in Zimbabwe, following its belated independence in 1980, requires a longer historical view, and the interrogation of a wider cast.

This book attempts to provide a context for the socio-political crisis of Zimbabwe in the first decade of the twenty-first century. There was among British historians in the middle of the twentieth century a 'Whig interpretation of history', which assumed that everything was getting better and better. More recent assertions that history had come to an end, in the global triumph of liberal democracy, shared the same complacency. But countries can also go backwards.

Here, therefore, I have sought to look at recent events with a mordant retrospective eye – to investigate how it was, in the territory and peoples in a specific geography in central Africa, that a tragedy of sad and serious proportions could develop. It is too soon to provide a definitive work of scholarship, which others are anyway better equipped to write. But this book seeks answers to questions that many ask. How could a country which emerged triumphantly only thirty years ago from a brutal civil war embark so defiantly on a suicidal course? Ownership was skewed, and there was much bitterness. But there was also much optimism.

Many have helped me in researching and writing this account. First of all I should like to thank my wife, Juliet, for her patience and loving support. Then I should like to single out Professor Stephen Chan, who had the kindness to read a draft; Lucy McCann, archivist at Rhodes House, for access to the Mark Rule papers; and Philip Murphy, director of the Institute of Commonwealth Studies, London, where I hold a Senior Research Fellowship; and my friends at Zed Books, London publishers.

Others I should like to thank for advice, assistance or information of various kinds are: Justice Mahomed A. Adam, Chief Emeka Anyaoku, Reg Austin, Philip Barclay, Rajiv Bendre, Wiz Bishop, Robin Byatt, Innocent Chofamba, Antonater Tafadzwa Choto, David Coltart, Luis Covane, Eddie Cross, Sir Brian Donnelly, Peter Fraenkel, Peter Freeman, Polly Gaster, Peter Hain, John Hatchard, Tony Hawkins, Sekai Holland, Derek Ingram, David Ives, Robert Jackson, Errol Kendall, Peter Longworth, Mark Lowcock, Emmanuel Makota, Simbarashe Makota, Vernon Makota, John Makumbe, Wilson Manase, Reyhanna Masters, Primrose Matambanadzo, Dewa Mavhinga, Gustavo Mavie, Wilf Mbanga, Wilfred Mhanda, Japhet Moyo, Sternford Moyo, Tabani Moyo, Andy Moyse, George Alex Muza, Douglas Mwonzora,

Matthew Neuhaus, Nomfundo Ngwenya, Denis Norman, Hasu Patel, P.J. Patterson, Richard Ralph, Sir Shridath Ramphal, Tony Reeler, Barbara Richardson, Patsy Robertson, Lloyd Sachikonye, Lauren St John, Edwin Sakala, Clyde Sanger, Eileen Sawyer, Keith Scott, Syed Sharfuddin, Clare Short, Leonardo Simão, Emelia Sithole, Derek Smail, Patrick Smith, Irene Staunton, Ingeborg Stofring, Robin and Janet Stott, Anna Umbina, Rindai Chipfunde Vava, Paul Verryn, Brendan Vickers, Patrick Wintour, John Worsley-Worswick, Carl Wright, Siphamandla Zondi, Simon Zukas.

PROLOGUE

TWO BIRTHDAYS

On 21 February 1924, Robert Gabriel Mugabe was born in the Kutama Mission, a Roman Catholic mission in Zvimba, in what was then Southern Rhodesia. His father was a carpenter, born in Malawi, who deserted the family when Robert was 10; his mother, Bona, to whom he was devoted, brought up the family. He would have had no expectation as a child that he might become executive president of an independent African country.

Just over two years later, Princess Elizabeth was born in Bruton Street, in London's smart Mayfair district, on 21 April 1926. Her father was Duke of York, second son of King George V. Although she was third in line for the throne occupied by a king–emperor, it was not until her uncle Edward's unexpected abdication a decade later that there was any likelihood that she herself would be a queen of the United Kingdom.

These two iconic individuals, both entering their eighties as the twenty-first century got under way, symbolise some of the conflicts which underlie the decline and fall of Zimbabwe. At their birth the British Empire was at its apogee.[1] It seemed indestructible, and part of the mental furniture for inhabitants of the British Isles and of much of Africa. But in his lifetime

Mugabe was to be a guerrilla leader, chairman of the Frontline States confronting apartheid South Africa. He was to walk out of the Commonwealth in 2003, having hosted its Harare meeting to applause in 1991.

Queen Elizabeth's controversial decision, as head of the Commonwealth, to attend the Commonwealth summit in Lusaka in 1979 ignored security anxieties voiced by the Conservative press in London. There was, after all, a civil war raging just south of the Zambian border, and the Rhodesians had attacked targets in Lusaka. But her presence made possible the start of negotiations which brought the war to an end, and the conversion of Rhodesia into an independent Zimbabwe ruled by its black majority.

A glance at the press at the time of the two births illustrates the extraordinary distance travelled during these lifetimes. The *Rhodesia Herald*, whose front page boasted that it was 'The Oldest Established Newspaper in Rhodesia',[2] naturally ignored the birth of another black boy to a carpenter's family. Its front page was filled with advertisements for cattle sales, furniture and general merchandise, of interest to a small, agriculturally biased settler community.

But behind the sense of security lay a whiff of concern, captured in the editorial printed three days before Mugabe's birth, which discussed the decision of the South African parliament to enfranchise mostly white women. The fact that some coloured voters in the Cape retained a vote could lead to 'thorny problems'. General Smuts, supporting the bill, stated that it would create a bad feeling among coloured people if they gave the vote to white women, but not to coloured ones. The more reactionary General Hertzog said he could not support the bill 'on account of the colour difficulty'. It has been our experience, he added, that when we have given the coloured man an inch he has demanded an ell.[3]

In London, by contrast, the birth of the new princess two years later was big news. Her parents had been staying at the London home of the parents of the Duchess of York, the Earl and Countess of Strathmore, and the King and Queen were woken up between 3 and 4 a.m. to be told the happy news. The Court Circular issued from Windsor Castle stated, 'The King and Queen have received with great pleasure the news that the Duchess of York gave birth to a daughter this morning.' Following what was then the custom for royal births, the home secretary, Sir William Joynson-Hicks, was summoned to Bruton Street for the birth, and informed the lord mayor of London by special messenger. The Duke of York, replying to a telegram from the lord mayor, asked him to convey to the citizens of London 'our sincere thanks for their kind congratulations'. The King and Queen were cheered in the street when they came to see the baby.[4]

What follows seeks to describe how Zimbabwe came to be what it is today, in a story which starts with conquest, and the arrival of the earliest white settlers, before either Mugabe or the Queen were born. For what went wrong in Zimbabwe is not just a tragedy made possible by Robert Mugabe, or the British, or the international community. It has its roots in Africa and the rest of the world's attitude to Africa; it is about race, land and nation-building; few of those involved down the years have entirely clean hands; and this account aims to show how easily the social fabric of a promising state can be destroyed.

ONE

CONQUEST

The occupation of Rhodesia, of what became Zimbabwe, at the end of the nineteenth century was not planned by the British government in London. Rather, it was the project of a single, powerful man – Cecil Rhodes, one of the few individuals to give his name to a country.[1] It was bloody, it involved lies and the deception of the Ndebele ruler, Lobengula, and the conquest was not quick. It formed part of a complex web of politics involving local freebooting whites and European powers in the run-up to the Anglo-Boer War, 1899–1902. Looked at from the vantage point of the middle of the twentieth century, when Harold Macmillan told South Africans that a 'wind of change' was blowing through their continent,[2] it was also surprisingly recent.

Cecil John Rhodes, born in 1853, was the sixth surviving child of an Anglican vicar, the Reverend Francis Rhodes, of Bishop's Stortford in Hertfordshire. He was only 17 when he arrived in Durban after a sailing voyage of seventy-five days to join his brother Herbert to grow cotton. His education was put on hold because it was thought that a long sea voyage would be good for his sickly health. After a year, when cotton was unrewarding, Rhodes joined the adventurers who were flocking to the New Rush diamond mines at Kimberley, a radius of some two and a half miles in an area hitherto occupied by Boer farmers and Africans.

The story of how Rhodes came to dominate the diamond business, while at the same time getting a pass degree at Oxford University, has often been told – initially he was seen as a hero of imperialism, later as an ogre. But he was not just interested in wealth for the sake of it. He saw it as an opportunity to obtain power, and to realise his vision for expanding the British Empire in Africa.[3] His maturity coincided with Disraeli's rebranding of Britain's ragbag of colonies and protectorates around the world as the empire on which the sun never set, and Queen Victoria as Empress of India.

In the 1880s Rhodes was operating in several fields simultaneously – as a businessman creating a diamond cartel and, after a cautious start, building a further fortune in the newly discovered goldfields of the Witwatersrand; as a politician in the Cape Colony parliament, where he would become prime minister in 1890; and as a lobbyist in Britain for imperial expansion who had the ear of ministers and journalists, while all the time needing to keep shareholders in his companies happy. Always worried about his health and longevity, he had prodigious energy, and showed increasing ruthlessness.

The country which is Zimbabwe was, in the 1880s, largely controlled by an offshoot of the Zulu warrior nation, the Amandebele – 'the people of the long shields' – whose illiterate but imposing king was Lobengula. Now the Ndebele, their name was anglicised at the time as Matabele. Lobengula, who had many wives, ruled from his royal kraal in the traditional African town of Gubulawayo, near what is now Bulawayo. White hangers-on and fortune-seekers, and Christian missionaries, were beginning to arrive.

The Ndebele had moved up from the south in the 1830s, conquering or obtaining tribute from the more numerous but often more peaceable Shona polities. The first moment of Shona glory, the Mutapa civilisation, with its remarkable stone buildings at Great Zimbabwe, had peaked over three centuries earlier. In the late sixteenth century the Mutapa rulers had accepted Portuguese suzerainty. The Ndebele expanded at the expense of a later Shona political system, the Rozvi confederacy, when they arrived in the nineteenth century.[4]

The Ndebele were led by a commander named Mzilikazi, who had helped Shaka establish Zulu power, but then fell out with him, crossing the Limpopo river after defeat in a nine-day battle by Boers who were on their Great Trek north to escape the British. Along the way they incorporated others, with lower status, in the Zulu-led army. The Ndebele were courageous, regimented, but extremely brutal in their raids on the Shona villages, slaughtering adults, enslaving children, and capturing cattle and supplies. Mutinhima, from a powerful Rozvi family was 'pursued ... under instructions from King Mzilikazi to pluck out his heart and deliver it to him'.[5] Some Shona became vassals. Some retained an insecure independence. Two years after Mzilikazi's death in 1868, Lobengula, one of his sons, established himself as his successor.

Lobengula was regal and tall, with a dreadful mien and elephantine walk, approached by his subjects on their knees. Praise-singers called him 'Eater of Men' and 'Stabber of Heaven'. European contemporaries who visited him were not sure whether he had sixty wives or two hundred.[6] Either way the wives kept an eye on his regimental kraals, while he ruled formally with the aid of *indunas*, or senior councillors. In modern terminology he was a micro-manager, who knew what was going on in his kingdom.

But his territory was coveted. The Germans had ambitions to take it, to link German South West Africa (now Namibia) with German East Africa (now Tanzania). The Portuguese, although they seemed indolent and absent-minded colonialists to northern

Europeans, published a foreign ministry map in 1887 which set out a claim from today's Angola in the west to today's Mozambique in the east; this simply absorbed the lands in the middle as Portuguese. The Boers had an interest too, and in 1887 Pieter Grobler, on behalf of the Transvaal republic, had renewed a treaty of friendship with Lobengula. And all this was to ignore the driving force, imperialist and entrepreneurial, which was Cecil Rhodes.

Rhodes's power in the 1880s was expanding on several axes. In 1884, three years after becoming an unpaid MP in the Cape parliament, he became the colony's treasurer and deputy commissioner of Bechuanaland, which he saw as 'the road to the North', bypassing the Boer republics. He lost a point the following year when Bechuanaland became a protectorate under Whitehall, fuelling his suspicion of 'the imperial factor'. But in 1887, with his partner Charles Rudd, he registered the Consolidated Gold Fields of South Africa Ltd in London.[7] This, like the De Beers diamond combine which he and Barney Barnato brought together as a monopoly the following year, was empowered to annexe and govern territories as well as conduct business.

In 1888 too, Rhodes won the support of Sir Hercules Robinson, British high commissioner in southern Africa, for his dream of expansion to the north. In July, Robinson agreed to try and obtain a concession from Lobengula of

> parts of Matabeleland and Mashonaland which are not in the use of the Natives, and to provide for the protection of the Natives in the parts reserved for them, as well as the development of the unoccupied territories surrendered to the Company by a Royal Charter somewhat similar to that granted some years ago to the Borneo Company.[8]

Although Rhodes remained ambiguous about the imperial factor, this was the go-ahead he needed. With fortune-hunters representing other syndicates surrounding Lobengula, Rhodes

sent Charles Rudd and two others to see the Ndebele king to
negotiate an exclusive mineral concession. Rudd was kept hanging
around in the insanitary quarters of the white encampment by
Gubulawayo and, in spite of a gift of 100 gold sovereigns to
Lobengula and of 200 to the Rev. Charles Daniel Helm of the
London Missionary Society, who was the king's trusted inter-
preter, the project seemed to be going nowhere.

Lobengula was right to be cautious. Whites were beginning
to infiltrate his territories. Some of his young militants would
have liked to kill the lot of them. He also needed to consult his
indunas, his senior councillors. He knew the military power of
the British, but he also knew they could not be trusted.

To break the stalemate, Rhodes and Robinson turned to Sir
Sidney Shippard, a Rhodes ally who as acting attorney general
had steered him through some tricky legal moments in the
diamond fields of Kimberley, and who was the first resident
commissioner in Bechuanaland. On 16 October 1888 Shippard
turned up at Gubulawayo, escorted by his mounted police, and
with the Anglican Bishop of Bloemfontein and other notables in
his party. Shippard refused to grovel to Lobengula, walking to
greet him across a carpet of goat dung, in a buttoned-up frock
coat in the heat. The British, he said, were not like the Boers who
wanted land; they only wanted to mine and to trade. Rudd had
earlier offered guns – although Rhodes was already planning a
military conquest – and a steamship on the Zambezi.

After a two-day meeting with the *indunas*, who were won over
by the white delegation, Lobengula agreed to put his mark to the
concession document. Of course he was deceived. The concession
gave Rhodes's new chartered company complete charge over the
metals and minerals in his kingdom 'together with full power to
do all things that they may deem necessary to win and procure
the same'.[9] Lobengula was promised £100 a month, 1,000 Martini-
Henry rifles and 100,000 rounds of ammunition, and the armed

steamboat. Verbal promises that there would only be ten diggers, or that white miners would fight for the king, were meaningless. Without fully appreciating it he had given away his country, including those parts occupied by Shona and others which had never come under his rule.

The situation remained difficult for Rhodes as information about the real scope of the concession got back to Lobengula, who wrote a letter denying the concession, which was published in the *Bechuanaland News*. He also refused to accept the first consignment of rifles, and sent two of his *indunas* on a mission to London to see Queen Victoria. The two *indunas*, Babayane and Mtshete, got a letter from the colonial secretary making clear that 'Englishmen who have gone to Matabeleland to ask leave to dig for stones have not gone with the Queen's authority' and warning that not too much power should be given to the concession-hunters who got to Lobengula first. There was considerable hostility to Rhodes in London, both from those concerned for Africans, from rivals, and from those appalled that a rich man had hijacked imperial policy.

But in an extraordinary turn of speed, using his money and gifts of persuasion, Rhodes chased after the *indunas* to London and overcame his main opponents. He won over the press – *The Times* and the financially pressed but reputable W.T. Stead of the *Pall Mall Gazette*. He offered prominent Liberals and Conservatives places on the board of a new company, the British South Africa Company, which got a royal charter, and to which the concession was transferred. This company harked back, in the grandeur of its powers, to those earlier instruments of trade and empire-building, the East India Company and the Hudson's Bay Company.

The new company was empowered to operate north of the Limpopo and west of the Portuguese possessions in East Africa. It could act as a government; set up banks and companies; build railways (always an interest of Rhodes); settle and cultivate land; carry out mining operations; and set up its own police force with its own flag, to keep order. Notwithstanding the disaster which had overcome the East India Company and British authority in South Asia only thirty-two years earlier, when the mutiny broke out, a British government had once again handed over a large region, and many thousands of indigenous people, to a private company.

Lobengula realised that he had been tricked. He had one of his trusted advisers, Lotshe, and some 300 of Lotshe's extended family put to death, for persuading him to sign the Rudd concession. By December 1889, Rhodes had decided to conquer Lobengula's lands. He commissioned Frank Johnson, a 22-year-old former quartermaster in the Bechuanaland mounted police, to raise a force of 500 men to defeat the Ndebele. If successful, Johnson would get £100,000, and the men would be rewarded with 3,000 acres of land and the right to look for gold.

Due to a leak, the invasion was postponed. It had reached the ears of the new high commissioner in the Cape, Sir Henry Loch, who was not as friendly to Rhodes as Sir Hercules Robinson. Johnson took the blame, not incriminating Rhodes. But less than a year later Rhodes made another contract with Johnson, under which he would skirt Matabeleland and take over Mashonaland to the north and east; the Shona lands would be handed to Rhodes's company, fit for civil government, by 1 October 1890. In principle a direct clash with the Ndebele, the strongest military nation in central Africa, might be avoided.

This time Johnson thought he could occupy the land with only 250 pioneers – good fighting men who might also be the nucleus of a civilian population. Rhodes, a bachelor with a penchant for handsome young men, added a dozen names of his own – 'angels' or 'lambs' according to contemporaries. And Sir Henry Loch insisted, in a row with Rhodes before he would sanction the expedition, that the Chartered Company needed at least 400 mounted men to hold the base. These were the forebears of the British South Africa Police, who policed Rhodesia until the independence of Zimbabwe. In the end there were 200 pioneers, a mixed bag from the Cape, accompanied by 500 charter company police, 350 Ngwato labourers and 2,000 oxen pulling 117 ox-wagons.[10]

Amazingly the pioneer column, which started from Bechuanaland and included Anglican clergy, got past the Ndebele lands, moving with wagons at 12 miles a day, without being attacked or ambushed. At a certain point Dr Leander Starr Jameson, a friend of Rhodes who had been one of his negotiators with Lobengula, decided on a demonstration of firepower to impress a deputation of suspicious *indunas*. A firing of nine-pounder guns and machine guns suggested that the white men should not be trifled with. On 13 September 1890 the Union Jack was hoisted at a place named Fort Salisbury, in honour of Lord Salisbury, the current Conservative prime minister in London. Within a couple of years the first issue of a newspaper, the *Rhodesia Herald*, was being published there.

Rhodes himself, by now prime minister of the Cape Colony, visited 'his' territory in October 1891 to find numerous complaints from the pioneers who had not found gold, had found agriculture difficult and company levies extortionate, and were ravaged by disease. Shona villagers, often mistreated, had staved off hunger for some by giving them food. At the same time the Chartered Company's claim remained insecure, for the following month Lobengula concluded a competing agreement with a German adventurer, Eduard Lippert, under which, in return for a down payment of £1,000 and £500 a year for a hundred years, he had the right to establish farms and towns in the territory of the Ndebele and the Shona. The Chartered Company was in danger of going bankrupt, and to save money Rhodes took the risky decision to reduce his police force from 650 to 150 by Christmas 1892.

Nevertheless it was in 1893 that Lobengula and his *impis*, or military forces, were challenged directly, and overcome. The story began with the cutting of a section of telegraph wire between Fort Victoria and Fort Tuli by the subjects of a petty Shona chief. Telegraph communications were vital for the company and Lobengula was prevailed on to send two regiments to massacre the miscreants, and burn their *kraals*, their traditional homesteads. He also wanted to punish Shona cattle thieves. The vengeance spread and other Shona, who had been working for white farmers, were killed or ran away. Possibly 400 Shona were hacked to death by the Ndebele, under the walls of Fort Victoria, frightening the whites with visible barbarism. There was minor damage to white property.

Dr Jameson, a medical doctor and Rhodes's representative – who had beguiled Lobengula by treating his gout – decided to provoke the Ndebele. He was acting on his own initiative, but knew that he had Rhodes's backing. He created a bogus incident outside Fort Victoria in which he claimed that troops under the command of a Captain Lendy, who believed in terrorising the African population by 'severe measures', had been attacked by Ndebele. Lendy then shot thirty Ndebele, who had offered no resistance. Lobengula had taken care to avoid conflict with the whites in the Shona areas, though he still wanted tribute and his suzerainty recognised. He was worried that the company would use any excuse to invade Matabeleland. Although Sir Henry Loch tried to put the brakes on the blatant war-making of Rhodes and Jameson – sealed by a passage from Luke's gospel in the New Testament[11] – Lobengula's efforts at appeasement failed.

The Chartered Company put a force of 1,400 troops in the field in three columns, supported by African wagon drivers. Though vastly inferior to the Ndebele in numbers, they were armed with the new machine guns invented by Hiram Maxim in London's Hatton Garden, and Lobengula's troops were unfamiliar with the rifles supplied by Rhodes. On the Shangani river, Jameson's army was surrounded by 6,000 Ndebele. But the company's guns were devastating, and some 500 Ndebele were killed. Soon after, on the Bembisi river close to Gubulawayo, the slaughter was worse: 500 out of 700 in Lobengula's royal regiment were killed, and 3,000 Ndebele altogether, with only one white killed.

It was all over quickly. An explosion and fire destroyed Gubulawayo, and Rhodes established a new town 3 miles away. Lobengula died shortly after.[12] In his last speech to his people, the Ndebele king, who had tried to avoid war, said: 'You have said that it is me that is killing you: now here are your masters coming.... You will have to pull and shove wagons; but under me you never did this kind of thing ... the white people are coming now. I didn't want to fight with them.'[13] Speaking to his troops in December, who were awarded land and loot, Rhodes threatened that if the imperial government tried to take away what they had won they might follow the example of the United States and declare a republic, free from the British Crown. It was an extraordinary foretaste of the whites' unilateral declaration of independence in 1965. The value of company shares soared in London. The British government, by order in council in July 1894, acknowledged Rhodes's triumph, the boundaries of the new state, and the company's right – already exercised – to allocate land, and gold claims.

But the cruelty of the new order, with dispossession of African cattle and land, and an iron fist, could not be denied. Forced labour, taxation and terrible revenge against any threat to white control were intrinsic to the occupation. For example, in 1894 the British South Africa Company police arrived at the Methodist mission farm at Zvimba, not far from the Jesuit mission where Robert Mugabe would be born some thirty years later. A white man had died. The police flogged three men in front of their families, took seven chiefs hostage and shot four of them dead. When two Methodist missionaries complained to the acting administrator, a Mr Duncan, they told him that anywhere else this would have been called murder. He replied that it was necessary to establish law and maintain order.[14]

As prime minister of the Cape, Rhodes had made it a matter of principle to work in cooperation with the Afrikaners, the long-established agricultural community which had stayed under British rule and not trekked north. With them he increased the property qualification which made it difficult for Africans in the colony to get the franchise, and he passed the Glen Grey Act, which began the process of providing reservations for Africans and limited 'industrial' schools – the start of what after 1948 would be known as the Bantustan policy in South Africa. In the towns of the Cape, Rhodes was promoting segregation.

But Rhodes, the visionary imperialist, was also a high-stakes gambler. At the end of 1895 he promoted the ill-starred Jameson Raid into the Transvaal, the independent Boer republic, which nearly brought down both his Chartered Company and his private territory of Rhodesia. The plan was for Dr Jameson and a small party of armed men to link up with the gold miners around Johannesburg in a rebellion. This would catch the Transvaal Boers unprepared, and bring them into a British-run South Africa. Many British officials, including Joseph Chamberlain, the colonial secretary, were complicit in the plot.

Jameson and his men suffered losses, were rounded up by the Boers, and handed over to the British for punishment in England. Disastrously for Rhodes, who had lost his Afrikaner support in the Cape and was temporarily demoralised, it opened up the prospect of a successful African rebellion in Rhodesia. For Jameson had been Rhodes's unpopular viceroy in Rhodesia, and had stripped the country of white police to join his adventure in the Transvaal. There were only forty-eight white police in the whole of Matabeleland, and the Ndebele *impis* remustered and gathered hidden weapons.

The news that Jameson and his white police had surrendered to the Boers triggered an Ndebele rebellion on 20 March 1896. It was led by prominent *indunas*, priests of the Mwari cult, and a former Ndebele slave named Mkwati. Nyamanda, eldest son of Lobengula, also took a commanding role. Around 200 whites, and a similar number of black servants, were hacked to death. But by the end of May, Bulawayo had been relieved. Contrary to the company line that the Shona had been rescued from subservience to the Ndebele, this rebellion was followed, in June, by a Shona uprising also; over a hundred settlers were killed in the first few days, and survivors retreated to Fort Salisbury. Paramount chiefs and spirit mediums inspired the Shona, although some Shona stayed neutral or even collaborated with the whites. But grievances were many, including white demands for forced labour and the sexual demands of young white men, who hugely out-numbered white women in the early stages of the colony.

The Ndebele, armed with modern weapons and with their military tradition, were the most feared. Their lands had been occupied according to alien European ideas of property, they had been subject to forced labour, a hut tax to push them into the money economy, and most of their prized cattle had been stolen.[15] When they rebelled in March, they rose up with ferocity; white farms and mining camps were attacked, and the remaining settlers, desperately frightened, retreated into laagers in Bulawayo and Gwelo. Rhodes, who had just got back from London after trying to dissipate the political damage of the Jameson Raid, made himself a colonel and led a relieving column. But crucially he was supported by imperial troops, and crucially the Ndebele did not coordinate with the Shona. In May the Ndebele suffered their first defeat, and when Rhodes arrived in Bulawayo on 1 June

– just prior to the Shona rising – a public holiday was declared in his honour.

Rhodes demanded utter ruthlessness in pursuing the Ndebele in what turned into a guerrilla war. He generated propaganda about African barbarism in London. The Ndebele defended a succession of hills, first the Mambos, then the Matopos, and Frederick Carrington, the imperial commander, sought to starve out the Ndebele troops in the Matopos. *Kraals* were burnt and food stocks destroyed, in a foretaste of techniques that the British would use against the Boers not long after.

But Rhodes, who had to overcome his own lack of personal courage, was moved by the deaths of the white soldiers. He underwent an epiphany. At considerable personal risk he negotiated a series of peace agreements with the Ndebele *indunas* in August, offering to reform the police and reduce the exactions of his administration.

The imperial officers – who included Robert Baden-Powell, founder of the Boy Scout movement – were not happy with Rhodes's private peacemaking. Indeed Baden-Powell appears to have broken the laws of war in executing a rebel, Uwini, who had surrendered on a promise that his life would be spared.[16] Yet Rhodes's peace deal with the Ndebele was crucial to the continued status of his Chartered Company. It made possible the withdrawal of the troops sooner rather than later, sparing British government expense, and permitting the company to retain its control through the British South African Police.

But the Shona war went on for another year. Rhodes, who had always taken the Ndebele more seriously as a military threat, was not personally involved. He led no peacemaking *indabas*, or consultations, with the Shona leaders. Shona people were gunned down. When they hid in caves, the caves were dynamited. There were hundreds of punitive expeditions across the country. Although many years later, in its nationalist propaganda, Zanu–PF would refer to the rebellion as the *chimurenga*, the first war of independence, it was more a series of separate community risings, not well coordinated.

The sheer horror of these revenge missions was illustrated by what happened at a Shona village called Shaungwe, on the top of a steep hill nearly 300 metres high. It had never been captured by the Ndebele, but the British cut off its water supply and set up machine-gun posts on all the slopes. They waited until thirst and hunger forced surrender, but 90 men were killed in a breakout where others got away, and when 200 women surrendered after a long siege they showed a stoical composure in sipping from their first calabash of water.[17]

News of this vicious war did reach the outside world, and missionaries who watched it were particularly appalled. John White, a Methodist who had been outraged by the Zvimba murders three years earlier, saw 'hundreds of men, women and children blown to pieces … it seems even more sad that a nation of civilisation and standing should be engaging in such work.'[18]

Rhodes, severely damaged by the Jameson Raid, and with ambitions to become Cape prime minister again, was not upset by what he would have seen as mopping-up operations against the Shona. A committee of inquiry in London on the Raid became a whitewash, in which Rhodes and Joseph Chamberlain, the colonial secretary, combined to defend each other. Rhodes was seen by many, both in Britain and in English South Africa, as a hero who had saved Rhodesia for the Empire. He was actively involved with those who wanted to crush President Kruger's independent Boer republic of the Transvaal, and four years after the Raid the British launched the Anglo-Boer War. He saw out the first phase of the war in besieged Kimberley, where he undermined and tried to take over from the British commander, Colonel Robert Kekewich. Rhodes died at his home near Cape Town, in March 1902, of heart failure. The war by then had moved into its final guerrilla phase.

Rhodes had been an imperial visionary, desirous of spreading British rule and colonisation up through the African continent. He wanted to see telegraph lines and a railway linking the Cape to Cairo. He had famously told Queen Victoria, who asked him what he had been up to lately, that he had added two provinces (what became Southern and Northern Rhodesia) to her dominions. But in the chessboard of African imperialism he, and his Chartered Company, had not had it all their own way. Bechuanaland and Nyasaland had escaped his clutches, remaining protected by the Colonial Office. He had been rebuffed in attempts to move westwards into King Leopold's Katanga, and eastwards into Portuguese East Africa, when he had sought access to the Indian Ocean.

He certainly loved 'his' Rhodesia, arranging to be buried in the Matopos Hills at a spot with a breathtaking view, in the area where he had made peace with the Ndebele. But in a sense the territory was contingent. It happened to be north of the Limpopo. His firm's propaganda about mineral or agricultural riches, designed to attract white settlers, might not be justified, and indeed the Chartered Company was never a great financial success. What was certain for him was that geography required its occupation by whites for the purposes of his vision, just as the African inhabitants were either an obstacle or a cheap labour force.

And his vision, at the acme of imperial ambition, was stupendous. As a 23-year-old he had envisaged a secret society which would promote British rule throughout the world. Dying under the age of 50, he left much of his fortune to endow scholarships to his old university, Oxford, to spread British values in a more acceptable fashion.[19] Like Lenin, he was a man who believed that the end justified the means.

But what was the nature of the white settlement in what is now Zimbabwe in the last decade of the nineteenth century? The first pioneers had been promised farms of 3,000 acres each while Sir John Willoughby, a baronet who had commanded their escort, acquired 600,000. Frederick Selous, who was a guide to the expedition, was given 21,000 acres in Mashonaland by Rhodes, as an inducement. Recruits for the war against Lobengula in 1892 were offered 6,000 acres to farm, twenty gold claims, and a share of looted cattle. In 1895 Rhodes gave Alfred de Fonseca 33,000 acres of Ndebele land, and he awarded Cape MPs tracts of land in Rhodesia as freely as he gave them shares in his Chartered Company, to buy support. By 1899, 15.7 million acres had been given to Europeans.

Land was given out to syndicates, and to young aristocrats, who in many cases had neither the desire nor the skill to master agriculture and overcome bush, rinderpest, malaria, locusts and drought. 'Lady Dudley's son, a youngster of the la di da class, has just been sent up here probably with an expression of Jameson's wish that half a county may be given to him', wrote William Milton, a disgusted imperial administrator to his wife in 1896.[20] He thought there was little good land left to be settled by working immigrants.

There were therefore distinctions, of class and money, among the early settlers. Many were adventurers of the kind who had flocked to Kimberley in the diamond rush, and to the Rand in the gold rush, young men on the make, sometimes with dubious backgrounds. Few had the patience or experience for agriculture. The offer of gold claims was more inviting to many than the award of the Africans' land. Yet they were not experienced prospectors, and they lacked the equipment to dig deep even where there were signs of gold-bearing rocks. Heavy rains, lasting for five months in 1890, bogged down the pioneers and were followed by mosquitoes, malaria and fever. Many died. Little gold was found, and in 1894 a mining expert named John Hammond told Rhodes that more was unlikely.

The whites had little understanding of Shona society, religion and political organisation. They dismissed the idea that earlier Shona had been responsible for the architectural wonders of Great Zimbabwe. They were strongly racist, and saw Africans as barbarians; it did not occur to them that the missionaries' slow progress in making conversions to Christianity reflected the survival of a powerful indigenous belief system. They did not appreciate that pre-colonial societies were full of complexity. There was also a bias in favour of the Ndebele, seen as having a warlike character, similar to that of the respected Zulus. 'Noone likes the Mashonas, dirty, cowardly lot. Matabele bloodthirsty devils, but a fine type', wrote an early diarist.[21]

Rhodes was strongly criticised for the expense of food and materials brought up from the Cape. The early settlers were ambivalent about his Chartered Company, which was seen as doing more for its shareholders in Britain and Europe than for those suffering hardships on the ground. Until the railway came up to Bulawayo ordinary imported necessities seemed very dear. And, until nearly the end of the nineteenth century, the white settlers remained fearful of insurrection, ambush or murder from the conquered blacks.

Seen from the African viewpoint, it was a tale of unmitigated dispossession. The cattle, symbol of wealth for the Ndebele especially, were taken from them. An alien approach to land ownership was foisted on them. Although previous overlords had demanded tribute, the whites' urgent pressure for them to pay tax meant they had to become labourers to earn money. As late as 1979, during the Lancaster House negotiations for an independent Zimbabwe, Joshua Nkomo was moved to tears in recalling how his mother had been pushed off her land. The best grazing was now in the hands of the Europeans.

A Land Commission set up in 1894 proposed limiting 'the Matabele nation and their slaves' to the two reserves of Guai and Shangani with a total area of 10,500 square kilometres – the origin of a policy that lasted for most of the twentieth century. Critics noted that the reserves were sandy, poorly watered and in unpromising locations. Yet, while the Ndebele and Shona were no longer free to roam wherever they pleased, many of the properties so flippantly distributed by Rhodes and the Chartered Company were not being actively farmed.

The company had monopoly powers. It was both a capitalist and an imperialist enterprise. When it was financially weak, Rhodes would back it with his De Beers shares. When he and his friends won a war, the value of its stocks in London would rise. But not all its shareholders were British; late in life, after the siege of Kimberley had been raised in the Anglo-Boer War and Rhodes was criticised for a speech, he defended himself by arguing that it was designed for his French shareholders.

Looking back a century later it is striking how Rhodes played 'the imperial factor' when it suited him. He did not want the government in Westminster to hobble his ambitions, or provide what he described as 'negrophile' protection for Africans. Yet he did want recognition for what he was doing – the British Post Office recognised his state as 'Rhodesia' in 1895 – and he wanted British troops and finance from the City of London whenever necessary. His threat of an early UDI, the unilateral declaration of independence actually carried out by the Smith regime in the 1960s, was essentially hollow. Empire-building in central and southern Africa was a vulnerable task, with Boers, Germans, Portuguese and Ndebele to contend with; the British South Africa Company needed backup, which only the British government could provide. When the machinations of Rhodes finally brought all-out war with the Boer republics, only the massive imperial army of Lord Roberts, with about 40,000 men and a hundred artillery guns, could rescue his dreams.

Another aspect of this early history worth dwelling on is the relationship of the territory north of the Limpopo with South

Africa. Of course South Africa, in its modern sense, did not exist. There was the Cape Colony, the conquered Zulu territory, the two Boer republics of the Transvaal and the Orange Free State and, rather to one side in the west, the Bechuanaland protectorate. Rhodes's aim was to join all these, and areas to the north stretching up to modern Uganda if he could, in an Anglo-Dutch federation in the British Empire.

However, the existence of the Boer republics, and the fact that Bechuanaland was not under the Cape or the Chartered Company, meant that Rhodesia had a certain geographical independence. It could not easily be swallowed up by the Cape. There is little doubt that Rhodes's policy, with respect to Africans as a subject race and a labour pool, was consistent in both the Cape and his new company territory. But the format was different. Furthermore the composition of the early settlers in Rhodesia was more 'British' than in either the Cape, where there was a well-established Afrikaner community, or certainly than in the Transvaal, where the motley group of miners and dependants were coming to outnumber the Boer population.

Rhodesia might be a tribute to the imperial idea, and the triumph of a particular imperialist, but it was also a somewhat independent fact in the congeries of southern African statelets and ethnicities.

Two aspects of the conquest era also cast a long shadow. It continued, and developed, a culture of violence which existed before Rhodes's pioneer column arrived in Salisbury. Whereas African disputes had been settled by assegais and knobkerries, the Europeans introduced the latest, most destructive equipment in modern warfare – heavy guns, machine guns and rifles. Death and threats of violence became an underlying discourse between Europeans and Africans, overlaying the periodic violence in relations between African groups.

Second, there was almost absolute impunity for the white conquerors. Neither Lobengula with his slaves, nor the Shona paramount chiefs, had been running liberal democracies. But the new arrivals claimed to stand for a civilising mission, as well as personal enrichment. Although they complained about the Chartered Company's expensive imports, the white settlers in the 1890s generally regarded Rhodes and those who protected them from African vengeance as demigods and heroes. Only a handful of missionaries and others could see that their cruelty was an affront to Christianity and peacemaking.

Cultures of violence and impunity were built into the DNA of the state created by Cecil John Rhodes.

TWO

WHITE SUPREMACY AND
THE SETTLER STATE

With Rhodes's death, the rebellions defeated, and British victory in the Anglo-Boer War, Rhodesia moved into an era of relative quiet and gradual colonial growth. In London's eyes it could seem a backwater. More important was the federation of the South African territories into the Union of South Africa in 1910. But this did not include the protectorates of Bechuanaland, Swaziland and the Sotho kingdom, and, although geopolitical strategists would already have liked to include Rhodesia, the anomaly of a company-run territory was an obstacle. The British Act which set up the Union of South Africa left open the possibility that Rhodesia might join as a fifth province.

The company's minutes and resolutions had to be sent to the Colonial Office, and the colonial secretary had the right to cancel them where they affected the administration of the colony; he could also remove directors and officials. A resident commissioner, paid for by the Colonial Office, was in charge of police and army, but did not have a staff. An administrator, responsible to the company, presided over an executive and a legislative council. Significantly, the settlers acquired an elected majority on the legislative council in 1907. There were two separate administrations – one for the whites and one for the Africans – so the administrator was both head of the civil service and secretary for native affairs. This complex system represented a compromise between the Colonial Office (the imperial factor), the company, white settlers, and a paternalistic gesture to limit the exploitation of conquered Africans.[1]

Friction between the settlers and the company continued. The colony was short of capital. The company, after a visit by its deputation from London in 1907, decided to give preference to agricultural development over mining, which increased the competition with Africans for land. In fact, after a disappointing start, Rhodesian gold mines had produced as much as 200,000 oz in 1902, but the British victory in the South African war exposed them to stronger competition from the south. Even in the 1890s there had been occasional strikes by African miners.[2]

The small white population, of 14,000 in 1907, jumped by nearly 10,000 over the following four years, as agriculture was promoted. When renewal of the company's 25-year charter was discussed in 1914, a ten-year supplement was agreed. For the British government, this was a cost-saving measure. But it left open two different options for the colony: merger with South Africa or 'responsible government' by the white electorate. A protectorate arrangement under the Colonial Office, as occurred in neighbouring Bechuanaland or Nyasaland, became less likely as the white population rose.

Land policy for the Africans was ambiguous. To begin with, the company sought to keep Africans on the white farms, where labour was badly needed, seeing the reserves as a temporary refuge for those who could not adjust to the European way of life. The philosophy was assimilationist, portraying Africans as a potential proletariat. By the 1920s the attitude to land was more clearly segregationist, and the reserves became the permanent share left to Africans. At a social level, of course, the attitudes of the white settlers to Africans had from the start been a mixture of fear, contempt and sexual anxiety. In 1903 the Legislative Council approved the Immorality Suppression Ordinance, which made extramarital sex between a black man and a white woman illegal. The man could be sentenced to five years' hard labour, the woman to two – but there was no equivalent punishment for a white man consorting with a black woman.

Pressure on Africans to earn money in the white economy was exercised through taxation, although African traders and individuals increasingly wanted access to European goods. In 1903 it was proposed to substitute a poll tax for the hut tax, and the settler interests wanted to set this at £2 a head. But, following lobbying by missionaries, the poll tax was fixed at £1. The missionaries, who had been in the country since before the conquest, but without much success in evangelism, hoped to win African souls after the defeat of their spirit mediums. They had a monopoly of African education until 1920, and after that were running some of the most prestigious schools. Nonetheless the progress of Christianity was slow; in 1928 it was estimated that less than a tenth of the African population of around a million had been converted.

De facto segregation applied to the towns as well as the countryside, with Africans placed in 'locations' at a distance from white housing, unable to own property, and deemed to be on temporary release from their homes in the reserves. It was a system destructive of family life and community traditions. It was supported by the requirement, which was introduced prior to the rebellions, that men should carry passes to legitimise their movements. By 1910 each African man had to carry a registration certificate, and be ready to show it. Hence two features of the South African apartheid system, so much criticised as National Party racism after it was formalised after 1948, were actually features of the Rhodesian colony over thirty years earlier.

Africans came under the jurisdiction of the Department of Native Affairs and native commissioners. Whereas elsewhere in the African empire the British had operated by indirect rule, using the chiefly and traditional authorities to govern, in Rhodesia the native commissioners had direct power and the traditional chiefs were subordinated. The native commissioners, keen to avoid the forced labour of the Jameson regime, faced criticism from white farmers who wanted more African workers at lower cost.

The 1914–18 war impacted sharply on Rhodesia. It created a boom for the agricultural and mineral commodities produced by the colony. It demonstrated that there was no new appetite for rebellion in the African population. It showed a patriotic loyalism in the white population. And it hastened the end of the rule by the Chartered Company.

In spite of the shortage of capital, and the smallness of the white population – only 27,000 in total – the war showed that the colony had built a diversified economy in less than a quarter of a century. As well as its farm products there were exports of coal, gold, copper, tungsten, chrome, zinc, antimony and asbestos. A high proportion of white males joined in the imperial armies which captured the German colonies. Around 5,500 white men served in German South West Africa (Namibia) and German East Africa (Tanganyika), suffering serious losses in the latter campaign where they were commanded by the South African General Smuts. The authorities were sufficiently confident of African attitudes to recruit two Rhodesian Native Regiments, which fought under white officers in East Africa.

Just prior to the outbreak of the war an important dispute over land was referred to the judicial committee of the Privy Council. The issue related to what was described as 'unalienated' land – land which had neither been given nor sold by the company to settlers, or Rhodes's friends; nor was it reserved to Africans. It was a resource which could either be sold to provide revenue for

the company or, in the view of the Colonial Office, it belonged
to the Crown.

The case was brought by the Legislative Council, by now
under settler control. But a group of missionaries, the Aborigines
Protection Society and Nyamanda – who continued to be active
in African politics with his status as Lobengula's heir – argued
that such land should go to Africans. Nyamanda asked the Crown
for the return of 'the so-called unalienated land to the family of
the late King Lobengula in trust for the tribe according to Bantu
custom'.[3]

The hearings were long-drawn-out and in the end the Privy
Council found for the Crown. This decision – which came after
the death of Dr Jameson, who as president of the company represented continuity with the founder – helped bring the end
of Chartered Company rule in Rhodesia. A commission was
established to value the work of the company in ruling as an
agent of the Crown, and in 1921 it assessed this at just over
£4.4 million.[4] The British South Africa Company did not leave
Southern or Northern Rhodesia, where it continued to have important land, railway and mining interests. Indeed as late as 1932
the *Round Table* journal could observe that 'The peculiarity of
the Rhodesian economic field is that it contains practically only
one capitalist – the powerful financial group which comprises
the B.S.A. Company and its subsidiary companies', and in the
mid-1920s they were responsible for at least 60 per cent of railway
traffic.[5] But the company was no longer a quasi-government.

This left open the question, what next? The two options were
'responsible government', a description of straightforward settler
rule on the model of the old Cape Colony, or absorption into the
Union of South Africa as a fifth province. The one option that was
not on the agenda was rule by the Colonial Office, which could
have led to a very different evolution for Southern Rhodesia in
the twentieth century. It was not on the agenda for two reasons.

First, the white settlers were already sufficiently numerous and had considerable political autonomy. Second, rule from Whitehall was likely to be more expensive for the British government.

The debates around the constitutional future for Rhodesia exercised the white community; they virtually ignored the blacks. Nyamanda and the surviving upper-caste Ndebele pressed fruitlessly for a protectorate status for part of Matabeleland. But they were ignored. Others, such as the Rhodesian Bantu Voters Association, the Rhodesia Native Association and the Gwelo Native Association, were more interested in sectoral issues, or getting Africans onto an electoral register, and in some cases the leadership came from black immigrants rather than Shona or Ndebele. The Africans were still recently conquered peoples, with little social intercourse with whites, and in no way regarded by them as partners or equals.

The struggle between the advocates of 'responsible government' and supporters of union with South Africa came to a head in a referendum on 27 October 1922. The campaigners for responsible government were led by Charles Coghlan, a Bulawayo lawyer who had made his name by litigation for settlers against the Chartered Company. He was a Roman Catholic of Irish ancestry. He led the 'unofficials' on the Legislative Council, and represented the white grassroots, which were now beginning to include an artisan class. His slogan was 'Rhodesia for the Rhodesians, Rhodesia for the Empire'.

On the other side were the richer, more respectable people in the colony, and its major institutions – including the company. Its effective leader was the prime minister of South Africa, General Jan Smuts. From his earlier incarnation as a Boer general in the Anglo-Boer War, he had become an advocate of reconciliation between Boers and Britons. He emerged from the First World War as a key imperial statesman, who had run the Germans out of their African colonies, and gone to the Versailles Peace Conference.

In 1921 he won a significant victory in a South African general election, over the Afrikaner nationalists, and was able to offer both Rhodesians and the Chartered Company attractive deals.

His approach had something in common with Rhodes, in that he envisaged a white-ruled, self-governing nation, part of the British Empire, stretching up into the heart of Africa. In its linking of national security to such expansion, it also looked forward to the strategy of the apartheid South African state in the 1970s and 1980s, which sought a protective ring of vassals to its north. Smuts, although an Afrikaner himself, had low politics in mind. He hoped that the Rhodesians, overwhelmingly of British stock, would provide a vote bank for him in South Africa.

But the result of the referendum was decisive: while the unionists got 5,989 votes, the supporters of responsible government won 8,774. Out of an African population of nearly 900,000 only 60 were on the register; out of a European population of 35,000, the register listed around 20,000. There were several causes for the unionist defeat, including a fear and dislike of Afrikaners, who were immigrating and taking low-paid white jobs. One of the conditions of Smuts's offer, required to get it through his own parliament, was that the Afrikaans language would have parity with English in Rhodesia; this annoyed the Rhodesians. Violence in South Africa in 1922, causing loss of life for both Africans and Europeans, made the country seem unsafe and unattractive to join.

Hence the years 1922–23 were crucial in establishing the identity of Rhodesia as separate from its powerful neighbour. There were echoes of the Irish settlement in the same period. Northern Ireland was carved out of the Irish Free State as a Protestant-dominated statelet, where for many years the large Catholic minority was kept subordinate. But whereas London had granted authority to a majority in Northern Ireland, in Rhodesia this authority was given to a small minority in the population of the territory, with few real checks.

Southern Rhodesia had a constitutional status which was almost the autonomy of South Africa, Canada and Australia – the self-governing dominions in the British Empire – but not quite. It was technically a Crown colony. But a convention developed under which the United Kingdom would never legislate for it except by agreement with or at the request of the Rhodesian government. The issue of land, in the 1920s, continued to be a source of friction. Dr Jameson had been ruthless in reducing the amount and quality of soil available to both Ndebele and Shona, and this helped to explain the rebellions in the 1890s; a decision in 1897 by Sir Richard Martin, the first resident commissioner, more than doubled the land set aside for the Ndebele, and increased the amount for the Shona. Nonetheless the land available for Africans was only 20.5 million acres, out of a total in Southern Rhodesia, in 1914, of 96 million acres.

Throughout the First World War the Chartered Company had been wanting more agricultural land for the whites, and the Native Department sought to resist, especially in Matabeleland. Significantly, especially in Shona areas, there was an African boycott of work on white farms and altogether the proportion of indigenous farm labourers more than halved between 1913 and 1922.[6] A Native Resources Commission under Sir Robert Coryndon proposed a net reduction of some 1 million acres for the African reserves. Furthermore, the changes would give the Africans land that was less fertile. The issue was tackled again in 1925 when Sir Morris Carter, a former chief justice in Uganda and Tanganyika, reported on behalf of a Land Commission.

It was not until a Land Apportionment Act was finally passed in April 1931, with approval from the British government, that there was some degree of finality. Leaving aside the tribal trust lands, for Africans not expected to be part of the European economy, 7.4 million acres were set aside for African purchase, and 49 million acres for Europeans. Almost every urban area was reserved for the Europeans, which meant that in theory no African could buy or rent housing there.

The whites persuaded themselves that this was a good deal for the Africans, and a Native Development Department was set up in 1929 to help Africans with agriculture and conservation. But in fact the deal was massively disproportionate – with 28 million acres, including the reserves, set aside for 1 million Africans, and 48 million acres set aside for 50,000 whites. Furthermore the African birth rate rose faster than had been forecast, while significant land set aside for the Europeans was not being farmed. As late as 1965, when UDI was declared, a quarter of 'white' land was not being occupied or used.

The impact on race relations was of course negative, especially as the towns began to grow. It was compounded by the dismissive way in which African males were treated as 'boys', with little recognition that they were or could be equals. Such attitudes were commonplace in Britain's African colonies in the interwar era. At a human level there were many Africans, like Joshua Nkomo, who carried around bitter memories of the loss of agricultural land. Stan Mudenge, Zimbabwe foreign minister in the late 1990s and early 2000s, told a British high commissioner how his grandfather had shown him the place where the family had formerly farmed.[7]

White Southern Rhodesia had fought off the possibility of merger with South Africa, but in the 1920s many of its politicians – including Charles Coghlan, who was the colony's first prime minister from 1923 to 1927 and had changed his mind on this – were keen to absorb Northern Rhodesia. This was partly a matter of trying to run a unified rail system in central Africa, and partly from a desire to acquire the newly discovered riches of the Copperbelt.[8] However, a British commission set up in 1929 under Sir Hilton Young, charged with reviewing boundaries and policy across east and central Africa, dashed these hopes.

Although the commission recommended that Kenya, Uganda and Tanganyika should join together, it did not wish to include Nyasaland or the Rhodesias in such a federation. London too wanted to hang on to the copper of Northern Rhodesia and was also persuaded by a 'trusteeship' argument that the interests of native peoples should be paramount. What this really meant was that there were not many whites living in the protectorate, compared with Southern Rhodesia where they had established their own power base.

After Coghlan the key white politician was Godfrey Huggins, prime minister of Southern Rhodesia from 1933 to 1953, and architect of the ill-fated Central African Federation. He was a doctor, born in Bexley, Kent, who arrived in the country in 1911 and practised as a surgeon, the first in Southern Rhodesia. Huggins was deaf but sociable, a skilful manager of conservative instincts, who came to power with the support of a radically pro-white Reform Party and then created a winning coalition called the United Party.

The racial radicals in the Reform Party were pushing for overt segregation and separate development, with removal of Africans from the common roll and protection for white artisans. They had a strange ideology of 'twin pyramids', with European and African pyramids side by side, but with the European pyramid containing the more important jobs and in control of the African pyramid with its lower skills base. This philosophy was a challenge to Cecil Rhodes's view, towards the end of his life, that southern Africa should recognise an equality and partnership between civilised men. The pyramids would never be equal.

Huggins was no ideologue. The Dominions Office in London, not the Colonial Office, liaised with the Salisbury government. It rejected both the idea of sending brighter Africans to Northern Rhodesia for promotion to more senior posts, and the proposal that Africans be removed from the common roll of voters. But

Huggins persuaded the Dominions Office to approve his Industrial Conciliation Act, 1934, which was far more important to the white artisan community in Southern Rhodesia.

This Act required firms in urban areas to pay the same wages to black as to white workers, which looked progressive to the Dominions Office. But in reality it had several consequences which damaged the prospects of African advancement.[9] Economically it destroyed the potential advantage of an African to an employer – that he could be hired more cheaply than a white man. Second, because it did not define an African as an employee, he could not have trade-union rights. Third, it left the African skilled worker to the ancient mercies of the Master and Servants Act, under which labour obduracy was met with criminal penalties. The total effect was to choke off the acquisition of higher skills at better wages for Africans, as well as the scope for African unionism. A Labour Party, representing the interests of white workers, was vigilant in preventing the progress of blacks.

Social change for Africans threatened the authority of the chiefs and older generation, and in the 1920s the white Native Commissioners sought to reconstruct a state-supported tribalism which had only a partial resemblance to Shona and Ndebele traditions. The Native Department was split between those who wanted to encourage African individualism, often influenced by Christian values, and those who wanted to restore communal practices. The efforts of the Lobengula family to persuade Britain to assume direct responsibility, to recognise the chiefly status of his grandsons, and to restore unalienated land to their trusteeship for the Ndebele, were firmly resisted.[10]

Southern Rhodesia between the wars operated to tight government budgets. It actively encouraged white immigration, but white numbers were still pretty small, climbing from less than 35,000 in 1922 to 65,000 in 1940; although African numbers had risen relatively less, from around 900,000 to 1.39 million in the same period, it meant that the ratio in the first year of the Second World War was 1:21.[11] Without substantial white immigration it was inevitable that more of the African population would become urbanised, and commercial and industrial growth would challenge ideological ambitions for segregation. Agricultural policy was sharply skewed in favour of white farmers rather than black, especially in prices for maize, the staple food crop for Africans.[12]

For the colony was doing better, in spite of the international recession in the early 1930s. Although it had its ups and downs, tobacco farming took off, particularly in the Shona areas north and east of Salisbury. Agriculture was dominated by big combines, and many small white farmers still lived close to the edge. Salisbury overtook Bulawayo in population and wealth. Transit freight brought income to Southern Rhodesia, and the coal mines of Wankie prospered on the back of the exploitation of the Copperbelt. The economy depended largely on mining, with gold, asbestos and chrome the principal exports.[13] While union with South Africa disappeared as an aspiration, Huggins – who was hostile to Afrikaners – continued with others to hanker for a merger between Southern and Northern Rhodesia.

In 1938 the two secretaries of state in London, for the dominions and for the colonies, set up a commission under a former governor general of New Zealand, Lord Bledisloe. Its task was to review British policy in Nyasaland, Northern and Southern Rhodesia, and to see whether there was a justified case for partial or total federation.

The upshot, debated in the UK parliament in July 1939, just prior to outbreak of the Second World War, was significant. The commissioners rejected the case for partial or total amalgamation, principally because the 'native policy' was too divergent. In Northern Rhodesia and Nyasaland it was the African interest which had priority in colonial policy, even if self-government still seemed a long way off. In Southern Rhodesia the Africans were subordinate to the white settlers. Furthermore, in each territory, the Africans were opposed to mergers, which they could see would lead to an extension of Southern Rhodesian practices. Commissioners were struck by the ability of Africans, who largely lacked a formal Western education, to recognise and speak up for their interests.

Although the Bledisloe report could not lead to major institutional change, and got buried in the debris of war, it hinted at long-term issues of importance. First, it showed that African opinion, though not well organised, was definitely opposed to settler rule; this was a thread that ran through to the Pearce Commission's sounding of African views on a deal offered by Ian Smith in 1972, following UDI, which fell short of one-man, one-vote, or independence before majority African rule. Second, it showed that Huggins and establishment whites in Southern Rhodesia were keen to extend their sway northwards, in spite of the demographic obstacles; this was to lead to the ill-fated Central African Federation of 1953–63. Third, it marked the start of an era when academics in Britain joined church people and left-wingers in anxiety about suppressing the African voice; by the 1950s this informed opinion was strongly influencing the Labour Party, then in opposition in Britain, which in government had granted independence to India.

African organisations gained in strength in the 1930s and 1940s, as welfare societies lost ground to more militant bodies influenced by South African examples and the cut and thrust of industrial struggle. 'Advanced' farmers, and a Christianised elite, had been at the forefront of organisations like the Rhodesian Native Association, founded in 1924, and the Rhodesia Bantu Voters Association. The Industrial and Commercial Workers' Union, launched in Southern Rhodesia in 1927 as an offshoot of a South African union, claimed 5,000 members only five years later.

But these secular groups were competing for African support, at a time of disruption to traditional Shona and Ndebele society, with millenarian religions such as the Watch Tower sect.

The combination of Christian and Africanist values in some of the leaders was epitomised by the career of Thompson Samkange, who had been born in 1893 as Mushore in the Chipata area of the Zvimba chieftaincy, not too far from the birthplace of Robert Mugabe in Kutama.[14] The atrocity recounted in Chapter 1 made evangelism, by Methodist missionaries, extremely difficult; Chief Zvimba and his Shona group initially fled the area, and were subsequently removed from the mission farm by the Native Department. Nonetheless, against family opposition, Mushore allowed himself to be baptised as Thompson and came under the influence of the outspoken pro-African missionary John White.

Thompson Samkange trained as a clergyman and teacher, was posted to the Wankie Colliery and learnt Ndebele in Bulawayo. In 1928 he was secretary to the first Missionary Conference of Christian Natives, when White was in the chair, and in Bulawayo was a mediator in clashes between Shona and Ndebele workers. A visit to India inspired him to press for the indigenisation of the Methodist Church in Rhodesia, and in the late 1930s he played a major role in federating 'native' and welfare societies in the Southern Rhodesian African National Congress, with the name borrowed from the South African ANC, which had been founded as far back as 1912. He was Congress president from 1943 to 1948, an era in which the main competition lay with Benjamin Burombo's African Voice Association, and the reformed Industrial and Commercial Workers' Union (ICU).

Southern Rhodesia, as a Crown colony, entered the Second World War automatically in September 1939; South Africa, as an independent dominion, only joined in on the British side by a narrow parliamentary majority, due to anti-British and pro-German sentiment among Afrikaners. The war led to heroic actions by patriotic Rhodesian whites abroad, particularly in the Royal Air Force – where Ian Smith was a fighter pilot, twice shot down – and considerable suffering for the black communities at home. All told some 8,500 white men and 1,500 white women served in the forces, with 14,000 Africans; white losses were significantly higher. Many white Rhodesians fought alongside South Africans, and were used to train Africans from other colonies.

There was, however, a distinction between African recruitment in West Africa, never an attractive region for European settlers, and southern Africa. In the Gold Coast, which as Ghana was to become the first independent African state in the Commonwealth, as many as 65,000 Africans were allowed to join up and two were commissioned as officers.[15] White memories elsewhere could recall the dangerous effectiveness of black Africans who had fought for the Kaiser in Tanganyika in 1914–18, and on both sides in the Anglo-Boer War.

However, inflation saw a rise of 140 per cent in the cost of living between 1939 and 1947, seriously outstripping the wages of most urban Africans. Growth of African populations in towns had led to overcrowding, slums and health problems; the government shelved plans to build a new clinic in the Bulawayo location in December 1939. 'The spirit of self-help must be preserved and any scheme must be contributory', said the chairman of Bulawayo's public health committee in 1945, in a Dickensian comment.[16]

Southern Rhodesia was used, with Canada, as a centre for the Empire Air Training Scheme and eleven air stations were built; Tony Benn, who became a leading figure in left-wing British Labour politics in the second half of the twentieth century, was one of those who trained there. The white population of around 65,000 in 1940 temporarily rose by 15,000. But the war effort was underpinned by black labour. A Compulsory Native Labour Act, 1942, made strikes dangerous, but they happened all the same, especially when the mealie meal ration was cut back. By 1943 it was estimated that around 11,000 Africans had been rounded up for forced labour on the military airfields, as well as on the farms and elsewhere.

As in Britain and the United States, the war led to industrial interventionism and some slightly more liberal attitudes. There was even a white communist cell in Southern Rhodesia, which swept up the youthful Doris Lessing.[17] In 1941 Godfrey Huggins produced a statement on Native Affairs, in which he foresaw a time in the future when land segregation and job reservation might end; and in 1945 he required local authorities to build housing for Africans, although the following year his duty on urban employers to provide free accommodation for their workers in the 'native area' was balanced by strict pass laws and rules on registration. He nationalised the iron and steel works in Bulawayo, and in 1947 he bought Rhodesia Railways from the old Chartered Company, even though much of the network ran through Northern Rhodesia and Nyasaland.

African representation in Southern Rhodesian electoral politics was tiny: only 136 out of a potential total of 6,000 who met the franchise qualification bothered to register after the war. But African muscle was displayed in the workplace. High inflation and overcrowded housing lay behind a strike, in October 1945, of over 2,000 black railwaymen. They were organised in the Rhodesia Railways African Employees' Association, formed a year before out of the old Bantu Benefit Society, to campaign for better wages and conditions.

The strike was precipitated by the introduction of a new system of overtime pay by the Chartered Company, which penalised better paid workers while offering more to others; the general manager dismissed representations by the union, saying that 'if they waited six months they would not be seen', and the strike rapidly spread from Bulawayo across the Zambezi to Broken Hill and the Copperbelt. In the end 8,000 workers were involved, the company was forced to negotiate, and the upshot was an increase in the starting pay for railway workers and official criticism of the housing policy of the company.[18]

This success electrified black trade unionism, and was recognised for its political importance. Jasper Savanhu, who was president of the Bulawayo African Workers Trade Union, which was set up a week after the successful conclusion of the rail strike, commented that it had proved that

> Africans have been born ... Africans realise as never before that united they stand and divided they fall.... We have found ourselves faced by a ruthless foe – exploitation and legalised oppression by the white man for his and his children's luxury.... The days when a white man could exploit us at will are gone and gone for ever.[19]

Very quickly the black workers in many trades in Bulawayo, from bakeries to breweries, formed unions; in Salisbury the ICU was rebuilt by Charles Mzingeli; other unions were formed outside these federations, and in 1947 there was a split in the union movement in Bulawayo, between those claiming to represent the unskilled migrant workers and those in skilled and semi-skilled occupations. A small group of wealthy African entrepreneurs, such as the Chidavaenzi brothers, who ran a transport company in Mashonaland North, was also beginning to emerge. Many union leaders were themselves small businessmen; Mzingeli had been editor of the *Bantu Mirror*. Such leaders found themselves pushed aside by popular pressure when local inflation, plus an awareness that the British Empire was in retreat from India to the Gold Coast, led to a general strike in April 1948.

The strike began with municipal workers in Bulawayo, and impatience overtook union leaderships, with activists demanding an immediate withdrawal of labour. Altogether 100,000 workers got involved, and the strike spread to domestic servants and small towns, as well as Bulawayo and Salisbury. Two wage increases in quick succession staved off a strike at the Wankie colliery. Houses and cars belonging to the black middle class were damaged in the locations but, although Huggins mobilised police and territorial soldiers, there were no deaths and the strike petered out quickly. In fact Huggins, as prime minister, responded calmly. He said that Southern Rhodesia was witnessing the growth of a proletariat which happened to be black, and it would be foolish to react with coercion in a showdown.

Half a century on, of course, another union movement would take on another government.

Shortly after the end of the general strike in Southern Rhodesia, there was a momentous development for the whole of southern Africa. Dr Daniel Malan's 'purified' National Party won a small majority of seats in South Africa's election on 28 May. Although Smuts's United Party had a plurality of the popular vote, the Afrikaner-based National Party became the government. So it remained until the first democratic, multiracial elections in 1994.

The success of the National Party, with its ideology of apartheid and suppression of black aspirations, had cultural and economic roots. In South African cities there had developed a poor white Afrikaner class, sandwiched between the Africans and the advantaged Anglos; a wave of cultural nationalism, asserting the Afrikaans language and the traditions of the *volk*, promoted pride; rural Afrikaners continued to resent the dominance of Anglo-dominated gold mining and industry; and, with the Anglo-Boer War less than fifty years in the past, there were festering resentments against the declining British Empire and hankerings for the old Boer republics.[20]

In London, and much of the world outside Africa, South Africa loomed large and its neighbours seemed mere appurtenances. Economically, and in its military contribution in two world wars, this was no more than the truth. Hence the election of the National Party government, which contained former sympathisers of the Nazis, caused widespread shock. It also cast the Rhodesias, north of the Limpopo, in the role of a pro-British, potentially more liberal, alternative. This somewhat misleading characterisation was supported by two other elections in 1948.

In August an election in Northern Rhodesia saw a victory for the 'unofficial' settler group led by Roy Welensky, a tough former railwayman whose mother was an Afrikaner and father a Lithuanian Jew. He was a charismatic figure, a voracious reader and heavyweight boxer, who had never gone beyond primary school in his formal education.[21] In spite of the purported paramountcy of concern for Africans in the colony, Welensky had parlayed the small settler interest – strengthened as a result of the copper boom and the growth of a class of white miners – into significant power. He negotiated successfully with the British South Africa Company and the Colonial Office to transfer a slice of mineral royalties to the Northern Rhodesian government.

In September, in Southern Rhodesia, Godfrey Huggins also won a solid victory. He had been ruling as prime minister of a minority government. But he was a cunning tactician, and used an arcane defeat in the legislature over a proposal affecting the Inter-Territorial Currency Board to win a dissolution. The governor, Sir John Kennedy, asked the leader of the opposition to try to form a government; when he failed, the governor permitted an election.

Hence, by the end of 1948 – the year of the Berlin blockade, when a European war between NATO and the Soviet bloc seemed a serious possibility – southern Africa appeared to be going in two different directions. In South Africa, the Nationalists were heading towards full-blooded apartheid. In the Rhodesias, two strong white leaders were beginning to think about bringing Cecil Rhodes's two offspring together.

It was not easy for Huggins and Welensky to get their project off the ground, and the struggles surrounding the birth, survival and death of the Central African Federation were crucial to the

development of African nationalism in each of the three territories that comprised it. Its failure led to Ian Smith's unilateral
declaration of independence and a brutal civil war. Its patrons
had extremely mixed motives. While many white supporters in
central Africa saw it as a way of confirming their dominant status
in an era of decolonisation, it was sold to the United Kingdom as
a partnership deal which would empower Africans, and a contrast
to apartheid.

Although the Bledisloe report was shelved, wartime needs
for economic coordination helped to create a permanent Inter-
Territorial Secretariat in Salisbury in 1941; three years later
this was turned into a Central African Council, though it was
still advisory. Currency and rail coordination continued to go
forward. However, when, in October 1948, Huggins and Welensky met Arthur Creech Jones, colonial secretary in the Attlee
Labour government, he made it clear that amalgamation between
Southern and Northern Rhodesia would not be allowed.[22] This
merger was their first preference, and the Conservatives also made
clear that it was a non-starter.

How was it that, when a merger between the Rhodesias was
ruled out in 1948, the more difficult concept of a Central African
Federation involving Nyasaland – where the white population was
tiny[23] – could come into existence only five years later? Much is
explained by the persistence of Huggins and Welensky, and the
fact that a Labour government almost lost the 1950 election in
Britain, and was replaced by a Conservative government the following year. The Conservatives were more sympathetic to white
opinion, and less responsive to the Africans than Labour.[24] The
Conservatives were willing to overrule the Africans, and believed
that they and white Rhodesian politicians were speaking the same
language when they talked of 'racial partnership'.

Nonetheless the process was not straightforward, and key
steps included a London meeting of officials of Britain, the two

Rhodesias and Nyasaland, to consider the feasibility of federation in March 1951; they came up with a complicated scheme under which the territories retained their different responsibilities for African affairs, and separate constitutions and relationships with the UK, but a federal cabinet and parliament would be responsible for defence, economic policy, European primary and second-ary education and other matters. Important functions, including mines, agriculture and law and order, would remain with the three territories. In theory African rights would be protected by an African Affairs Board, which would review all federal legis-lation, but it was unlikely that more than one of its ten members would be an African.

This conference was followed by a high-powered meeting at Victoria Falls, in September, including both Commonwealth and Colonial secretaries of state. This basically endorsed the officials' scheme, although by then it was obvious that African opinion was hostile. Three Africans from Northern Rhodesia and two from Nyasaland opposed it in the meeting; there were no Africans in the Southern Rhodesian delegation, which included the white minister for native affairs. Two further conferences took place in 1952, and a final one in April 1953; this was boycotted by Africans from Northern Rhodesia and Nyasaland, but, perhaps surprisingly, Jasper Savanhu and Joshua Nkomo were included in the Southern Rhodesian delegation. Nkomo said he would argue for Federation in Southern Rhodesia.

The final deal, when the Rhodesia and Nyasaland Federation Act received the royal assent in July 1953 in the UK, following a favourable referendum in Southern Rhodesia in April, embodied a few changes from the officials' original scheme; law and order, for instance, would stay with the territories. But seventeen out of the thirty-five seats in the legislature were allocated to Southern Rho-desia, and it was hard to imagine that this would have an African majority any time soon. The preamble to the Act suggested that the Federation could expect to join the Commonwealth in due course. While Huggins talked positively of racial partnership in the UK, he told his right-wing supporters at home that it would be like a rider partnering a horse.[25]

If Labour opinion in Britain had largely swung against the Federation, even though Andrew Cohen, the influential permanent secretary at the Colonial Office, had come round to the idea, what was happening in central Africa? In 1948 two key nationalists, Dr Hastings Banda of Nyasaland and Harry Nkumbula from Northern Rhodesia, had written a powerful statement against federation in London. Although Nyasaland had few Africans with a Western education, opposition from traditional leaders was widespread. In 1953, for instance, Chief M'Mbelwa II travelled to London to express the hostility of his nearly 200,000 people of Mzimba.

In Northern Rhodesia, modern nationalism was just getting under way. A Northern Rhodesian African National Congress was formed in 1948, an amalgamation of existing welfare societies, and took wings in the struggle against the Federation. An Anti-Federation Action Committee was set up in Ndola, heart of the Copperbelt, and its white secretary, Simon Zukas, was deported by the colonial authorities in 1952. Congress was led by Harry Nkumbula, a graduate of the London School of Economics. He took over from Godwin Lewanika, and was the dominant figure in African politics in the territory until the late 1950s, when Kenneth Kaunda and Simon Kapwepwe led a radical breakaway. In the course of the decade, as the Federal experiment foundered on its incompatible purposes, African nationalism found expression in opposition to fancy Federal franchises, and a recognition that 'partnership' was a ploy to delay African majority rule.

In Southern Rhodesia, African politics started from a weaker position than in its two northern neighbours. The leaders were less militant, and more willing to play along with the Federation, in hopes that this would lead to creeping Africanisation. The fire-breathing former union leader Jasper Savanhu turned into a docile member of Huggins's United Federal Party, elected MP on white votes. Joshua Nkomo, a former social worker on Rhodesia Railways who became secretary of the African Rhodesian Railways Union, was the key figure in the 1950s. He came to be seen as Ndebele, though sometimes described as a Kalanga, a member of an ethnically Shona group that lived alongside the Ndebele, with which there was mutual assimilation.[26] He became president of the Southern Rhodesian African National Congress when it was resuscitated in 1957 by activists in the City Youth League of Salisbury, who had organised a bus boycott in protest at fare increases. He went on to be president of its successor, the National Democratic Party.

Nkomo liked the good life, and, when the going got tough later and nationalist leaders were arrested, he was sometimes out of the country, arguing that he was building international support. While pushing African arguments on land, and against the social restrictions in cities, he was always a relatively moderate figure. For a while he hoped that the federal experiment would lead to African advance at many levels, and the election of more African MPs.

The heyday of the Federation was brief. It was going downhill as a viable concept from around 1956, when Britain and France failed in the Suez adventure, and especially from 1957, when the independence of the Gold Coast was recognised in the new name of Ghana. As seen by African nationalists in the three territories, there was no reason why they should not have the same freedom to govern themselves enjoyed by Kwame Nkrumah. Indeed a pan-African conference for independence movements, hosted by Nkrumah in Accra in 1958, gave a fillip to nationalists in central and southern Africa.

The economy of the Federation was expanding from 1953 to 1956, and its capital was sited in Salisbury. This was one of many factors which made Africans in Northern Rhodesia and Nyasaland worry that they were being subject to a takeover by reactionary whites to their south. The generating plant for the Kariba hydroelectric dam, the most spectacular industrial investment in the Federation, was set on the Southern Rhodesian shore and did not start producing power until after the unilateral independence of 1965; many thousands of Africans who were displaced, as a long artificial lake was created, were removed to less fertile land without compensation.

One reason for the hesitancy of African politicians in Southern Rhodesia, as against their friends to the north, was that Garfield Todd, prime minister of the territory from 1953 until 1958, seemed to mean what he said when he talked of African empowerment. He made small changes, insisting for instance that those who had been called 'boy' should be known as 'Mr'. He raised African wages. He talked to Joshua Nkomo and to Guy Clutton-Brock, a white idealist who had joined Congress. He made a marginal adjustment to the franchise so that an African with ten years of schooling could register to vote. A former missionary, born in New Zealand, he made speeches which went down well with African audiences. He obviously irritated conservative whites, who thought he had dictatorial tendencies.

But he was not hell-bent on African majority rule, and he took a strong line when African miners at the Wankie colliery went on 'unofficial' strike in 1954; he declared a state of emergency, and called out territorial troops. Yet the conservatives in his own party, the United Rhodesia Party, staged a coup which dismissed him in early 1958. Nathan Shamuyarira, who went on to become a Zanu–PF minister and close associate of Robert Mugabe, wrote in 'Crisis in Rhodesia' in 1965,

The years of hope for peaceful cooperation and swift progress towards racial equality – or better, a non-racial state – were over.... A sad but perhaps treasured compliment was paid to Todd at that time when an African composed a song which became a best selling record.[27]

In the 1950s white Southern Rhodesians had one of the highest standards of living in the world, and their incomes were around ten times those of unskilled or semi-skilled Africans. The white population rose sharply after the Second World War – from 82,000 in 1946 to 135,000 in 1951; white numbers nearly doubled again, from 135,000 to 223,000 between 1951 and 1960. The benign climate, the sense of space, low taxation and the cheapness of labour, especially of domestic servants, were all attractions. In spite of the beauties of the landscape, with its exotic game, and the continuing availability of farmland, most of this migration went to the towns. Here whites could live in the equivalent of London's garden suburbs, in a style that few could have afforded in Europe.

Most of these arrivals were coming from an austerity Britain, which was just recovering from the bombing, loss of life and heartache of the Second World War. For them Southern Rhodesia seemed more 'British' and secure than South Africa, which was now coming under Afrikaner hegemony, with its overt oppression of the black population. Not always politically wise, they could hope that the Federation might be a big state in the making. Some of the British immigrants were also hostile to the post-war Labour government, seeking 'freedom' in the middle of Africa. Others were beguiled by the talk of racial partnership into supposing that their own advantages could coexist with African advancement, without a clash between the two.

But there were complexities in this white influx. Some observers doubted how committed to Southern Rhodesia the new arrivals really were – there was an emigration concealed in the net figures for immigration. Also, the relationship with South Africa was ambiguous. Its economy and institutions were much stronger, and whites north of the Limpopo looked south for shopping, for education and in their attitudes. While spoken English was a requirement for white immigrants it was also the case that, particularly in rural areas, there was a significant population of Afrikaner origin.

In retrospect the Federation was built on a series of illusions, and when they came crashing down the fallout was dramatic. It opened the way to the go-it-alone independence of Southern Rhodesia's white minority government in 1965, and the bush war which followed. Britain's strategy for extracting itself from empire – it also promoted federations in the West Indies and Malaysia – failed on the unwillingness of indigenous nationalities to join shotgun marriages. And in Central Africa the weak link was always Nyasaland, which was poor, with a small white population, and a special relationship with a religiously and politically distinct part of the United Kingdom, Scotland.[28]

Early in 1959 there was a coordinated crackdown on African nationalists in Nyasaland and Southern Rhodesia. By March there was a state of emergency in both territories, with federal troops flown to Blantyre, the Nyasaland capital, and Sir Edgar Whitehead, the new Southern Rhodesian premier, ordering the arrest of 500 Congress members in his country; the Southern Rhodesia African National Congress was proscribed; to complete the picture, Kenneth Kaunda and his colleagues in the Zambian African National Congress in Northern Rhodesia were also arrested.

What was the justification for this? It was alleged, on what turned out to be slender evidence, that there had been a plot by Nyasaland Congress leaders to organise a massacre of whites and 'Uncle Toms'. Dr Hastings Banda and others were arrested and flown to Salisbury; their imprisonment was followed by twelve days of rioting in Nyasaland in which fifty people died. Although the Congress parties in the three territories were not closely coordinated, it would appear that the colonial authorities in Northern Rhodesia, and Whitehead in the south – who had been facing African unrest over previous months – took the opportunity to smack the more radical nationalists everywhere. Whitehead's Preventative Detention Act, which permitted detention without trial, and his Native Affairs Amendment Act, which limited rallies by black nationalists, offset measures to integrate cinemas and end separate black and white queues at post offices and banks.

The row in the United Kingdom was enormous. The Labour and Liberal parties, and the Church of Scotland, demanded an inquiry. The Conservative government appointed a commission under a High Court judge, Lord Devlin; later in the year Harold Macmillan appointed a commission under Sir Walter Monckton to look at the whole future of the Central African Federation, and when he himself visited Salisbury the following year he concluded that the future of the Federation looked desperate. It was on this tour, when he visited West Africa also, that he told the South African parliament that a 'wind of change' was blowing through the continent.

Most African leaders boycotted the Monckton commission. Dr Banda, released from prison and with 250,000 members of his Malawi Congress Party – which was given permission to police his meetings – made it clear that he was not interested in a future for the Federation. Nyasaland, to be called Malawi, wanted to leave.

The events in central Africa could not be separated from what was happening in the rest of the continent, and in London. Iain Macleod, a new Conservative colonial secretary, had concluded that there had to be a drastic speeding up of decolonisation; that was the context for an African tour by the British prime minister,

Harold Macmillan. In 1960 the UK's biggest colony, Nigeria, became independent. So too did Cyprus, which had seen fighting with Greek militants in EOKA, and which had been regarded as too small in population to become an independent state. A Lancaster House conference recommended independence for Kenya, where the British had put down the Mau Mau rebellion, and arrangements were made to buy out white settlers.

Closer to central Africa, and causing alarm to whites in particular, there had been the chaotic independence in the neighbouring Belgian Congo; at Sharpeville, in the Transvaal, 69 Africans were killed and 180 injured when South African security forces put down a protest over pass laws and oppressive apartheid. Blacks and whites drew different conclusions from what seemed a rapidly changing order. In Nyasaland/Zambia and Northern Rhodesia/Zambia, Africans could see little excuse for not having independence at once. In Southern Rhodesia/Rhodesia the whites wanted to bring back from London the reserved powers intended to protect Africans, and were increasingly talking of independence, whether London wanted it or not; this was the cry of the chief opposition party, the Dominion Party.

Along the way the advocates of federation, Sir Roy Welensky, who had taken over from Huggins as prime minister, and Sir Edgar Whitehead, who had pursued some liberal measures as well as a crackdown, came to be utterly overtaken. Nevertheless, Whitehead's Law and Order Maintenance Act, and Emergency Powers Act, both passed in 1960, gave the government and police draconian authority, of a kind most democracies would only justify in wartime. Robert Mugabe, at home after teaching for two years at a secondary school in Ghana, and studying at the Kwame Nkrumah Ideological Institute, made his first political speech. It was in protest at the arrest of leaders of the National Democratic Party, which had been set up to replace the proscribed Southern Rhodesia ANC.

In the middle of 1960, before the Monckton commission reported, Africans obtained a majority of seats in Nyasaland's legislative
council. Dr Banda's Malawi Congress Party won twenty-two out
of the twenty-eight elected MPs in the first elections that followed,
in 1961. Although technically Malawi did not become independent until 1964, it had effectively left the Federation; a rearguard
action by Welensky stalled an African majority in the Northern
Rhodesian legislature until October 1962, when Kenneth Kaunda's United National Independence Party took the lead. Northern
Rhodesia, becoming Zambia, was also on its way out.

In Southern Rhodesia, the fallout from the Monckton commission saw rioting and division among Africans, and a hard-won
victory for Sir Edgar Whitehead in an overwhelmingly white
referendum. The referendum was on a new constitution for the
territory. This involved an increase in the assembly to sixty-five
seats; a complex franchise with A roll and B roll seats; the most
modest increase in African voting;[29] and a declaration of rights
which supposedly protected Africans. In July 1961, Whitehead
won the referendum by a 2:1 majority. The African NDP ran its
own referendum, in which over 372,000 voters – most disenfran-
chised by the new constitution – voted against it.

The contrast between what was happening in the three
territories caused an upsurge in militancy among Africans in
Southern Rhodesia. An NDP congress in Bulawayo agreed to
boycott the next elections, although the Federals were running a
public relations campaign, called 'Build a Nation', to try to get
Africans to register. The NDP was significantly more radical, and
more pan-African, than its predecessor, the Southern Rhodesia
ANC. It wanted one-man, one-vote and talked of violence to
disrupt the settler economy. Violence and arson, in the towns
and the countryside, broke out. As many as 30,000 demonstrators
gathered in Harare township, on the edge of white Salisbury,
and were roughed up by police and armed soldiers; in Bulawayo

the security forces established a 6-mile cordon between the city and the African townships. By the end of several days of rioting and police brutality, twelve Africans had been killed and several hundred injured.[30]

Whitehead banned the NDP on 9 December 1962 – ironically the date of Tanganyika's independence. Nkomo claimed that the NDP had a paid-up membership of 250,000, and it reformed ten days later as the Zimbabwe African Peoples Union, with Joshua Nkomo again the president, and Ndabiningi Sithole as chairman. Robert Mugabe was the publicity and information secretary. Out of the country, Nkomo had managed to get the UN General Assembly to pass a resolution requiring a new constitution for Southern Rhodesia. When he returned, his arrival triggered a new wave of militancy, and in September ZAPU also was banned, and its leaders restricted in their movements.

Africans boycotted the Southern Rhodesian election in December 1962, which was unexpectedly won by a new party formed that year – the Rhodesian Front. Whitehead was not a charismatic character. He was a bachelor, and partly deaf. He had become suspect to the largely white electorate as someone who seemed too keen on African advancement, and who was prepared to repeal the Land Apportionment Act.[31] Violence in the townships worried the whites. The key Rhodesian Front leaders were farmers. Winston Field, a farmer who had been part of the conservative Dominion Party opposed to Whitehead, became prime minister. His deputy was Ian Smith, the one-time RAF airman who had spent five months fighting alongside communist partisans behind enemy lines after being shot down in Italy; he was also a farmer. D.C. 'Boss' Lilford, the wealthiest of these farmers, had helped to set up the new party, which was supported on a grassroots basis by many lower-middle-class and artisan whites who felt threatened by Africans. The main aim of the Rhodesian Front was to achieve independence for a white-ruled territory.[32]

In March 1963 the British government accepted the inevitable: the Federation would dissolve. Welensky was so bitter that he refused to sit down at meals with British ministers. A meeting to discuss the division of federal assets took place at the Victoria Falls Hotel, on the Rhodesian side of the Zambesi, at the end of June. Winston Field threatened to boycott the meeting unless the United Kingdom accepted independence for his country on the basis of the Whitehead constitution. In London, in the Conservative cabinet, there were some who would have permitted this; Field and Smith believed that R.A. Butler, the minister put in charge of central African affairs by Macmillan, had made a verbal promise to this effect, but there is no documentary evidence.

There was therefore a stand-off between London and the white Rhodesians from 1963 on; whereas Malawi (Nyasaland) and Zambia (Northern Rhodesia) both became independent in July 1964, the allegedly 'civilised' Europeans in Rhodesia were stuck in a continuing colonial status. Although the Macmillan government was dying, to be replaced when Sir Alec Douglas-Home became prime minister in October 1963, it was unlikely that any British government could move far from the position set out by Macmillan in his diary on 28 March 1963:

> Southern Rhodesia demands (with a certain show of reason) that if the Federation is to break up S Rhodesia must also be independent and Welensky will support this claim. Actually HMG have no *physical* power to take any part in the affair. But we have a *legal* position and some *moral* influence. S. Rhodesia is a Government of several million Africans ruled by 200,000 whites. Are we to give this country with this constitution and now under Field formal independence...?[33]

Macmillan was aware that the UK would run into serious international opprobrium if it granted independence on this basis; on the other hand he worried about forcing Southern Rhodesia into the hands of apartheid South Africa. When Winston Field came to see Douglas-Home in February of the following year he got no real comfort either from him or from Harold Wilson, leader of the Labour opposition, which had a real chance of defeating the Conservatives in the election that had to be called in 1964. Douglas-Home was concerned about the response of the Commonwealth, whose anti-racist attitudes had led South Africa to withdraw in 1961. But Field's failure led to a coup against him in the Rhodesian Front cabinet. In April 1964 he was ejected, to be replaced as Rhodesian prime minister by Ian Smith, who was committed to independence – whether or not the British or international community approved.

Hence in 1964 the situation involved a kind of checkmate. African opinion in the territory would be satisfied by nothing less than majority rule, as was being achieved in Malawi and Zambia, and demanded action by Britain. White Rhodesians wanted independence, or at least dominion status of the kind that South Africans had had. And the British, with legal responsibility but minimal actual power, really did not know what to do, apart from expressing aspirations for unimpeded progress to majority rule, which they were unable to enforce.

The struggle between the Rhodesian Front and African nationalists continued, with the Whitehead ban on ZAPU maintained when Field became prime minister. Initially some restrictions were eased. Nkomo had taken his executive into exile in Tanzania and it was there that a group of four – Robert Mugabe, Ndabaningi Sithole, Leopold Takawira and Moton Malianga – tried to overthrow him. Nkomo had been talking of setting up a government in exile. President Nyerere and leaders of newly independent states felt strongly, like these four, that the nationalists should be doing more inside Rhodesia to build resistance.

Nkomo denounced the plot against him and, after he had returned to Salisbury, suspended the plotters at a press conference. The rest of the executive met in Dar es Salaam the next day, and voted by four votes to three to depose Nkomo. After two failed attempts at mediation the group of four then founded a rival movement, the Zimbabwe African National Union, in August. This was an elite manoeuvre, carried out above the heads of the ZAPU membership. But it was a definitive split in the nationalist ranks, with crippling consequences over the next two decades.[34]

The political differences were not profound, although ZAPU came to lean towards Moscow, and ZANU towards Beijing, in their interpretations of socialism. However, there were strong underlying clashes of personality, and ZANU was led by people of Shona origin, while Nkomo was defined alongside the Ndebele. ZANU wanted a policy of 'confrontation' against the Rhodesian Front. There was violence, intimidation, petrol-bombing and murder in the locations, as the two groups fought for the allegiance of urban Africans.[35] Nkomo, still popular but accused of a being a 'sell-out', had little of the martyr spirit about him. Nkomo also accused the ZANU group of being 'stooges' who had 'sold the country to the Americans'.[36] The African trade-union movement split. In August 1964 Ian Smith banned both ZAPU and ZANU, and detained as many leaders as his police could catch. Teachers, of whom Mugabe had been one, were prohibited from political activity.

A new development in the United Kingdom, in October 1964, gave hope to the nationalists and anxiety and irritation to the white electorate. Harold Wilson's Labour Party was returned to power, with a tiny House of Commons majority of four. Although Wilson himself had shown little interest in Africa hitherto, he was a supporter of the Commonwealth, hostile to racism, and his party was overwhelmingly opposed to granting independence to a white minority regime.

Smith had been pushing the Douglas-Home government to accept the 1961 constitution as the basis for an acceptable independence, so long as he could demonstrate African support for it. But his proposal for an *indaba* of chiefs did not impress Douglas-Home and when Labour's new Commonwealth secretary suggested visiting Salisbury in October 1964, after attending the celebrations of Zambia's independence, he wanted to meet Nkomo and Sithole. Both were in jail. When Smith refused to let them out to see him, he did not go to Rhodesia. This prompted Wilson to issue a tough warning about the risks the Rhodesia Front would run with a unilateral declaration of independence (UDI).

The scene was set for UDI, and civil war. The contradictions in the Central African Federation had produced a combustible atmosphere. It had radicalised Africans. It had initially increased the confidence of whites, as Salisbury became the capital of a proto-dominion and investment poured in; then their illusions of partnership were exposed, and their fears of African violence – whether in the Congo or their own townships – appeared real. In the break-up of the Federation, what had been Southern Rhodesia hung on to the federal military forces and equipment, the Kariba generating plant, and a relatively high standard of living for whites. But it was all more fragile than it appeared.

Could the Federation ever have 'worked' – in the sense of providing a direct path to an African majority government in Central Africa? In retrospect, given the position of advanced African opinion in Nyasaland and Northern Rhodesia, it was always unlikely. It would also have required an abandonment of perceived self-interest by Southern Rhodesian whites in the early 1950s, for which they were simply unprepared.

The degree of turnabout in white opinion was illustrated at a by-election in Arundel, in a wealthy white Salisbury suburb, in September 1964. It was won by a 2:1 majority by Clifford Dupont, for the Rhodesian Front, over Sir Roy Welensky, now standing for the Rhodesian Party, which argued for a negotiated independence. Sir Roy was subjected to anti-Semitic abuse, and was so heckled at the count that he was unable to speak. Rhodesian Front supporters drowned his voice, singing:

Good-bye, Sir Roy.
Good-bye, Sir Roy.
We'll see you in our dreams...
Good-bye, Sir Roy.[37]

FROM UDI TO LANCASTER HOUSE

The process leading up to the unilateral declaration of independence (UDI), by white Rhodesia in 1965, was convoluted. The Rhodesian Front government had made it plain to its electorate that it wanted independence on the basis of the 1961 constitution. But it also prevaricated, talking of a 'negotiated' independence, in the knowledge that many were reluctant to break the British connection, and anxious as to how easy it would be to survive in a state that would be an international pariah. It was unwilling to test African opinion in an open way, and instead set up an *indaba* of 622 chiefs and headmen in October 1964. Many were placemen, on government stipends. This group approved of independence on the 1961 basis, as did a white referendum the following month, where the Rhodesian Front slogan was significantly cautious – 'Yes means Unity, not UDI'.

The British Labour government was not keen to push the Rhodesians into UDI. At the same time it could not condone handing over an African majority to a white regime which had already departed from democratic norms and locked up nationalist leaders. It was more sensitive than the Conservatives to anti-colonial and Commonwealth opinion. It was suspicious of

Ian Smith, who was seen in London as slippery and duplicitous – exactly the image that Smith had of Harold Wilson, the Labour prime minister, and promoted in Salisbury.[1] Wilson and his colleagues were alarmed when Smith fired the Rhodesian chief of staff, Major General Anderson, who had made it clear that he was opposed to UDI.

Wilson had heard reports from Salisbury that Smith intended to declare UDI on 27 October 1964, and issued a sharp warning at 8 a.m. Rhodesia time that morning. It is unlikely that Smith was quite ready, and over the following twelve months a variety of constitutional schemes were discussed, with both sides realising that breakdown was very near. There was talk of altering the 1961 constitution and the franchise, and talk of a new Royal Commission. Smith visited London to attend the funeral of Sir Winston Churchill in January 1965 and, in a last-ditch attempt to see if agreement could be reached, Wilson himself visited Salisbury that October, insisting that Joshua Nkomo and Ndabaningi Sithole be brought from detention so that he could meet them.[2] In early elections in May 1965, when Smith still denied that he wanted UDI, he had destroyed any vestige of white opposition in the A roll electorate. The following month, at a Commonwealth conference in London, Wilson staved off calls for immediate British military intervention to promote majority rule.

The bottom line for Wilson was African consent and, in the final abortive negotiation, he had suggested that a Royal Commission could test African opinion. He also saw no reason why the Rhodesian Front could not continue with its 1961 constitution, without moving to independence. But this was contrary to the ideology of the Rhodesian Front, and seen as demeaning. Yet Smith and his colleagues had a justified fear that, in an open canvass of African opinion where nationalist leaders were free to argue their case, Africans would reject their scheme. On 11 November 1965, in a weird allusion to the Armistice timing at the end of the

First World War, and in a document with archaic language, the Rhodesian cabinet declared the country's unilateral independence, UDI. Tanzania broke off diplomatic relations with Britain, for failing to crush the rebels, and the Queen's governor general, Sir Humphrey Gibbs, was left in a constitutional limbo.

Why was it that Wilson, like the Conservative cabinet before him, so publicly ruled out military intervention against the rebels? Was it a matter of an unwillingness to move against white 'kith and kin' – awareness of the racist card that Smith himself was playing? In fact Michael Ramsay, Archbishop of Canterbury, had sent an unusual message to Wilson in Salisbury, on behalf of the British Council of Churches, which said that 'a great body of Christian opinion would support you' if Britain had to use force.[3] *The Round Table*, the London-based journal of Commonwealth commentary, argued that Britain should be willing to impose direct rule for a generation.[4] Some observers[5] felt that the threat or use of force would not have been challenged by the British military, and could have dispelled the bluster in Salisbury; Kenneth Kaunda, by now in charge in Zambia, would have provided logistical support and there were British air force planes to hand.[6] But with an infinitesimal majority in the House of Commons it would only have needed three pro-Rhodesian members of the Labour Party to have brought down the government.

London had, in the post-war period, been quite prepared to use force when its colonies displeased the British government. The classic case was in British Guiana (now Guyana), where in 1953 the UK had sent a cruiser, two frigates and 700 troops to suspend the constitution and overthrow the Marxist government of Cheddi Jagan. The issue had arisen again there in the 1960s, where the British colluded with a covert anti-Jagan programme of the United States, now worried by the threat of 'Castro-communism'. This succeeded in getting rid of Jagan in 1964 after a delay to independence and the switch to a system of proportional representation. As in central Africa there were underlying issues of race.

UDI brought to a head the question of who was going to rule Rhodesia, whites or blacks, and, more surreptitiously, which African party would in due course come to power. The next fourteen years, in the period between UDI and the Lancaster House settlement, saw almost constant manoeuvring. To make sense of this period, which saw a gradual build-up in a civil war in the bush, and the crucial collapse of the Portuguese empire in 1974–75, it is necessary to look in turn at the African nationalists, the Smith regime, the regional neighbours and the British government; yet the interplay between each of these parties was continuous.

The immediate effect of UDI was more rhetorical than real. Britain cut off trade and finance and UN sanctions were declared,[7] yet the Rhodesian Front was able to import and export through South Africa and Portuguese East Africa; companies were able to launder Rhodesian tobacco onto world markets. False certificates of origin were used for Rhodesian exports; Britain's trade rivals, including the United States, France and Germany, were not squeamish about taking her place in the Rhodesian market.

An oil embargo, which was one of the reasons why an over-confident Wilson thought the regime would collapse in weeks, failed because fuel was transported by road through South Africa. Britain's Beira patrol, a naval force to prevent oil being piped into Rhodesia from that port, was therefore redundant. An angry Nigeria nationalised BP, accused of colluding in sanctions-busting, and Wilson was forced to defend Britain's ineffectiveness at the first Commonwealth summit to be held outside the UK, in Lagos. Symbolic of the gesture-making by the British was Radio Francistown, a propaganda exercise, broadcasting from Botswana.[8] Newly independent Zambia and Malawi, dependent on communications through Rhodesia, were in no position to impose instant sanctions, and Zambia's vital copper industry needed coal from Wankie and hydroelectricity from Kariba.

The Rhodesian nationalists, severely repressed and with their leaders in prison, took a while to adjust to the gravity of the situation. Whereas only a few years earlier they had hoped that power would fall into their hands, as it had in Northern Rhodesia and Nyasaland, they were now faced with a grinding struggle against resolute enemies. They were divided, quarrelsome, violent, and sought to pursue both diplomatic and military strategies.

In the 1960s, ZAPU trainees went to the Soviet Union for military preparation, and potential commanders in the ZANU army went to China; Josiah Tongogara, who became the best-known ZANU military leader, went to China in 1966; as a child he had grown up on a farm owned by Ian Smith's parents. Although some then in the Rhodesian forces acknowledged 'a few hairy moments' in the late 1960s, it was not until the 1970s that the guerrilla war really got under way. But in April 1966 a group from ZANU's Zimbabwe African National Liberation Army (ZANLA) was involved in a battle in Sinoia – leading to 28 April being marked as Chimurenga Day. A combined force of Zimbabwe People's Revolutionary Army, ZIPRA (ZAPU) and ANC guerrillas was destroyed in Wankie, soon after UDI, and led to the temporary break-up of ZIPRA in 1967.[9] A more serious and successful attack by a group from ZANLA took place on Altena Farm, in northern Rhodesia, in December 1972.[10]

The period of burgeoning war, with a certain fluidity of personnel between ZIPRA and ZANLA, and an armed struggle developing which was independent of the imprisoned political leaders, had lasting consequences. In the divided world of communism, ZAPU and ZIPRA were patronised by the Soviet Union, which was also supporting the ANC in South Africa. ZANU and ZANLA were leaning towards the Chinese. ZIPRA was being trained for a conventional war. ZANLA, following Maoist principles, was preparing for a peasant-oriented guerrilla war. Both organisations were largely based in Zambia until 1975, when the Mozambican liberation movement, FRELIMO, took power in Mozambique and ZANLA shifted its base there. Smith's agents stirred up suspicion within and between the guerrillas.

To begin with, ZAPU and ZIPRA were seen as the stronger parties. But as time went on it became clear that ZANLA was doing more of the fighting inside Rhodesia. This was partly a matter of geography, as the Zambesi river was a barrier to ZIPRA, trained for conventional war, whereas ZANLA was raising consciousness in peasant villages on the north-east and eastern side of Rhodesia, populated by Shona. Even before Mozambican independence there was cooperation between FRELIMO, an experienced guerrilla force fighting the Portuguese, and ZANLA. Further, while Ndebele were still represented in ZANLA and Shona in ZIPRA, a closer identification grew between ZANU/ZANLA and the Shona communities, and ZAPU/ZIPRA and the Ndebele. Given the preponderance of Shona in the total population – there were roughly four Shona to every Ndebele, although some groups lay outside this classification – this evolution was significant for the long-term outcome between the rivals.

The friends of the nationalists, Zambia's Kenneth Kaunda and Tanzania's Julius Nyerere, recognised that their divisions were disastrous, and urged them to unite.

Zambia in particular was suffering from Rhodesian reprisals. The end of the 1960s and beginning of the 1970s saw a series of British negotiations with Smith, starting with HMS *Tiger* in 1966 and HMS *Fearless* in 1968, which involved complex electoral arrangements which were designed to produce an African majority, but not in any hurry. The choice of warships with impressive names for this diplomacy reflected public relations and security concerns. ZAPU and ZANU had no direct role in these talks.

Instead the arguments of the nationalists were presented via the Commonwealth, which got Wilson to commit to NIBMAR – No Independence Before Majority African Rule. Smith rejected the British proposals at these shipboard meetings.

But in 1970, unexpectedly, the Conservatives under Edward Heath won a British election. It was clear that his party – which had opposed UN sanctions against Rhodesia – was much more friendly towards Smith. Furthermore it was committed to resuming arms exports to the apartheid regime in South Africa, which led Heath into a major battle with other Commonwealth leaders at their 1971 summit in Singapore. The Rhodesian Front, not yet severely inconvenienced by the bush war, had an unprecedented chance to do a deal with the former colonial power. In November 1971 Sir Alec Douglas-Home, as foreign and Commonwealth secretary, signed a provisional agreement with Ian Smith.

This agreement, with more fancy franchises and no broad-based interim government or appeals to the Privy Council, was much better for Smith than anything on offer from Harold Wilson. Arguably it just met the five principles that had been laid down since 1964: unimpeded progress to majority rule; guarantees against retrogressive amendment of the constitution; an immediate improvement in the political status of the African population; progress towards ending racial discrimination; and a test of acceptability by the Rhodesian population as a whole. But it certainly did not provide for No Independence Before Majority African Rule, and was instantly criticised by African and Asian governments in the Commonwealth, and by the Labour opposition and others in Britain.

The sequel demonstrated the almost total rejection of this agreement, and of the Rhodesian Front government, by the African population. A team under Lord Pearce, a British law lord, spent two months travelling around Rhodesia in early 1972, testing the acceptability of the deal. With other leaders in prison, public opposition was coordinated by Bishop Abel Muzorewa, a mild Methodist. The team concluded that the majority of Africans rejected the agreement because they mistrusted the government: they resented the humiliations of the past, and the limitations of government policy on land, education and black advancement. Indeed, since UDI, several members of the Front had denounced multiracialism. The death of the 1971 agreement knocked out the British for the time being as interlocutors for change in Rhodesia, and swung attention back to the regional dimension, and military prospects.

Awareness of the unpopularity of the white government led to gradually increased support for the guerrillas, and a spread in the war; though still relatively small, the number of Rhodesian security forces and guerrillas killed doubled between 1973 and 1974.[11] Guerrilla deaths rose from 179 to 345, and Rhodesian deaths from 44 to 96. But these numbers hurt the Rhodesians more. They began to recruit mercenaries to make up for the shortage of white troops, called up in regular rotation. Infighting among the guerrilla armies, increasingly confident that they would win in the longer term, grew more intense.

In late 1974 President Vorster of South Africa, President Kaunda of Zambia and Dr Kissinger, President Nixon's secretary of state, began to work together in an attempt to head off the war. The period was known as detente, and its high point was a Lusaka Accord in December 1974. Vorster, Kaunda and Kissinger feared that, with three wars running simultaneously in Angola, Rhodesia and Mozambique, it was probable that three Marxist, pro-communist governments would come to power through the barrel of a gun. The military coup in Portugal in April 1974 had shown that the Portuguese were no longer willing to fight for their colonies. The United States was looking at the region from a Cold War viewpoint. The South African government was principally concerned with the survival of apartheid, wanted to stop ANC attacks at home, and the SWAPO war in Namibia, and could live with a friendly black-run government to its north. President Kaunda, a Christian humanist who preferred negotiation to war, was unsympathetic to revolutionaries.

Smith was unwilling to give much ground. Delays to supplies bound for Rhodesia via South African railways were one of the pressures used against him, and in 1974 he released imprisoned African leaders, including Ndabaningi Sithole, Robert Mugabe and Joshua Nkomo. This exacerbated personality and other disputes at a time when the Frontline States, the independent African states close to Rhodesia, were crying out for nationalist unity. ZAPU had had an internal conflict in 1971, which led to a short-lived FROLIZI group, the Front for the Liberation of Zimbabwe, which included Nathan Shamuyarira, a one-time correspondent for the *Manchester Guardian*, who became a minister and apologist for ZANU after 1980.

There was a serious leadership struggle going on within ZANU, not fully resolved until 1977. In 1974 and 1975, Nkomo and Abel Muzorewa, the better-known leaders, were competing for African support. Bishop Muzorewa, free to organise, had been given status as a black spokesman by both parties during the Pearce test of opinion. The Lusaka Accord detente talks in November–December 1974 led the Frontline States to give recognition to the Bishop and his United African National Council, and to withdraw support from ZANU and ZAPU.[12] Strong pressure was put on these two, with their armies, to agree to a ceasefire, which they did not.

It was the struggle within ZANU that was of lasting importance to Zimbabwe. Essentially the fight was between three elements: the leaders who had been imprisoned for eleven years; the external political leadership under Herbert Chitepo, the popular party chairman; and the ZANLA army, led by the charismatic but poorly educated Josiah Tongogara.

Six of the ZANU central committee, including Mugabe and Ndabaningi Sithole, nicknamed 'Rubber dinghy' by his Rhodesian warders, had been kept in prison in Gweru (then Gwelo). At a certain point they decided to vote on the leadership and Sithole was ousted as ZANU president in favour of Mugabe, by three votes to one, with Sithole and Mugabe not participating. There were several reasons why the cooler, younger and more intelligent Mugabe was preferred. Mugabe, as secretary general of the party, was second in line of succession. Sithole had been prepared to renounce violence, was destabilised by his years in prison, and was the victim of stool pigeons. Mugabe was much more sympathetic to the military route to power, and less willing to compromise with other nationalists. He had become seriously embittered.

Mugabe, with other political prisoners, was locked up for twenty-three hours a day. He himself studied for degrees and, still a professional teacher, encouraged others to follow lessons at whatever level was appropriate. He maintained a spirit of optimism and positivity. But his own attitudes were coloured by an immense personal tragedy. In late 1966, when he was in the Salisbury remand prison, he was told that his 3-year-old son Nhamo had died suddenly in Ghana, where he was staying with his in-laws and his wife, Sally. He had hardly seen his son, and was not allowed out on compassionate grounds to mourn.[13] His sister Sabina broke the news to him, and he was inconsolable.[14] Nhamo was short for Nhamodzenyika, or 'suffering country' in Shona.[15]

Sally Mugabe had herself spent six weeks in a Salisbury prison earlier, after being given a five-year suspended sentence for sedition, and after Nhamo's death she moved from Ghana to London, where she worked as a secretary at the Africa Centre. There she campaigned for her husband's release. In 1970 she was threatened with deportation. Mugabe, from prison, appealed to

James Callaghan, as home secretary and then to Harold Wilson, as prime minister, to let her stay. There was a dispute between the Home Office, which wanted to deport her, and the Foreign Office, which thought it would be politic for her to remain. In the end, after a high-profile media campaign on her behalf, the new Conservative government which took office in 1970 permitted her to remain. The experience did not endear the British government to Mugabe, still much in love with Sally and aware that she had been hit hard by Nhamo's death.

Yet the rise of Mugabe came through a coup, not a constitutional change voted on by all ZANU members. Kaunda, Nyerere and Machel did not recognise Mugabe, and insisted that Sithole should continue to lead the ZANU delegation in the Lusaka talks. They ordered that he, and Moton Malianga, who had come from Rhodesia with him, should be returned to Que Que prison and that Sithole should come instead. It took two years before Mugabe succeeded in getting acceptance, both within ZANU, ZANLA and from the regional players. During this time he acquired a special animus against Kaunda. There was also an undemocratic legacy of top-down authority within ZANU, from an event which was only explicable in the complex, treacherous conditions of the time.

In Zambia, where Kaunda was putting the squeeze on the guerrillas in the interest of a negotiated peace, there were violent clashes within ZANLA. These had ideological and educational as well as purely personality aspects. The ZANLA army, with bases in Zambia and Tanzania and Maoist inspiration, included peasants who had been abducted from their villages to join the struggle, young idealists who had run away from the University of Rhodesia, and a handful of spies and turncoats. There were Marxist revolutionaries, and those who just wanted to get their land back from the whites. There were convinced secularists, and those who worshipped with traditional Shona spirit mediums.

There was a gender dimension, with some men abusing women and keeping them in traditional roles.

Chains of command within ZANU were further disrupted when a car bomb killed the respected Herbert Chitepo, party chairman and leader of the exiled wing, when so many were locked up in Rhodesia. He was assassinated in Zambia in March 1975. It is now fairly certain that he was murdered by Ian Smith's Central Intelligence Organisation, whose sabotage operations were designed to stir up conflict and suspicion between the nationalists.[16] At the time it was not unreasonably thought that he was the victim either of vicious internal ZANLA feuding, or of a plot by Zambia, which wanted to push its strategy of detente. Kaunda set up an inquiry by a doubtfully independent international commission, and cracked down harder on ZANU.

The assassination followed close on the heels of a rebellion within ZANLA, organised by Dakarai Badza, formerly the field commander in north-eastern Rhodesia, and a political commissar, Thomas Nhari, who had once been in ZIPRA. Both had been demoted to the ranks in around October 1974 for insubordination. Although their mutiny has been described as ideologically driven, with the backing of young Marxists, they had also had contacts with Rhodesian intelligence and their uprising was timed to weaken ZANU's hand in the detente talks.[17] They criticised corruption and mismanagement in the high command, led by Tongogara.

This was a brutal episode. The rebels kidnapped a number of senior commanders, as well as Tongogara's wife and small children. They executed around seventy fighters who refused to join them, and captured Chifombo, a ZANLA transit camp in eastern Zambia. However, drawing on troops from Tanzania, Tongogara skilfully recaptured the camp and a trial was held there, presided over by Herbert Chitepo. Most of the rebels were to be demoted, but Tongogara and the high command summarily executed many, including persons not directly involved in the mutiny. It appeared as if the ZANLA high command was not under the control of the party leadership. A belief that Chitepo was too lenient, and could even have sympathised with the rebels, was one reason why some thought that Tongogara was implicated in his assassination.

The issue of justice and human rights inside liberation armies, and in their treatment of prisoners, arose throughout southern Africa during the struggle against racism. In general the liberation committee of the Organisation of African Unity took the view that the camps and practices of liberation movements were their own affair, and not usually the concern of the governments on whose territory they operated. Exceptionally, the African National Congress of South Africa agreed human rights guarantees for prisoners of its armed wing, Umkhonto we Sizwe, and controversially enabled the Truth and Reconciliation Commission set up after 1994 to investigate allegations against the ANC.[18]

The sequel to Chitepo's assassination was drastic. The Zambians arrested all the ZANU and ZANLA people who came to his funeral, and a thousand trained guerrillas were detained at a place called Mboroma. A number of ZANLA prisoners were beaten up and Tongogara was put on trial. Zambian troops shot ZANLA fighters; ZANLA and ZIPRA fighters shot at each other; only a handful of guerrillas were left inside Rhodesia, almost unsupported; and, but for crass security tactics by the Rhodesians which turned rural Africans against them, detente would have triumphed. The period of 1974–75 was perhaps the lowest point of the armed struggle.[19] The OAU had withdrawn recognition from ZANU and ZAPU in January 1975. In Mozambique – where FRELIMO was taking over in 1974, but independence was not recognised until the following year – FRELIMO's Samora Machel joined Kaunda in anaesthetising ZANLA. Tongogara had been put on trial in Zambia, accused of Chitepo's murder, and other military leaders were imprisoned.

However, the efforts of the Frontline States to achieve unity among the nationalists, and the efforts of Kissinger and Vorster to get Smith to share power, were equally unavailing. The Frontline States were a loose alliance between the governments of Tanzania, Zambia and Botswana and FRELIMO in Mozambique, which wanted a black majority government in Rhodesia, and an end to the war. But they could not get ZANU, ZAPU, FROLIZI and Muzorewa's African National Council to agree. Ian Smith decided that Joshua Nkomo was the leader most likely to enable whites to continue pulling the strings, and he continued to negotiate with him secretly after a failed Victoria Falls conference in August 1975. The conference had failed because Smith refused to accept racial parity in the government straightaway, or majority rule in five years – which of course is what actually happened.[20]

In 1975–76 there was an attempt by guerrillas from both ZIPRA and ZANLA to create a joint army called the Zimbabwe People's Army, ZIPA. This had some encouragement from the Tanzanian and Mozambican governments; it had a strongly Marxist flavour; it represented a critique by younger, better-educated fighters of their political and military leaders; it was hostile to detente, as the detente phase seemed to be going nowhere, while involving a selling out by people like Nkomo and Sithole; and it broke up partly on ZAPU–ZANU frictions. The ZIPA period overlapped with the *Vashandi* (workers') movement within ZANLA, which shared these attitudes, and which was treated as a rebellion by Tongogara and Mugabe.[21] Activists at ZANLA's Mgagao camp in Tanzania had issued a declaration in November 1975 which defined the liberation struggle as a revolutionary war, and rejected Sithole as ZANU's leader. Implicitly the Mgagao declaration recognised Mugabe, describing him as 'outstanding.' *Vashandi* leaders were to be detained by Machel in Mozambique after ZIPA collapsed.

However, the detente era had one striking result. Robert Mugabe was released from prison in Rhodesia in 1975, and escaped into

Mozambique near Troutbeck Inn with Edgar Tekere, assisted by Chief Tangwena. This was not simple, because he took three months to cross the border, and it has been alleged that this was because Samora Machel did not particularly want him.[22] These high-value ZANU figures were then taken to camps in Manica for 'clearance'. Certainly Machel was wary and critical of the Rhodesian nationalists, with their endless infighting, and, although sympathetic to ZANU, was initially supportive of the policy of detente. He was also uncertain of Mugabe's status. Around the end of 1975 Mugabe and Tekere were 'restricted' by Machel to a hotel in Quelimane, although they were able to communicate with ZANU colleagues. The Mgagao declaration, subsequently confirmed by a ZANU committee meeting in Mozambique, cleared the way for recognition of Mugabe's leadership.

Ironically it was a BBC broadcast in January 1976, when Mugabe was allowed to leave Mozambique for a visit to London, that commended him to the ZANLA fighters in the camps, and in detention in Zambia. In the interview he declared his dissatisfaction with the 'unity' African National Council imposed on the rival Zimbabwean movements by detente. He said that the freedom fighters were ready for action, and that in reality ZANU dominated the ANC. Three of the ZANLA leaders in detention – Tongogara, Kangai and Gumbo – wrote from their imprisonment in Mpima to congratulate him and offer support.[23]

But it was the Geneva conference, chaired by Ivor Richard on behalf of the United Kingdom, which allowed Mugabe actually to meet other key players – both political and military – in his party, ZANLA and more widely. This effort was promoted by Henry Kissinger, in a final effort at peacemaking before he was removed from office as US secretary of state, following the election of Jimmy Carter as president. Working with the South Africans, the British and the key African governments, Kissinger persuaded Ian Smith and the different nationalist movements to meet in Geneva at the end of 1976 in another attempt at a negotiated solution.

The conference failed, but it marked a turning point. It demonstrated the leadership skills of Mugabe, who succeeded in weaving together the warring elements within ZANU and ZANLA. He did so partly by seeming democratic and neutral, listening to the fighters and external leaders without being in the pocket of anyone. He was uncompromising in pursuing the interests of ZANU, and opposed to any suggestion of a merger with Zimbabwean rivals. However, as a result of the arguments for unity from the Frontline States and the fighters of ZIPA, he was to agree to a loose alliance – the 'Patriotic Front' – with ZAPU.

The conference also marked the beginning of the end for the Smith regime. With full Mozambican independence, Samora Machel had implemented UN sanctions, confiscated Rhodesian assets, including a large amount of railway rolling stock, and opened a border of 764 miles to guerrilla incursions. Rhodesia had become far more dependent on South Africa, and South Africa was losing interest.

While ZANLA was becoming more optimistic about a military victory, white Rhodesia was beginning to lose heart. More white males were going south, to avoid the frequent call-ups for military service; whereas there had been net white immigration in the 1960s, more families were starting to leave in the mid-1970s, and there was net emigration; Rhodesian security services were increasingly dependent on mercenaries, although it was not until 1978 that there was an attempt to conscript blacks. Looking back in his autobiography over thirty years later at the situation in early 1977, Ian Smith wrote, 'Regrettably, there were signs that our white community, for the first time, was beginning to have doubts about our future.' He blamed the changing, more negative attitude among white South Africans.[24] Behind the scenes, Vorster was pressing Smith to come to terms with some of the nationalists.

The Geneva talks also brought the British, now with a Labour government since 1974, back into the picture. The UK was an ally of the USA, had strong commercial interests in southern Africa where 140,000 Rhodesians also retained British passports, and was constantly harried by other Commonwealth members to do more to achieve majority rule. Shridath Ramphal, the Guyanese who became Commonwealth secretary general in 1975, was emphatic that he wanted to end racism in southern Africa on his watch. Legal independence, for a state which had been a British colony, would have to involve the UK. Significantly, Geneva also saw the USA and Western nations dangle a possible US$2 billion development fund before Smith and the nationalist leaders, as a lure to get them to agree. This was the financial inducement which lurked like a will-o'-the-wisp around the 1979 Lancaster House talks and led to ZANU cries of betrayal into the twenty-first century.

The Geneva conference was rapidly followed, after the change of administration in the USA which brought Jimmy Carter to the presidency, by another Anglo-American initiative involving Cyrus Vance, US secretary of state, and Dr David Owen, UK foreign and Commonwealth secretary. In March of 1977 they developed a scheme which included a United Nations peacekeeping force for Zimbabwe, and a Zimbabwe Development Fund worth US$1–1.5 billion, to which the British would contribute 15 per cent, up to a maximum of £75 million.

These proposals also failed, but contained an important commitment to finance black empowerment. Though hedged around with the language of the British civil service, the drift was clear.

> The Fund could also provide support for, and take into account the balance of payments implications of, programmes designed to encourage skilled labour and managerial personnel to contribute to Zimbabwe's development and to effect a smooth transition to a more balanced pattern of access to ownership of farms, houses and businesses.[25]

How was it that white Rhodesians, with a population of fewer than 200,000, managed to hold on so long? Their leaders' talk of defending Christian civilisation on the Zambesi from communists was not a mantra that could easily convince their own supporters.[26] White Rhodesia was not a particularly Christian or devout community, and among its opponents there were many who had been educated at Christian missions. What the Smith regime was fighting for, with a bloody-minded determination which became increasingly ruthless as the war went on, was a pleasant white lifestyle supported by cheap labour, and a number of illusions about the modern world.

This was a rather provincial society, in an era before global television and the Internet, where many attitudes were mediated through the bigger white communities of apartheid South Africa. It was also driven by fear. The implosion of the Congo, when the Belgians withdrew in 1960, coloured the run-up to UDI; the Nigerian civil war, from 1967 to 1970, provided a frightening scenario of ethnic bloodshed; the victory of FRELIMO, in adjoining Mozambique, had seen the overwhelming majority of white Portuguese settlers simply run away; the mid-1970s witnessed the bloody despotism of Idi Amin in Uganda.

The regime demonised the guerrillas as 'terrorists', or 'terrs', and indeed some of their actions against peasants as well as white farmers were as much to do with spreading fear as attacking military targets. The regime was operating a police state, with censorship, many informers, and a policy of divide and rule among an African population which was more than 90 per cent of the total. African trade unions were stamped on, with sixty-eight leaders in detention by 1973.

Initially Smith's government was quite successful in its economic policy, with a process of import-substitution for manufactured goods, and reduced dependence on agriculture and tobacco exports. Manufacturing output rose by 12 per cent a year in the early UDI period, and parastatal marketing organisations were responsible for evading sanctions in the export of tobacco and minerals. Significant countries, including West Germany, Switzerland and China, and even North Korea (subsequently, like China, an important ally for Robert Mugabe), never ratified sanctions against Rhodesia.[27]

However, in the 1970s the economy worsened. Droughts, and the world recession provoked by the oil price rise in 1973, provided external shocks. Fuel, expensively imported to evade sanctions, was rationed. Manufacturing output fell by 27 per cent between 1974 and 1978, and there was a net loss of 50,000 urban jobs in the private sector.[28] Although the war was largely confined to the rural areas, its cost was hitting everyone. By 1979 it has been estimated that it accounted for 40 per cent of the gross domestic product. Commercial agriculture was severely damaged by call-ups of white farmers, and abandonment of the most exposed properties; call-up which had started as seven days a month in the Police Anti-Terrorist Unit became twenty-eight days on and twenty-eight days off in a regiment. Smith's decision to close the border with Zambia in 1973 meant a loss of freight revenue for copper. By the second half of the 1970s the UDI economy was becoming unsustainable.

It was after the failure at Geneva, with a fierce resumption in the war, steady progress by the Patriotic Front, and darkening prospects for his economy, that Ian Smith launched an 'internal settlement'. In 1978 he struck a deal with three African leaders who did not have armies at their command: Bishop Muzorewa, Ndabaningi Sithole and Chief Chirau. Like Smith they were also hostile to the Organisation of African Unity, which had recognised the Patriotic Front as the authentic representative of Rhodesian Africans. The deal shared an impulse with Margaret Thatcher's Anglo-Irish Agreement of 1985, which sought to end the long-running insurgency in Northern Ireland by bringing together men and women of goodwill against 'terrorists'. But like that, and similar efforts, it suffered from the overwhelming flaw that it failed to accommodate those who held the weapons, or bring peace to non-combatants.

Nonetheless, although the resulting coalition between Muzorewa and Smith gave Smith the real power over a weak partner, the creation of 'Zimbabwe–Rhodesia' was the death knell of racist white supremacy. Whites were in a minority in the new parliament, with 72 black MPs, 20 whites on a separate roll and 8 more on a common roll. Smith kept control of the security services and the war, and property rights were protected. But white morale suffered and senior officers resigned. The green and white Rhodesian flag had come down. What were the whites fighting for now? It was far from clear. Net emigration was 11,000 in 1977, rising further in the two years of Zimbabwe–Rhodesia; higher taxes and the conscription of all white males under 38 brought home the unpleasant and essentially hopeless consequences of the quixotic UDI of 1965. Government was breaking down in much of the countryside.

But there was an interesting insight into African opinion. An election won by Muzorewa, with 64 seats, saw a large voter turnout of an estimated 1.8 million, or 64.8 per cent. It was this election that a British Conservative team, led by Lord Boyd (formerly a colonial secretary, as Alan Lennox-Boyd) described as 'free and fair'. The Patriotic Front had called for a boycott, decrying Muzorewa and company as 'sell-outs'. There was almost certainly coercion by the Rhodesian security services to get people to vote. However, the relatively high turnout was a strong hint that Africans too were getting fed up with the war. The fact that the Bishop did very badly in elections just over a year later may be interpreted by disappointment that the internal settlement failed to bring peace.

The final phase of the war was cruel. White opinion was outraged when ZIPRA shot down a Viscount airliner near Kariba

with a Sam-7 missile, in September 1978, killing thirty-four passengers in the crash; ten of the survivors were killed by guerrillas whom they thought were rescuers in the Urungwe Tribal
Trust Land near the Zambian border. The dean of the Anglican
cathedral in Salisbury, John da Costa, gave vent to the resulting
anger in a sermon, and 38,000 copies of its recording were sold.
He said:

> Nobody who holds sacred the dignity of human life can be any-
> thing but sickened at the events attending the crash of the Viscount
> *Hunyani*.... The horror of the crash was bad enough, but that
> this should be compounded by the murder of the most savage and
> treacherous sort leaves us stunned with disbelief.... This bestiality,
> worse than anything in recent history, stinks in the nostrils of
> Heaven. But are we deafened by the voice of protest from nations
> which call themselves 'civilised'? We are not. Like men in the
> story of the Good Samaritan, they 'pass by, on the other side.' One
> listens for condemnation by Dr David Owen, himself a medical
> doctor, trained to help all in need. One listens, and the silence is
> deafening. One listens for loud condemnation by the President of
> the United States, himself a man from the Bible-Baptist belt, and
> once again the silence is deafening. One listens for condemnation
> by the Pope, by the Archbishop of Canterbury, by all who love the
> name of God. Again, the silence is deafening.[29]

ZIPRA subsequently shot down a second Air Rhodesia Viscount,
killing all fifty-nine passengers.

But of course the Rhodesian security forces had been equally
if not more ruthless in their own country, and in launching re-
prisal raids into Mozambique and Zambia. Rhodesians attacked
ZANLA camps in Mozambique at Nyadzonia in 1976, where 600
refugees were killed, and Chimoio in 1977. These were terror raids
on camps which, although they provided succour for guerrillas,
were largely for refugees, with schools and hospitals. Fay Chung,
who survived an attack by Rhodesian paratroopers on Chimoio,
thought they had deliberately targeted refugees to avoid taking

casualties by attacking guerrillas nearby. Of the eighty-five who died, fifty-five were children, and she believed that the Rhodesians had taken away their white dead and wounded, leaving their black soldiers to be buried by the ZANU refugees.[30] Senior ZANU and ZANLA figures had left the area ahead of the raid.[31]

Rhodesians knew that ZANLA guerrillas, less well equipped than ZIPRA, were coming across the frontier from Mozambique, poorly trained. But they also recognised that ZANLA had huge human resources. They started arming Mozambican rebels to take on FRELIMO, and interdict ZANLA invasion routes, the origin of RENAMO and the immensely damaging fifteen years of civil war in Mozambique. If ZANLA was relatively weak in arms, it was strong on ideology, using commissars, purges, slogans and political rallies where Maoist-style self-criticism sessions came together with pre-colonial traditions of public confession in *pungwes*.[32] Words of Portuguese – *chefe* for leader, *povo* for the people – entered the vocabulary of ZANLA and ZANU, as part of an overt commitment to revolutionary Marxism.

The Rhodesians also attacked ZIPRA camps in Zambia in 1978. In a raid on 19 October their fighter planes took over Zambian air space and killed 1,600, with their commander calling himself 'Green Leader' in contacts with the Lusaka control tower, which were also made into a recording. Rhodesian attacks caused deaths and substantial destruction of property in Lusaka; on one occasion Joshua Nkomo, a large man, had to squeeze himself through a lavatory window to escape an assault on the house in which he was living. Questions were raised in Zambia as to whether it was ZAPU or the Zambian defence forces which were supposed to be defending the country.

But some of the worst fighting, and abuses, took place in the Rhodesian countryside in the last two years of the war. Roads were mined and people and vehicles blown up. Peasants were coerced and beaten by both the Rhodesian forces and the guerrillas.

The Selous Scouts and civilian volunteers on the Rhodesian side had some of the worst reputations; cattle were poisoned by anthrax and crops burnt; Africans were cruelly beaten to death in public places in a way that anticipated techniques used by ZANU militias in the early years of the twenty-first century. Police stations, railway bridges and Rhodesian convoys were attacked by guerrillas, so that by late 1979 the Muzorewa–Smith government's writ did not run in the tribal trust lands or in countryside remote from the towns.[33]

It was against this background that the final act of the UDI drama was played out, in Lusaka and Lancaster House in 1979, and in Zimbabwe in 1980. This was an act with four scenes: the Commonwealth summit chaired by Kenneth Kaunda in Lusaka; the winter negotiation at Lancaster House in London, chaired by Lord Carrington, the Conservative foreign minister; the anxious electoral period, in which guerrillas inside Rhodesia gathered in assembly areas during a ceasefire for the elections; and the final denouement in which Robert Mugabe's ZANU section of the Patriotic Front won a comfortable victory and, in spite of some plotting among irreconcilable whites, took power.

Each stage of this process involved real tension. Mistrust, fear of backsliding, and the risk of renewal of the war hung over all participants. When the Union Jack – not the flag of Rhodesia–Zimbabwe – was lowered at midnight on 17–18 April, there was enormous African excitement at the Rufaro stadium, where the flag of independent Zimbabwe was raised. President Nyerere of Tanzania told Mugabe that he had inherited 'the jewel of Africa', echoing a sentiment that Mugabe had expressed to Smith in March. With the new prime minister making conciliatory statements to the white population there were many, both in Africa and outside, who felt that the new state was set fair.

The first scene in the drama was in some ways the most remarkable. Margaret Thatcher, the first woman prime minister in British history, was a conviction politician who was also a conservative Conservative. She had played an occult race card in the election campaign which she won, referring to her fear that the United Kingdom was being 'swamped' by immigrants. Her instinct was to recognise the 'Government of National Unity' of Muzorewa and Smith. But Peter Carrington was a patrician, 'one nation' Conservative, a peer by inheritance. He was keen to rebuild the United Kingdom's status in a world which had been massively changed by decolonisation. He succeeded in persuading Thatcher to hold off from a unilateral recognition of Muzorewa–Smith, in the hope that an internationally acceptable deal could be found. After all the failures since 1965 he relished the prospect of claiming a diplomatic triumph.[34]

The choice of Lusaka for the Commonwealth summit in August 1979 was not uncontroversial. While it gave a special opportunity to Kenneth Kaunda, as chairman, and to Shridath Ramphal, as Commonwealth secretary general – both of whom were keen for a settlement on the basis of African entitlement – it ran into criticism from the right-wing press, especially in Britain and New Zealand, where there was also a conservative government. Margaret Thatcher, in the presence of Robert Muldoon, the New Zealand prime minister, said she was minded to advise the Queen not to go. The press worried that the Queen, the head of the Commonwealth who traditionally hosted a banquet for leaders at the summit, would be in danger. Had she not attended, the value of the occasion might have been undermined.

Yet while it was true that the Rhodesians had been mocking the Zambian defence forces with raids on Lusaka, the last thing they were likely to do was to endanger the Queen's person. Fourteen years after UDI the Rhodesian Front elite, and their commanders, were still royalist ultras, even though they had declared a republic. Further, Ramphal took the precaution of persuading Nkomo to declare a ceasefire during the royal visit, which meant that Bishop Muzorewa did likewise.[35] There are no constitutional responsibilities attached to the headship of the Commonwealth, but it can exert influence. The Queen had only once before visited the Rhodesias, as a princess, during the royal tour to southern Africa in 1947.[36] But her commitment to the survival of the Commonwealth was and is unequalled. Buckingham Palace made plain that the Queen would go to Lusaka. She was cheered by large crowds in the streets of Dar es Salaam when she touched down there en route. Although an anxious Margaret Thatcher climbed down from her Royal Air Force plane on arrival wearing dark glasses – she told Lord Carrington she feared that acid would be thrown at her – the Lusaka summit was going to happen.

The Lusaka summit has entered Commonwealth folklore as the place where Mrs Thatcher danced with President Kaunda. But in fact it involved some extremely tricky diplomacy in which several players were involved. Ramphal, who had placed the Rhodesia debate on the agenda for the third day of the meeting, to allow for prior negotiation with Mrs Thatcher and the Front-line States, told the press that 'it would be an achievement if the week-long conference avoided splits.' Just prior to the conference, in early July 1979, a group of leaders including Malcolm Fraser, the prime minister of Australia, presidents Nyerere and Kaunda, Prime Minister Manley of Jamaica and General Obasanjo of Nigeria had been brought together with Thatcher by Fraser to work out proposals. This and other pressures had an effect on Thatcher, who told the British House of Commons on 25 July that she wanted a constitutional conference; she was backing away from her manifesto commitment to recognise the internal settlement.

In her opening speech in Lusaka, Thatcher said that the internal settlement was defective, and that it was Britain's aim to hold a constitutional conference and bring Rhodesia to legal independence 'on a basis which the Commonwealth and the international community as a whole will find acceptable.' While most of the leaders went off on an excursion to Victoria Falls, Kaunda and Ramphal arranged for a small group to stay behind: Thatcher and Carrington, Nyerere, Fraser, Manley and General Adefope, the Nigerian commissioner for external affairs in the military government which had nationalised BP and Shell to put pressure on the British.

Ramphal had been working on heads of agreement, and this small group, meeting in Kaunda's study, assented to the following points: that there had to be genuine black majority rule; that it was the constitutional duty of the UK to grant independence; that all parties to the conflict had to be involved; that there had to be 'appropriate safeguards for minorities'; that the British plan for a constitutional conference attended by all parties should go forward; that elections should be held under British authority, but with Commonwealth observers; and that it must be a major objective to end hostilities and sanctions (where the British faced a parliamentary vote on sanctions renewal in November, and right-wing Conservatives might baulk this).

The scheme bypassed previous Anglo-American proposals for an interim government, or United Nations oversight, and said nothing about land ownership, or any fund to rebuild Zimbabwe after the war. But it placed responsibility squarely on the United Kingdom – something it had arguably never had in the history of the colony. It would be the British who would have to manage the constitutional conference, the elections and the transition to a recognised independence. Neither ZAPU nor ZANU were directly represented in the Lusaka talks and the Commonwealth leaders had to take it for granted that the Frontline States could deliver their acceptance. Other players such as unions and civil society were not present, although the white commercial farmers sought to lobby in the background. 'We were all gambling', Ramphal commented in retrospect.[37]

The deal was nearly wrecked at the last moment. Although it was supposed to be kept secret until a final executive session of all Commonwealth leaders, Fraser decided to brief some British and Australian journalists on a Sunday.[38] Thatcher and Ramphal were at a service at the Anglican cathedral in Lusaka when Carrington informed his prime minister of the leak. An angry Carrington, worried about potential Conservative opposition in the British parliament, advised Thatcher to call off the agreement. However, scribbling on an order of service, Ramphal persuaded her to keep her nerve and that it would be possible to bring forward the announcement. So, at an Australian barbecue that evening, attended by all heads of government, they confirmed the agreement. It was duly announced to the whole press that evening.

For the combatant Zimbabwean parties the Lusaka Accord meant that they were now moving from an endgame to the war and into a climactic power struggle. This was a struggle to be umpired by the British, with the rest of the Commonwealth looking over their shoulders. The governments of the Frontline states, seriously damaged by the war and with the bigger problem of apartheid yet to tackle, were relieved that there was the prospect of a final settlement. For the Conservative government in the UK, annoyed as ministers were with Fraser, the accord could be portrayed as a British triumph, leaving the British in charge of the denouement. There would be no United Nations military involvement, as had been suggested in the Vance–Owen proposals.

The Lusaka agreement was in August. Lord Carrington, as foreign and Commonwealth secretary, was in charge of taking the constitutional talks forward, and they began before the end of September. He was determined to maintain the momentum, so he resolved to drive the London negotiations hard. His strategy was to present the British proposals by stages to three parties which were extremely unwilling to compromise – the Muzorewa–Smith delegation, ZANU and ZAPU. He was not a neutral chairman, sitting back and trying to weave together agreements. Buoyed up by Commonwealth support in Lusaka, suspecting that the Rhodesians could not go on resisting much longer, he also knew that Kaunda and Machel were ready to cut off support for the warring nationalists if they missed this chance for a settlement.

He was also unwilling to be sidetracked from the constitution, and was not concerned with longer-term issues of reconciliation. In his opening address he pointed out that a quarter of the population of Rhodesia had been born since UDI and that, while there were 'other aspects of a settlement which must in due course be resolved', the constitution is 'the fundamental problem to which we must address ourselves'.[39] The British were pushing very hard, but were reluctant to acknowledge that Shridath Ramphal, with whom the two Patriotic Front delegations were in close contact, was also doing his utmost to keep the negotiation on track.[40]

In his opening address Joshua Nkomo, speaking on behalf of the Patriotic Front as its more senior figure, complained at the vagueness of Carrington's initial proposals. He asked nine essential questions, of which the ninth was 'What will be the future of the people's land?' For Bishop Muzorewa the issue was simple, although in a sense belied by the fact of his presence in London. He claimed that his government, which had taken office on 1 June 1979, had been duly elected and should therefore be recognised; sanctions, including US sanctions recently renewed by President Carter over congressional opposition, should be removed. Throughout the talks, Muzorewa was under fire from his alleged partner, Ian Smith, who had more control over the military and sought to undermine any compromise.

Lancaster House is a grand house at the end of Pall Mall, used for many British government functions. It adjoins St James's Palace and Buckingham Palace and is a short walk from Marlborough House, a former royal palace made over by the Queen for use by the Commonwealth Secretariat. Its choice for the talks was a deliberate reference to the many independence negotiations for other former British colonies which had been agreed there. In spite of the idiosyncratic history of Rhodesia, the venue was hinting that actually this was, after all, a British colony which required British approval to get a proper independence.

The talks lasted three and a half months, until an agreement was signed on 21 December, which allowed delegations to return home for Christmas. Hundreds of journalists followed the twists and turns. Joshua Nkomo complained that the British were giving him a stingy meal allowance of £25 a day; Robert Mugabe was at one point living modestly in a poorly heated bed-and-breakfast hotel. Mugabe, and his ZANU delegation, were regarded by Carrington – who privately gave him a Yorkshire-style nickname 'E-ba-gum', reversing the letters of his name – as the principal obstacle. Mugabe had an image as an irreconcilable Marxist, and was suspicious that the other parties were trying to stitch up an agreement to his disadvantage. He threatened to walk out on several occasions, and once got as far as Heathrow airport before Samora Machel persuaded him to return.

Ramphal's biggest contribution was to prevent a Patriotic Front walkout on the tricky question of land, and the recognition of private property rights. His deputy, Chief Anyaoku, saw Mugabe, Nkomo and Tongogara, who complained that they were being asked to concede both on land and on white seats. How could it be democratic for 8 million black Zimbabweans to get only 80 seats in parliament, while 200,000 whites would get 20? They said that land was a main reason for the liberation war, and that as recently as 1969 Ian Smith had been expelling black families from their homes and land; some of their fighters had been pushed off their land when they were children. Anyaoku persuaded the Patriotic Front to drop their objection to what Carrington had proposed would be a temporary franchise for a decade, arguing 'What is ten years in the life of a nation?'[41]

But this still left the land issue. At a meeting in his official residence, with Mugabe and Nkomo, Ramphal told them:

> First of all, you cannot let Lancaster House break up, or worse still, end without you. Secondly, you are not going to be on good ground if the reason for the break-up is attributed to your refusal to have a clause protecting private property in the constitution of Zimbabwe. This is a clause that is in every constitution. So we have to find another way.[42]

What Ramphal came up with was a US guarantee of funding for an independent Zimbabwe government, which would enable it to acquire land compulsorily, and start a process of resettlement. He spoke to the US ambassador in London, Kingman Brewster. Brewster got clearance from Cyrus Vance and President Carter to make an offer to Nkomo and Mugabe that US funding would support an agricultural development fund for this purpose. This satisfied the two Patriotic Front leaders. However, there were no numbers attached to this offer; this was a deal to be done outside of Lancaster House; and Carter left the White House in January 1981 to be succeeded by Ronald Reagan, a president with very different views on southern Africa.

On 3 October the British tabled their proposed independence constitution, which included 20 seats for the white community out of 100 – too small to block an African majority, but an acknowledgement of race with long-term implications, and a rejection of the multiracialism claimed for the Central African Federation a quarter of a century earlier. On 17 October the British proposed that a British governor should assume responsibility in Rhodesia, for a short transitional period to include the elections. Commenting on Carrington's aggressive approach, the British diplomat Robin Renwick wrote: 'The most criticised aspects of British diplomacy at Lancaster House ["authoritarian", "high-handed", "arbitrary"] were in fact the key to its success.'[43]

By mid-November, with the involvement of Kaunda in getting agreement from the Patriotic Front delegations, they were being told that there would be a ceasefire commission with equal numbers of Patriotic Front and Rhodesian commanders, and a ceasefire monitoring force. The British were also pushing an enabling bill through Parliament, and threatening to do a deal with 'internal' parties if the Patriotic Front prevaricated. Renwick wrote:

> Each successive phase of the conference was more difficult than the last. The problems which, from the outset, had appeared certain to cause most difficulty were the military arrangements for the cease-fire and the separation of forces. Hence the strategy of tackling these only after agreement on the political issues had created momentum, and some expectation of success.[44]

The Rhodesians continued with attacks while the negotiations continued, and there was real concern that any agreement could be destroyed by a renewal of the fighting; the British were suspicious of how far their discipline would hold in the guerrilla forces. In the second phase of the Lancaster House talks Renwick was holding detailed military talks every morning with Peter Walls, the Rhodesian military commander, and every afternoon was talking to Dumiso Dabengwa, the commander of ZIPRA, and Josiah Tongogara of ZANLA. Given the British hostility to Mugabe, so strongly felt by Carrington, it was positive that General Farndale, the director of military operations in the Ministry of Defence, struck up a good working relationship with Tongogara.[45]

The arrangements for the ceasefire involved fifteen assembly points for the guerrillas, agreement between the Rhodesian and Patriotic Front commanders, and monitoring troops from the relatively few Commonwealth states which had not overtly supported the Patriotic Front – the UK (850), Australia (159), New Zealand (75), Kenya (51) and Fiji (24). There was a late row between the

British, Ramphal and other Commonwealth governments over
the observing of the planned election; the British wanted to
control the selection, while Ramphal insisted successfully that
his secretariat must choose the observers.

The British representative, briefing other Commonwealth
countries over the progress at Lancaster House, told them that
the UK was inviting observers from Canada, Australia, New
Zealand and one Caribbean state. But Ramphal pointed out that
the Lusaka Accord envisaged a collective role for Commonwealth
observers. When the British hinted that the UK would not fund an
observer team selected by the Commonwealth secretary general,
Nigeria stepped in to pay for it. On 13 December 1979 Ramphal
gave the Commonwealth Observer Group its terms of reference,
making it clear that, although the British would supervise the
election, it would be the Commonwealth which would adjudicate
the result.

The Lancaster House agreement provided for a constitution,
a ceasefire, an election, and arrangements to integrate guerrillas
within the Rhodesian military in a new Zimbabwe army. But it
also provided that the new state would inherit a debt of $200
million, and it agreed to pay pensions to all Rhodesian civil servants, including those who had left the country. The Muzorewa
government had offered white civil servants a generous deal on
pensions, as an incentive for them to stay. The area of greatest vagueness concerned land ownership, explored later, where
property was to be traded on a 'willing buyer, willing seller' basis,
and the UK never offered to fund a large-scale purchase of white-
owned farms of a kind that it had done at Kenyan independence.
There was talk of US and European funding for land purchase, as
with the US offer referred to above. But nothing was committed
to paper, and, while guaranteeing property rights, the agreement
made no mention of land. The new constitution was supposed to
last unchanged for ten years.

The deal was not signed by all parties in London until 21 December. But before then, as part of the drive for momentum in peacemaking, the British had appointed Christopher Soames as governor. He actually arrived in Salisbury on 12 December – via the Portuguese Azores and Britain's Ascension Island, because no African country would grant clearance prior to the formal agreement.

The appointment of Soames, Winston Churchill's son-in-law and a member of the British cabinet, was a masterstroke in a difficult situation. The first name suggested for the governorship was that of a senior official, Antony Duff, who had been running the Africa department at the Foreign and Commonwealth Office. But Carrington and Thatcher thought a political heavyweight would be better. The Churchill connection, to a Rhodesian Front leadership for whom the heroism of the Second World War still loomed large, was important. Ian Smith had attended Winston's funeral; Soames's wife Mary could supply Churchillian perorations;[46] Soames in Salisbury was able to offer guests the Pol Roger champagne of which his father-in-law had been so fond.

A big man, both physically and in reputation, Soames had the political knack of striking up relationships with people of varied backgrounds, the confidence of the British government and of his own experience, and a willingness to take decisions and to stand up to lobbying. Like Ian Smith he had seen war service, before becoming a Conservative MP. He was a former minister of agriculture in the UK, had been vice president of the European Commission and responsible for foreign affairs 1973–76, and was made a life peer in 1978.

Interestingly, although Soames was a former Conservative minister and a grandee, Harold Wilson had appointed him as ambassador in Paris in 1968. An anecdote from that time illustrated his character. He was told that a British trade fair in Marseilles was lacking in fizz. Using personal contacts unavailable to most diplomats, he rang Lord Sieff, then heading the Marks and Spencer retail chain, and requested a glamorous and high-powered participation from the store. This made all the difference.

The Soames governorship, signalled when the Union Jack was raised once more in Salisbury after his arrival, was a classic piece of British bluff. Many historians, particularly those of the Indian Raj, have argued that there was always a strong element of bluff in the ideal and operation of the British Empire; in India a thousand members of the Indian Civil Service administered 300 million people. Throughout the Empire there were never many British administrators and soldiers involved, and imperial ambition was often constrained by lack of funds. The story of Rhodesia, with the running of the colony outsourced first to a company and then to a handful of white settlers, was an egregious example. Westminster and Whitehall had never really been in charge.

But now the pretence was that the British, for a few months only, were going to manage a country which had endured war for over a decade, and arrange a transition to peace via elections. Rhodesian civil servants and military, responsible for UDI and its dire consequences, would have to take British orders. Nationalists and their armies, who had been suspicious of the British since before UDI and were starting on a final struggle for power, would have to observe a ceasefire. Everyone was jockeying for position. Rumours of coups and bad faith abounded. The British were keen to get South African troops which had been helping Smith back across the southern border, and FRELIMO troops assisting ZANLA to return to Mozambique. (Soames could not make the South Africans withdraw entirely, but accepted the fiction that they were on Rhodesian soil to protect the bridge at Beitbridge.)

The election was set to start on 27 February, but on 30 December, the day before the parties were required to register, ZANU tore up the Patriotic Front pact with ZAPU and decided to campaign on its own. The decision was announced by Enos Nkala, who was heading its internal wing. It reflected the view of the leadership that unless there was massive rigging of the poll[47] ZANU could win on its own. Furthermore Nkala, an Ndebele in the largely Shona ZANU, was violently anti-Nkomo. Yet ZANU had just suffered a serious blow. In the early hours of Boxing Day, 26 December 1979, Josiah Tongogara had been killed in a road accident north of Maputo; he had been en route to his headquarters near Chimoio to inform guerrillas of the cease-fire.

Inevitably, conspiracy theorists who know that ZANU has subsequently used a 'road accident' as a cover for political assassination have wondered about this death. Tongogara was popular with his troops and a charismatic figure, who could have embarrassed or challenged the political leadership now vested in Mugabe. It was known that he had seen Nkomo shortly before leaving London, and that he was in favour of the Patriotic Front fighting the election as a coalition. Many years later, Emmerson Mnangagwa told a young journalist at a family event that some things were better left unexplored. By then Mnangagwa, who had received a secondary education in prison with Mugabe as his tutor, was one of the key faction leaders in ZANU–PF. It is also significant that Tongogara's brother and sister, who subsequently joined the MDC, believe he was murdered. A recent report in *The Zimbabwean* stated that both the US and Soviet embassies in Lusaka were convinced that he had not died accidentally, and quoted a former Zimbabwean detective as having seen three wounds to his body, consistent with gunshots.[48] However, the one witness who survived the crash has said it was an accident. Murder or accident, his departure was certainly convenient to Robert Mugabe in removing a potential rival.

The US Air Force airlifted 20,000 tents to Rhodesia to accommodate the ZIPRA and ZANLA guerrillas in their assembly areas, and everyone watched nervously to see how many would come in, and whether the ceasefire would hold. The process started slowly, with only 1,800 men coming in by the end of the third day. But by 9 January 1980 over 20,000 men had assembled, 14,000 from ZANLA. The elections were not due to start for another seven weeks, which was a long time to keep guerrillas cooped up under the eye of a small Commonwealth monitoring force; in the Sabi tribal trust land, for example, 6,000 guerrillas were being watched over by just fifty British troops.

There were several problems. Rhodesian forces were itching to hit the sitting ducks, and for an excuse to say that the ceasefire had broken. There were confrontations between guerrillas and monitors. There were comings and goings between the assembly areas and the surrounding countryside; some armed bands did not come in; and arms were being cached for a potential war between ZIPRA and ZANLA if the election result disappointed one side or the other. ZANLA troops staged victory processions as they marched into their rendezvous, and intimidation of the peasantry continued in the run-up to the election. It has been claimed that as many as two-thirds of the ZANLA forces never entered the holding areas.[49] Sir John Boynton, the election commissioner who had run Cheshire County Council, was faced with a challenge quite different from any poll he had conducted in his peaceful county in north-west England.

While 200 foreign observers came to see the election, by far the largest group was organised by the Commonwealth. Led by ambassador Rajeshwar Dayal of India the eleven observers were supported by fifty-two assistants; arriving on 24 January they visited two-thirds of the static polling stations and over half the mobile ones between them. The only party leader who refused to see them was Bishop Muzorewa, who complained that Dayal had described the Rhodesian troops as 'not impartial'. When it reported on 8 March the Commonwealth group implied that the administration had shown bias against the Patriotic Front.

The campaign was full of incident. Two attempts were made to assassinate Mugabe. Soames resisted demands from the Rhodesians to call off the elections, on the grounds of intimidation by the Patriotic Front, and especially ZANU. However, he disallowed Enos Nkala, one of the more excitable ZANU leaders, from taking any further part in the campaign; Nkala had threatened that if ZANU did not win, the war would continue. Bishop Muzorewa was generously funded from South African sources, in hopes that he would repeat his success of the previous year and form a 'moderate' government.

British officials tried to control the information getting to Soames, who was somewhat isolated. They were hoping that a post-election majority could be put together involving the twenty white MPs and the MPs elected for Muzorewa and Nkomo.

However, Soames had brought with him a former Conservative MP, Robert Jackson, who had worked with him in Brussels. Intelligence reaching Soames via Jackson, who was in touch with Fernando Honwana of FRELIMO, was backed up by information from MI6, the British intelligence service. This gave Soames an insight into the real strength of ZANU, and enabled him to resist the suggestion of other officials that some ZANU candidates should be debarred in a pre-emptive putsch.[50]

Nonetheless the results, declared at the beginning of March, came as a brutal surprise to the South Africans, to the white Rhodesians and also to those British politicians who had been hoping either for a Muzorewa win or for a Muzorewa–Nkomo coalition. In an estimated 90 per cent turnout of a black electorate of 2.6 million, ZANU won 71 per cent of the votes and 57 of the 80 common roll seats. It could form a government on its own, with Robert Mugabe, perceived as a dangerous Marxist, as prime minister. The voting largely followed ethnic patterns, with the majority Shona overwhelmingly voting for ZANU and the Ndebele backing ZAPU, which won 20 seats. Muzorewa, with less than 4 per cent of the votes and only 3 seats, was humiliated.

What had happened? The sharp ethnic division, with roots going back to the pre-Rhodesian history of the nineteenth century, might not have been forecast. But the ZANU win over most of the country reflected more than success for its strategy of propaganda and coercion. Muzorewa's Zimbabwe–Rhodesia had failed to bring peace to a war-weary and exhausted people. Victory for Mugabe meant peace at last. Without coercion ZANU might not have won an overall majority, but Soames was in no position to prevent intimidation by any of the competing parties.

Although the Rhodesian Army commanders, led by Peter Walls, appealed to Margaret Thatcher to countermand the results, Soames moved rapidly to recognise them. The Commonwealth observers said that the result did reflect the will of the people. Soames had little choice but to agree. Soames met Mugabe, and encouraged him to speak of conciliation, and to form a broad-based government. The era which had started with Rhodes's conquest, and the bitter fruits of UDI in 1965, was at an end.

FOUR

ZANU IN POWER: THE 1980s

Independence came to Zimbabwe at midnight, between 17 and 18 April 1980, at the Rufaro football stadium, Harare, in a huge gathering of 40,000 people, thrilled with emotion. Up and down the country there were 'independence *pungwes*', parties that were also political celebrations. In the stadium the Union Jack, absent for so many years since 1965, was run down as the new flag of Zimbabwe went up, and Prince Charles gave Robert Mugabe the insignia of office. A roar rose from the crowd. Many world leaders, including Indira Gandhi from India, Malcolm Fraser from Australia and Kurt Waldheim, UN secretary general, witnessed the occasion. Bob Marley, the Jamaican lead singer of the Wailers, sang one of his hits, 'Free Zimbabwe'. There was a march past by troops from the new Zimbabwean Army, the product of Rhodesian, ZANLA and ZIPRA soldiers drilled together.

But there were empty seats in a section of the stands reserved for whites; and, hidden away behind benches reserved for junior ministers, sat Joshua Nkomo, who had hoped to be star of this show, along with his wife, humiliated.[1] In fact Mugabe had offered Nkomo the consolation prize of the presidency. He had asked Chief Anyaoku, then the Commonwealth's deputy secretary general, to convey an invitation to Nkomo to be president on the basis that he could see all cabinet papers, be able to intervene, and represent Zimbabwe at the UN and other international meetings. Nkomo took Anyaoku into his garden, and introduced him to two men with big wounds, the result of ZANU assaults during the election. 'I can't let them down', said Nkomo, refusing the offer. When the news leaked out to the ZANU executive, it was furious, knowing that Nkomo had been party to a potential coalition deal with Muzorewa and Smith's MPs.[2]

The period between declaration of the election results and the moment of independence had been nervous. Ultras in the Rhodesian military had actively considered a putsch, using the password 'Tally Ho the Fox', but General Walls, their commander, dampened the project after failing to get Mrs Thatcher to reject the results. Fernando Honwana, Samora Machel's enlightened representative in Harare, persuaded Walls to visit Maputo to discuss merging the three military formations which had been so recently at war. South Africa offered jobs and asylum to the Selous Scouts and Rhodesian intelligence personnel, most at risk from a new order.

But the key to stabilising the post-election scene was the remarkable personal rapprochement built by Lord Soames with the new prime minister, Robert Mugabe. Whatever Soames's personal preferences prior to the election, he threw himself into peace-building at the highest level, inviting Mugabe to a reception the day after the results and providing him with friendship and advice, even on constructing his cabinet. Mugabe made a series of conciliatory speeches, both to whites and to African opponents.

Mugabe's most famous speech, looking to build a new Zimbabwean personality, he gave at the Rufaro stadium. In it he said:

> If yesterday you hated me, today you cannot avoid the love that binds you to me and me to you. Is it not folly, therefore, that in

these circumstances anybody should seek to revive the wounds and grievances of the past? The ways of the past must now stand forgiven and forgotten. If ever we look to the past, let us do so for the lesson the past has taught us, namely that oppression and racism are inequities that must never again find scope in our political and social system. It could never be a correct justification that because whites oppressed us yesterday when they had power, the blacks must oppress them today because they have power. An evil remains an evil whether practised by white against black or black against white.[3]

More recent events have suggested to conspiracy theorists that these speeches were a sham, a facade for a long-term Marxist manipulator. But observers at the time saw Mugabe as almost bewildered by the suddenness of his power and accepted that his intentions were genuine. Back in 1974 he had been interviewed by Michael Nicholson, for Independent Television News, who asked him whether he had been embittered against whites by his lengthy imprisonment. 'No', he replied, 'We are fighting a system that is wrong. We don't hate the whites. We will have no racial discrimination in an independent Zimbabwe.'[4]

Although suggestions that Soames helped draft some of these speeches seem improbable, he was not the only one to promote a tone of reconciliation. Honwana and Machel warned Mugabe that a wholesale withdrawal of whites, as had happened in Mozambique in 1974–75, could be disastrous for the economy. Mugabe took several steps to calm fears. He appointed Walls to command the armed forces in the process of amalgamation; he kept on Ken Flower, as head of the Central Intelligence Organisation; he appointed David Smith, from the Rhodesian Front, as minister of commerce, and Denis Norman, president of the overwhelmingly white commercial farmers' union, as minister of agriculture; he persuaded Joshua Nkomo to be minister of home affairs, and Enos Nkala, banned from campaigning by Soames, became minister of finance. He recruited Chris Anderson, who had been a law and order minister for Ian Smith.

Mugabe was keen for Soames to stay on in Zimbabwe, seeing him as a valued counsellor, but Soames and the British were clear that there should be no conflict of authority. Once he was no longer governor, he should no longer be there. The British were thankful, as they saw it then, to be shot of any more responsibility, although a military training team was assisting the formation of the new unified army. The UK government had had various fall-back options. Robin Byatt, the new high commissioner, had been told that he might go as deputy governor; indeed he might be an ambassador if Zimbabwe did not rejoin the Commonwealth, which Rhodesia had left. As Soames climbed the steps to his plane to return home on 18 April, he suddenly turned back to have a word with Byatt. He was instructing him to get rid of the bomb-proof governor's car, built like a tank, not appropriate for the UK high commissioner in a Zimbabwe at peace.

But how far was Zimbabwe at peace? While the international community and media were basking, relieved, in thoughts of a risky job well done, enormous challenges faced the new ZANU–PF government. Inside the country there was a host of problems. How to meet the raised expectations of the people in areas like education, health and land ownership, and to Africanise the administration? How to cope with the aftermath of a war in which an estimated 27,000 people had died, perhaps five times as many had been seriously injured, and yet other lives had been disrupted and traumatised?[5] How to deal with the continuing friction between ZANU and ZAPU, and their armed auxiliaries?

Furthermore, the new Zimbabwe was a state surrounded by wars – in Mozambique and Namibia, and in South Africa too, where Zimbabwe was a transit for the fighters of the ANC's armed wing, Umkhonto we Sizwe (MK).[6] These were liberation wars, where Zimbabwe was now a beacon of success for liberators.

In Mozambique there was only a short hiccup in a civil war as patronage of RENAMO was transferred from white Rhodesia to the securocrats in Pretoria, with their ideology of 'total war' against anti-apartheid guerrillas and communism. SWAPO, the liberation force in what South Africans still called South West Africa, was well dug in in northern Namibia, where the South Africans had lost the support of the country's largest ethnic group, the Ovambo. These wars did not respect frontiers. In the final stage of the Rhodesian war, ZANLA and FRELIMO were fighting under joint command inside Zimbabwe, and ZANLA and FRELIMO forces fought ZIPRA and MK guerrillas in Matabeleland.

The Zimbabwe government had to assume that the apartheid government would do everything possible to disable it. At the same time, as the ANC's traditional alliance had been with ZAPU, ZANU had to build a new friendship with the liberation movement which was doing most of the fighting to its south. Oliver Tambo, the president of the ANC, worked with his chief aide Thabo Mbeki to establish cooperation with Mugabe and ZANU. But many others in the ANC leadership, particularly among those who had been locked up for years on Robben Island, were less sympathetic.

The greatest immediate challenge lay in pacifying the new country, Zimbabwe. Both ZANLA and ZIPRA had been cheating during the election period, keeping troops outside the assembly areas to influence or intimidate voters, and in readiness for possible further combat against each other or the Rhodesians. It was reckoned that only a third of the ZANLA force had entered the assembly areas to disarm, with another third propagandising in rural areas, and a third with their weapons in Mozambique and elsewhere.[7]

The new combined army would not have room for all the former combatants, and there were immediate rows about compensation for former fighters, including those who had fought for Rhodesia. A War Victims Compensation Act was passed in 1980, with claims to be handled by a commissioner; but the grounds were tightly drawn, and corruption alleged; nine years later, the Zimbabwe National Liberation War Veterans Association was founded, to fight for their rights. A few NGOs tried to help ex-combatants, including the disabled. But a proposal that all who had had to leave school or university to join the guerrillas should get privileged re-entry to education, on the lines of the GI Bill in the United States after the Second World War, was not adopted.[8] At the renamed University of Zimbabwe in Harare, where the overwhelming majority of staff were still white, there would have been resistance, and black students faced socio-cultural difficulties. By the end of 1980, for instance, only 15,000 out of 65,000 former combatants had been integrated in the army.[9] A few of the rest turned to banditry. There was suspicion that arms were being hidden on a large scale.

Mugabe and ZANU worked on two tracks simultaneously. On the one hand there was a strategy of reconciliation, simplified as a significant number of Rhodesian diehards left the country. This included the creation of a unified army, and certain gestures, such as encouragement for black Zimbabweans to take up the white sport of cricket, where the Barbadian batsman Gary Sobers was invited to coach. On the other hand, there was a strategy of force which assumed that victory was incomplete, that a revolutionary party and its military would face a showdown, with enemies inside and outside the country, at any moment. RENAMO, the anti-FRELIMO insurgency now supported by Pretoria, threatened eastern Zimbabwe and showed what the apartheid commanders could do. For ZANU, the two approaches cancelled each other out.

In fact the strategy of reconciliation was never pursued with sufficient energy and, as shown below, quickly broke down with the campaign against 'dissidents'. In Kenya, after independence in 1963, Jomo Kenyatta launched 'Harambee' – a policy in which all were encouraged to pull together in nation-building. In South Africa, President Mandela authorised a Truth and Reconciliation Commission after 1994. The absence of a proper strategy for reconciliation in Zimbabwe, following the end of the civil war, became a curse. Not surprisingly, the children and grandchildren of those who had been in ZAPU and ZIPRA, or who had worked or fought for the Muzorewa–Smith regime, became a source of recruits for the MDC, thirty years after independence.

ZANU had not magically changed into a civilian political party of the European type with success at the polls. Like FRELIMO it was structured as a Marxist party, with a politburo, and a top-down organisation reflecting the tenets of 'democratic centralism'. Although the central committee was elected by party members, the more powerful politburo, which aimed to supervise both party and state, was selected by Mugabe. He and other officials were addressed as 'comrade'. Furthermore, Mugabe was highly dependent on the military leaders of ZANLA for his power base. Fay Chung, who had been with the ZANLA guerrillas and was to be minister for education from 1988 to 1993, described Mugabe's relationship with the senior veterans as follows:

> In the person of Mugabe they found someone with a brilliant intellect, who could be a highly effective spokesman for the liberation movement, but who was inherently in a weak position. He could not use them as 'cannon fodder' and 'gun carriers' as former leaders had done. The military were suspicious of being utilised as instruments and weapons to achieve political goals, and then sacrificed and discarded once these political goals were achieved.[10]

The close relationship of Mugabe with ZANLA veterans, and especially the former commanders, would be an enduring element in his rule.

It was not paranoid of Mugabe to see the new state, where initially there was only a thin ZANU overlay of settler officialdom, as surrounded by enemies. Before and after independence there were outbreaks of violence close to the assembly areas, and in November 1980 there was a battle between ZANLA and ZIPRA guerrillas who had been moved to Entumbane, near Bulawayo; more than 300 died in a more serious shoot-out there and in the Midlands, three months later. Significantly, in July 1980, Mugabe renewed Ian Smith's state of emergency, originally introduced at UDI in 1965, for another six months; it was regularly renewed until July 1990.

The strategy of force was pursued by the establishment of a Shona, ZANU-loyal military formation which was additional to the unified army being trained by the British. In October 1980, following a visit to North Korea – the most Stalinist of the communist states but which, like ZANU, had followed the Chinese line – Mugabe made an agreement for the training and arming of a brigade of troops. This would be known as the Fifth Brigade, not constrained by the Geneva Conventions, and commanded by Colonel Perence Shiri, who was a cousin of Mugabe's and was to become chief of the Zimbabwe Air Force, and victim of an assassination attempt in the twenty-first century. It was answerable only to Mugabe. He called the Fifth Brigade 'Gukurahundi' – 'the rain which washes away the chaff before the spring rains' in Shona – which became the name for its subsequent massacres. Significantly, the ZANLA loyalists who overcame the Badza/Nhari rebels in Zambia had been given the same nickname. North Korean instructors started training this brigade in the last few months of 1981, and it passed out in September 1982.

There were opponents of the new government from three quarters: in South Africa, from irreconcilable whites inside Zimbabwe, and among the former ZIPRA guerrillas, particularly the minority Ndebele speakers. This opposition overlapped. South Africa was angry that ZANU had come to power, recruited the Selous Scouts to its own recce forces, and embarked on a strategy of destabilisation. South African intelligence aimed to exacerbate the frictions between ZANU and ZAPU, to stop supply lines for the MK, the ANC's guerrillas, and ideally to create a civil war comparable to the one which had developed in Mozambique. The South Africans established 'Operation Drama',[11] designed to create a 'Super ZAPU' guerrilla force to oppose the ZANU government and in 1981 were already destroying a Zimbabwean arsenal at the Inkomo barracks (in August), and attempting to kill Mugabe (in December). But how far there ever was a 'Super ZAPU' as claimed by Zimbabwe government propaganda – rather than South African subversion which was not well coordinated with the banditry of some ex-ZIPRA combatants – remains uncertain.

The report on the Gukurahundi massacres, first published by the Catholic Commission for Justice and Peace and the Legal Resources Foundation in 1997, emphasised that much of the South African strategy lay in misinformation, which succeeded in upsetting the insecure ZANU–ZAPU coalition:

> South African intervention in Zimbabwe in the 1980s was basically two-fold: it consisted of the systematic supply of misinformation to the government, and also of military attacks on the government and on the country's infrastructure. Many ex-members of the Rhodesian army, police and CIO became integrated into the South African armed forces. Some remained in the country after independence and actively recruited people for sabotage duties or to act as double agents. Some became government informers, ideally placed to exacerbate tensions between ZAPU and ZANU–PF by the use of misinformation. ZAPU was often blamed for various events which were in fact, at least partly, the work of South African agents.[12]

The crisis which broke the fragile ZANU–ZAPU coalition, and led to widespread deaths and suffering in Matabeleland, was precipitated by the discovery of arms caches. In February 1982 Mugabe announced that huge arms caches had been found on ZAPU-owned farms, and said there was a plot to overthrow the government. In fact a cross-party group of leaders, including Mugabe and Mnangagwa from ZANU and Nkomo and Dumiso Dabengwa, a key ZIPRA commander representing ZAPU, had been meeting to discuss the problem of arms hidden by both the guerrilla armies. But a combination of meddling by South African intelligence and a decision by ZANU to crack down on ZAPU gave this discovery a partisan flavour. It seems likely that at least some of the arms belonged to the African National Congress, en route for the MK in South Africa.

The sequel was vicious. ZAPU leaders were fired from the government, or arrested and tried for treason; the two former ZIPRA leaders, Dabengwa and General Lookout Masuku (who had become deputy commander of the new unified army), were tried for treason, acquitted and arrested again; a significant number of ZIPRA fighters went back into the bush, where they were responsible for banditry, rape and pillage; six foreign tourists from Britain, Australia and Canada were kidnapped and murdered by supposed 'dissidents', as they were known, damaging the precious post-war tourism industry.[13] After the kidnap the government passed a law granting freedom from prosecution to officials and security forces for any action taken 'for the purposes of or in connection with the preservation of the security of Zimbabwe'. Similar to a law passed by the Smith government in 1975 this was a clear signal that a liberation government still thought it was at war, and that it would not allow human rights concerns to stand in its way.

Starting in January 1983 the Fifth Brigade was unleashed on Matabeleland, with orders to wipe out the dissidents. This they did with unparalleled ferocity, lumping together the bandits and ex-ZIPRA fighters with innocent Ndebele villagers, in a total onslaught. They beat, killed, raped, tortured and burnt homes. They sought to make Ndebele speakers talk in Shona. There were mass detentions and disappearances. Bodies were buried in mass graves. Horrified observers were unwilling to recognise that this was government policy, sanctioned by Mugabe himself. But it was. He brushed off protests. After Mike Auret, director of the Catholic Commission for Justice and Peace, went to see Mugabe with two Catholic bishops and details of the abuses on 16 March, he publicly reprimanded 'sanctimonious' priests. In six weeks alone, in Matabeleland North from January to March 1983, 2,000 civilians had been killed, most in public executions. Ministers made threatening speeches. Emmerson Mnangagwa said, 'Blessed are they who will follow the path of the government laws, for their days on earth shall be increased. But woe unto those who will choose the path of collaboration with dissidents for we will certainly shorten their stay on earth.'

In 1984 the Fifth Brigade was sent into the neighbouring province of Matabeleland South, using largely similar tactics, although there was also a food embargo and 2,000 people were detained at one time at the Bhalagwe camp. The Fifth Brigade was supported by other army and police units. By the time it was withdrawn, later that year, a total of some 20,000 had died in Matabeleland, some 7,000 were suffering from the after-effects of torture, and hundreds of thousands of Ndebele had been intimidated. A significant chunk of Zimbabwe had been subject to curfew, and was being treated as occupied territory. People fled into neighbouring Botswana. Catholic bishops protested, criticism in the Western media was muted,[14] and the report of an inquiry commission, chaired by Simplicius Chihambakwe, was never published. Ironically the murders attributed to dissidents actually increased after the ravages of the Fifth Brigade, from 165 in the eighteen months between January 1983 and July 1984, to 264 in the two years from January 1985 to the end of 1986.[15]

Matabeleland, which apart from Bulawayo and Wankie had been less favoured economically during the settler era, suffered a new setback.

Why was it that this extraordinary internal repression did not reverberate more in the outside world? It was, in its violence and disregard of human rights on a huge scale, a link between the civil war of the 1980s, the second *chimurenga* in ZANU terminology, and the third *chimurenga*, with its assault on the opposition and the commercial farmers in the first decade of the twenty-first century. Only Sweden, which had provided aid to the African liberation movements for years, made a public protest.

In fact a number of Zimbabweans did not appreciate what was going on. Denis Norman, then travelling through Matabeleland as minister of agriculture, and meeting farmers, never heard a whisper of the gravity of this crackdown, although farmers were allowed to retrieve weapons they had handed in, to defend themselves against 'dissidents'; a culture of fear and a media blackout prevented internal discussion.[16] At the time the international concern with human rights, which became more salient after the end of the Cold War, was not so pressing. So-called allies of the West in Latin America had committed equally ghastly crimes. Sympathisers with the liberation of southern Africa from racism either did not wish to criticise ZANU, or would see the end – the destruction of a super-ZAPU in alliance with the apartheid regime – as justifying the means. The British High Commission in Harare, for example, was reporting to London what it could find out about events in Matabeleland, but was not making protests on the spot.[17] The international community badly wanted Zimbabwe 'to succeed' – as an example to facilitate a transition in South Africa, which was seen as far more important and difficult. Furthermore there was some complicity by former Rhodesian officers in the unified Zimbabwe Army, and the destruction by sabotage of thirteen planes in the Zimbabwe Air Force in July

1982, blamed on former Rhodesian air-force men, added to the sense that ZANU was indeed still at war.[18] Air Vice Marshal Hugh Slattery, deputy commander of the Air Force, was arrested and tortured.

In retrospect many observers consider that a serious error was made in the lack of pressure or international outcry to confront the Mugabe government at that time. Concerns expressed at Lancaster House in 1979–80 about the human rights of a smaller white minority did not extend to the Ndebele minority, only a few years later. The idea that outrages in war may be justified is as old as human conflict, and was given new currency in the 'war on terror' after 2003. At an early stage in the institutional and cultural development of the new state, when veterans of the independence struggle like Enoch Dumbutshena were trying to promote a 'culture of human rights', there was abuse on a large scale, a spirit of ethnic revenge, and the inculcation of fear and impunity. Former domination of the Shona by Lobengula and his family might have been avenged, and the risk of Ndebele secessionism nipped in the bud, but the long-term cost for Zimbabwe was enormous.

The upshot of the attack on super-ZAPU and the dissidents was the effective creation of a one-party state. Although Nkomo had been appealing to former ZIPRA fighters to surrender, ZAPU was hounded into submission. Surprisingly, given the levels of coercion, ZAPU succeeded in winning all the Matabeleland seats in the 1985 election; this was an election won comfortably elsewhere by ZANU, with the party of Ian Smith still controlling the 20 white seats. ZANU, while continuing to threaten ZAPU, also embarked on tortuous unity talks. In September 1987 Enos Nkala, the minister for home affairs, who had always been hostile to ZAPU, closed all of the party's offices and structures and said, 'From now on ZAPU would be viewed in the same manner as the MNR bandits in Mozambique.'[19] But the Roman Catholic hierarchy and the Catholic Commission for Justice and Peace appealed to both parties to make it up, in the interests of pacification. In December 1987 Robert Mugabe for ZANU and Joshua Nkomo for ZAPU signed a Unity Accord, creating a single party. In April the following year the government issued a clemency order, under which all dissidents, and those who had aided them, were given a full pardon for any crimes they had committed.

The new combined party was called the Zimbabwe African National Union – Patriotic Front (ZANU–PF), and its creation coincided with the elevation of Mugabe to the new status of executive president. Joshua Nkomo became one of two vice presidents. For the first seven years since independence, Mugabe had been prime minister, and Canaan Banana, a clergyman who had joined ZANU, was a largely ceremonial president. As prime minister, Mugabe was virtually all-powerful; President Banana, protected from jokes about his name by a law passed in 1982, was not a significant figure. But it was customary in African states since independence for the chief of the government to be president. While the old ZANU called most of the shots in the unified party, Mugabe's hold over politburo and government was strong, and while there were demands in ZANU–PF to create a formal one-party state, Zimbabwe never quite got that far. The constitutional change also wiped out the twenty reserved seats for whites which had been agreed at Lancaster House, and allowed the president to nominate them instead. Mugabe had been infuriated that, in 1985, the white electorate had continued to vote overwhelmingly for Smith's party.[20] Initially he used his patronage to bring a number of women, otherwise under-represented, into parliament. The Lancaster House commitment, that the constitution should last for a decade without change, was abandoned.

Aside from the dangers inside the country and its unsettled region, the 1980s seemed an exciting time for Zimbabwe. New schools were being opened at the rate of almost eight a week, and with double-sessioning the rates of literacy rose sharply. During this decade the number of primary schools rose from about 1,800 to over 4,500, and the number of secondary schools increased from fewer than 200 to over 1,500.[21] Secondary schooling in the Rhodesian era had been of a good standard, but only 2 per cent of blacks had had the opportunity. Everywhere there was an enormous hunger for schooling. The expansion was based on community support, backed by financial and technical assistance from the Ministry of Education. At the secondary level over half the age group was able to get tuition. Growth at the tertiary level was enormous. Whereas only around 300 black students were going to university annually prior to independence, the number jumped to around 10,000 within a few years. In schools the children were taught to chant ZANU slogans; in the University of Zimbabwe, where numbers almost doubled between 1980 and 1984, the students were as willing to criticise the government as they had been during the Smith era.

Social and health services were expanding in parallel. Doctors and other Zimbabwean professionals, who had qualified abroad in other African countries such as Nigeria, or in the UK or the United States, came home to help the new country make up for skill deficits. Maternal and infant mortality fell, aided by a version of the Chinese 'barefoot doctor' model, though it was sometimes hard to persuade newly trained Zimbabwean doctors to work in the district hospitals and rural areas. In spite of at least two droughts in the early 1980s, the economy was doing well, and international support was generous. The British backed an aid pledging conference, for which Lord Soames returned. Nigeria funded a new government news agency, Ziana. Pakistan supplied air-force technicians to train Zimbabweans to service the new MiG planes from China, to make up for the ones blown up at the Thornhill air base. The Commonwealth, which had worked so hard to achieve Zimbabwean independence, provided technical assistance from its Commonwealth Fund for Technical Cooperation.

Administration presented an enormous challenge. Within three years of independence most white civil servants had left, taking with them the guaranteed pension packages arranged by the Muzorewa government which were now an incentive to depart. African ministers, many of whom had been out of the country for some years, were suspicious of these officials anyway, and themselves were having to learn on the job. The white officials had worked by means of an old-boy network, with few written procedures. Because of security concerns, in the UDI period, there was an absence of statistics.[22] Government during the settler era had been primarily concerned with the small white population: a new machine had to be created, out of slender educated resources, balancing struggle loyalties with hoped-for competence, to meet the excited expectations of the whole population.

While social attitudes among the ZANLA guerrillas had been extremely mixed, combining patriarchy, Marxism and a belief in spirit mediums, the 1980s saw the government promote progressive family and gender legislation. Joice Mujuru, a former fighter who was said to have shot down a helicopter and who was married to Solomon Mujuru, the second-in-command to Tongogara, helped push through new laws. A 1982 statute on the legal age of majority gave equality to women at the age of 18. Before then, black women were treated as minors, for whom husbands or male relatives were responsible. Before then, women could not open a bank account. After 1982, daughters could inherit property and women could be guardians of their own children. The Sex Disqualification Removal Act gave women the right to be appointed to any post in the civil service. A burgeoning women's movement and activist judiciary promoted a new deal for women, overcoming opposition from traditionalists and routing unpleasant cultural practices, such as the pledging of young girls to appease angry spirits.

There was a gradual run-down in the white population in the 1980s, to approximately 100,000 by 1990. Not many white farmers left, and those who did were largely from the Afrikaner community. But there were still issues of race. These were not exclusively to do with land use, discussed below. There was a rapid growth in African employment in the civil service, and an expanding middle class, yet control of the commercial private sector remained largely in white hands. While the poorer, over-crowded African townships close to the cities were rebranded as 'high-density suburbs', and efforts were made to improve basic services, some of the low-density suburbs in Harare, with their jacaranda trees, neat English gardens and separate staff quarters, remained obstinately white.

Independence, therefore, was not followed by a rapid end to the spatial segregation which Zimbabwe inherited from Rhodesia. Nor did attitudes between blacks and whites change quickly, in spite of Mugabe's initial effort at conciliation. Among Africans there was a hierarchy of recognition, with Shona at the top, descending via the Ndebele to the smaller ethnicities, and descendants of those from Malawi, Zambia and Mozambique at the bottom.[23] There was a complex, underlying racism in ZANU's definition of a Zimbabwean which pulled against the policies of nation-building. As disappointment grew in the late 1980s and early 1990s, over the performance of the economy and the slow rate of black empowerment, Africans began to question the continuing status of whites.

This was exacerbated by the unreconstructed attitudes of too many of the white-Rhodesians-become-Zimbabweans. Mixing with each other, sending their children to private schools, they retained a settler mentality, and did not try too hard to slough off their sense of superiority, entitlement and self-defined 'civilisa-tion'. In 1980 white officials had shown how hard it was to change gear. When the Commonwealth Trade Union Council organised a conference for African trade unionists in Harare in June, two months after independence, white immigration officials deported them on arrival to Kenya, and it took an apologetic phone call from Mugabe to the foreign minister of Kenya to get them entry to Zimbabwe.[24]

There were, of course, considerable differences between what was happening in the urban areas and what was happening in the countryside. The ideology of ZANU, borrowed from Maoism, gave revolutionary precedence to the role of a rural peasantry. With victory, as supporters saw it, there were widespread expectations of land transfer and an improved standard of living. For years there had been overcrowding and soil erosion in the communal areas, and Shona inheritance customs – which meant that land was passed to brothers before it went down to the next generation[25] – exacerbated the sense of land hunger.

There was in fact a lot of land available for resettlement at independence, perhaps 3.8 million hectares,[26] the result of abandonment by white farmers in the final stages of the war or purchase by the Muzorewa government. The compromise at Lancaster House was that the land should be transferred on a 'willing buyer, willing seller' basis, with the costs shared equally between UK and Zimbabwe governments. A key element at Lancaster House had been in section 16, 'freedom from deprivation of property', which sought to prevent compulsory land acquisition at anything less than 'adequate compensation', with right of appeal to the Zimbabwe High Court. This, opposed by Mugabe and Nkomo, was one of the points at which the talks almost broke down. That they did not was thanks to the intervention by Shridath Ramphal and the US administration of President Carter, described in the previous chapter, whose ambassador in London was authorised to make a vague promise that 'the Americans would help with land development'.

Lord Carrington, whose overriding purpose at Lancaster House was to drive through a constitution and peace settlement, had acknowledged that land was one of the issues. He said, in a plenary session in October 1979:

> We recognise that the future government of Zimbabwe, whatever its political complexion, will wish to extend land ownership... The British government recognises the importance of this issue to a future Zimbabwe government and will be prepared, within the limits imposed by our financial resources, to help.[27]

But he was careful not to offer carte-blanche funding to buy out white farmers, and cast his offer in forward-looking terms of technical support for settlement and agricultural development. The British at Lancaster House did not see land as the crucial issue that it became; indeed the key negotiators either misunderstood its significance or, recognising its capacity for upending a deal, sought to sidestep trouble. They hoped that an unstated moratorium of ten years, the predicted life of the Lancaster House guarantees, would buy time for negotiation.

After independence, the UK set aside £20 million as a land resettlement grant, and a further £27 million as budgetary support to the Zimbabwe government, to enable it to cover its 50 per cent.[28] Both ZANU and ZAPU thought that this was unfair for a newly independent country, with other social demands, and that the UK alone should bear the cost of buying out the white farmers. Indeed Mugabe, as prime minister, was pressing both Soames and the British High Commission for aid for several purposes. But there were political difficulties for the Thatcher government, carrying out public spending cuts at home, in seeming to subsidise a group that had been in rebellion against the British Crown. Development aid, not then as popular with Conservatives as it was to become after David Cameron became leader, five Conservative leaders later, was a prime target for cuts. A significant minority of the farmers, of Afrikaner origin, did not hold British passports; commercial farmers, as a class, had been a backbone of UDI.

There was a sharp contrast in Kenya, which had become independent in 1963. There the British had funded the buyout of white commercial farmers in the so-called 'white highlands' at the time of independence. President Kenyatta's family was one of the beneficiaries. But there were important differences with the situation in Zimbabwe. The number of farms, and therefore the cost to UK taxpayers, was much smaller. The farmers concerned were generally UK citizens. There was a combined pressure on the British government from Kenyatta and the nationalists, the Colonial Office and the High Commission in Nairobi.

The arrangements in Zimbabwe after 1980 covered more than land purchase, to include financing related infrastructure, of water and power supply, clinics and schools. Care was taken to identify the original owners, who had often left Zimbabwe, for payments, and altogether 2 million hectares were transferred to thousands of small farmers. While the British and Zimbabwe governments were directly involved, with their agricultural advisers, other donors such as the European Union ($6.3 million) and the African Development Bank ($27 million) played a complementary role in paying for resettlement, though not land purchase. Kuwait provided £7.8 million ($12.5 million). The United States, which had made favourable noises to keep the Patriotic Front from walking out at a point of impasse during the Lancaster House talks, was not a significant agricultural donor; the arrival of Ronald Reagan as president, in early 1981, marked a rightward shift in US policy in southern Africa.

With independence, Mugabe insisted on a logical merger of the Ministry of Agriculture, which had dealt with the white commercial farmers, and the Native Affairs agricultural department, which had looked after the communal lands. Veterinary, extension and other services began to serve the whole country. With recovery after the war there were some striking increases in production from communal areas. Maize output, the key staple, rose from 41,390 tonnes in 1980/1 to 480,613 tonnes in 1985/6, and output of cotton, a cash crop, went up from 32,834 tonnes to 131,930 tonnes in the same period.[29] Yet real understanding of peasant agriculture was in short supply, especially among donors, and the World Bank pursued a model that added to frustration. By 1987 it had financed 94,000 small loans to peasant farmers who could not trade the surplus necessary to service the loans. Agriculture in Zimbabwe, going back to the earlier colonial era, had been geared to large-scale commercial output or immediate peasant subsistence. The market would have needed structural change to make the model work. In 1988, 80 per cent of borrowers funded by the World Bank defaulted, even though there had been a good rainy season.

Land transfer was a slightly bureaucratic process, slow to get going, and ZANU ministers would turn to rhetoric for political purposes. In 1981 they suddenly proposed a transfer of 180,000 families over three years, significantly beyond the capacity for the measured transfer, with infrastructure backing, on which the joint governments' officials had been working. Had this radical scheme been implemented its results might not have been unlike those of the chaotic 'fast track' land reform which actually took place at the end of the 1990s. At the time, however, Mugabe was not much interested in either the gradual or the radical transfer, and this scheme was dropped. His personal priority, as a former teacher, appeared to be the expansion of education. He did not turn out at events celebrating the settlement of new farmers, where he could have got political credit.

As the 1980s wore on there was a slowing of the movement for land reform, the government's technical capacity ran down, and some of the UK's allocated funds were unspent.[30] Commercial farms changed hands with the apparent security of 'certificates of no government interest', implying that the government had no intention of taking them over. Only 52,000 households had been resettled by 1990, and less than a fifth of the land set aside for them was of the best agricultural quality. Nonetheless, the resettled farmers did see considerable increases in their income over time. A longitudinal study showed that, between 1982/3 and 1993/4, these farmers had more than doubled their real income, which had also become less variable.[31]

Many considered that a key reason why Mugabe did not press the land issue in the 1980s was out of concern for its impact on white South Africa; it was important not to frighten South African whites with a violent takeover when there was a chance of a negotiated end to apartheid. Mugabe and others were conscious of his status as exemplar of a liberation leader taking over from a white-led regime. This consideration applied even more strongly after the release of Nelson Mandela, and the start of negotiations which led to the transfer of power in South Africa. Chief Anyaoku, who became Commonwealth secretary general in 1990, told Mugabe, after a conversation with Mandela then, that he should delay land reform even though the supposed ten-year moratorium on expropriation had expired; this meant that the bulk of the best arable land would continue in white hands.[32]

While the government was successful in providing safe water and sanitation in rural areas, and some richer peasants did well post-independence, there was still land hunger in the communal areas. Jealousy of the successful, largely white commercial farmers was not appeased. Further, ZANU strengthened its political hold through a system of Village Development Committees (VIDCOs) and Ward Development Committees (WADCOs), which were top-down and authoritarian in their approach to development. The district administrators who replaced the district commissioners of the colonial era were, like them, responsible to ministers rather than to their communities. The roles of state and party were fused, and ZANU's rural support in Mashonaland, built during the liberation struggle, was consolidated in peacetime.

Rapid economic growth and substantial external finance in the first two years of independence did not continue, and, although there was an air of optimism about the 1980s, it was pressure from the International Monetary Fund and the World Bank that caused the government to rein in some social programmes. Zimbabwe had borrowed massively from the World Bank in the early 1980s, hoping that repayments would fall from 16 per cent of export earnings in 1983 to just 4 per cent; however, by 1987 the repayments had jumped to 37 per cent, and the Bank had forced cutbacks in the education programme and food subsidies.

If 100,000 young people were leaving secondary schools in the mid-1980s, the formal economy was only creating 10,000 new jobs a year, and GDP growth was only 1.3 per cent a year.[33] Looking back from the disaster years at the start of the twenty-first century, many now consider that this betrayal of an eager youth was one of the underlying causes of subsequent bitterness and disillusion. Most of the pressure on formal employment was felt in the urban areas, where, as late as 1989, 62.5 per cent of senior management and 35.5 per cent of middle management in the private sector was still in white hands. At a certain level, with the former trade routes to South Africa still cut off, there was continuity between the economic autarchy of the UDI period and the 'African self-reliance' of ZANU.

There had been a history of friction between the nationalist parties and the labour movement prior to independence, although Joshua Nkomo had emerged from the trade unions. Organised labour was weak and divided, playing no part at Lancaster House; this, as pointed out by the Zimbabwean scholar Brian Raftopoulos, was in stark contrast to the situation in South Africa, where under apartheid in the 1980s the role of labour in a tripartite post-apartheid structure of government, employers and unions was clearly agreed by the African National Congress.[34] The Zimbabwe government initially introduced legislation on minimum pay and to restrict dismissals. It also imposed a new union structure in 1981, creating the Zimbabwe Congress of Trade Unions (ZCTU), which it largely controlled until 1985. Albert Mugabe, Robert's brother, was the first secretary of the ZCTU. However, a new Labour Relations Act of 1985 restricted the right to strike, and gave more power to the minister of labour.

It seems as if the government's interest in the organisation of labour was largely motivated by the desire to prevent strikes, which had flared in the post-independence euphoria. It brushed aside claims for union nominees to take the place of the white MPs when the constitution was changed in 1987, and the disappointing economic performance of the decade, when the real value of wages was falling, ended the fragile alliance between government and labour. In 1988, after a leadership struggle which turned on the need to establish a more authentic union movement, and end co-option by the government, Morgan Tsvangirai was elected secretary general of the ZCTU. Tsvangirai was then a ZANU member. It could not have been predicted that he would take on the government, as its most persistent and courageous opponent, in the 1990s. His own background was one of struggle, though not of involvement in the war; he was the oldest of nine children, who were deserted by their bricklayer father; he was unable to take up a mission school scholarship, and had climbed to become foreman and trade union rep in a nickel mine through sheer ability.

Following the Unity Accord with ZAPU, ZANU–PF was running an effectively one-party state. The media were largely under government control. As early as 1982, foreign journalists needed monthly permits from the government, and although a Mass Media Trust took over South African-owned papers alleg-edly to protect the independence of editors, it came under state control, and 'the turnover of editors between 1980 and 2002 at Zimbabwe Newspapers was the highest anywhere in the media world.'[35] Moves to socialism and formal one-party status were widely discussed within the party. That they did not go further was partly the result of a successful popular mobilisation by Edgar Tekere, the erratic secretary general of ZANU–PF, who had been expelled because he did not agree with the single- party proposal. His Zimbabwe Unity Movement contested the 1990 presidential and parliamentary elections. Facing similar intimidation and demonisation to what ZAPU had suffered in the 1985 election, and the Movement for Democratic Change would encounter in the twenty-first century, ZUM nevertheless won 18 per cent of the vote, though only 2 seats out of 120.

Another factor lay in developments in other countries. While Zambia still had a one-party state, this was coming under stress, and President Kaunda first had to concede multiparty elections, and was then rejected by voters in favour of the Movement for Multiparty Democracy (MMD) in late 1991; the leader of the MMD was Frederick Chiluba, a trade unionist who had been imprisoned by Kaunda, and who as president would be accused of serious corruption. In South Africa it was obvious that the anti-apartheid alliance of the ANC, the South African Communist Party and the Congress of South African Trade Unions (COSATU) was a multiparty affair. FRELIMO, which had made the unsuccessful Nkomati Accord in a compromise with the apartheid regime in 1984, hoping to end the civil war with the MNR, was beginning its slow retreat from Marxist purism. And, far more influential than these regional developments, was the impact of the fall of the Berlin Wall in 1989.

Lord Acton's comment, that all power corrupts, and absolute power corrupts absolutely, began to apply as Zimbabwe hovered on the edge of total one-party control. Critics, both inside and outside ZANU, complained that it was beginning to act like a business conglomerate, not a vehicle for the empowerment of poor Zimbabweans. A major scandal broke in 1988, nicknamed 'Willowgate', which concerned the purchase and resale of cars from the Willowvale assembly plant through political influence. Ministers broke price control regulations to resell cars, which were in great demand, at a premium black market price; one disgraced minister, Maurice Nyagumbo, committed suicide after a show trial. Nathan Shamuyarira, then a minister, sued Geoffrey Nyarota – editor of the *Bulawayo Chronicle*, which had broken the story – for defamation. Student demonstrations, in which a potential Rhodes Scholar called Arthur Mutambara played a leading part, led to the first post-independence closure of the University of Zimbabwe in October 1989.

So what were relations with the British government like in the 1980s? At one level they were strained, at another remarkably friendly. In a sense both feelings were encompassed in the unusual relationship between Margaret Thatcher, a Conservative who was fiercely anti-communist, and Robert Mugabe, who had not abandoned the Marxism with which he had emerged from his Jesuit upbringing. Both leaders were highly ideological. Mugabe, for instance, was far more ideologically driven than Julius Nyerere of Tanzania, of whom Ramphal said 'Nyerere's pragmatism always trumped his ideology.' Thatcher worked with her friend President Reagan to overthrow world communism and resisted attempts at successive Commonwealth conferences – particularly at Nassau in 1985, Vancouver in 1987 and Kuala Lumpur in 1989 – to force Britain into imposing sanctions on South Africa. Mugabe, by contrast, was a leader of the Frontline States opposing the apartheid regime, and provided troops inside Mozambique to guard the oil pipeline to Beira from the South African-backed MNR; indeed Zimbabwean soldiers fought alongside FRELIMO in attacks on the MNR base in Gorongosa.

But, rather like her hero Winston Churchill, who had worked with Stalin and Tito, Thatcher was ready to do business with ideological opposites. Famously she said she could deal with Gorbachev, the up-and-coming Soviet leader. Like Mugabe she also relished an argument. In March 1981 an international donors' conference was held in the UK, designed to raise funds for investment in independent Zimbabwe. The position of the Overseas Development Agency, then the UK's aid body, was that Zimbabwe was basically a rich country; only transitional support, for post-war reconstruction, could be justified in donor terms. However, Thatcher honoured the rather limited financial promises by the British on the land issue. She was also persuaded that, in the first couple of years of her government – unpopular because of sharp spending cuts – Lancaster House and Zimbabwe's independence were real foreign policy triumphs.[36] So in spite of disagreements over South Africa she respected Mugabe and wanted the new Zimbabwe to succeed.

For Mugabe, who had complicated feelings of attraction and repulsion towards the UK – he was particularly warm to the British royal family – there was also gratitude to the British prime minister. In the end he had won power partly thanks to her, and at less cost than might have been expected. Some of his critics thought he was too friendly to the British at the start of his government.[37] Ramphal, slightly aggrieved that the Commonwealth Secretariat had less access to the new administration, commented, 'They encumbered him with friendship – he became a darling of the British government.'[38] Lord Soames's family was almost embarrassed that, following the former governor's death in 1987 at 66, the same age at which his father-in-law Winston Churchill had first become prime minister, Robert and Sally Mugabe flew to England, uninvited, for the funeral. While the warmth of Mugabe's relationship with Soames was exceptional, his attitude to Thatcher also helped underpin a practical and not antagonistic collaboration with the United Kingdom. Early in the decade a significant number of idealistic British volunteers had taught in Zimbabwean schools; there was some business investment from the UK.

Internationally the Zimbabwe government had good standing in the 1980s. In the continuing Cold War, and with neighbouring liberation movements like the ANC and SWAPO, which were friends of the Soviet bloc, it still had fences to mend. It was not until 1983 that a Soviet embassy opened in Harare. It was, however, a key member of the Non-Aligned Movement, had a rotating membership of the UN Security Council, and a strong place within the Southern African Development Community (SADC), which was a regional body for economic development, set up with support from the Commonwealth Secretariat. SADC allocated portfolios to countries; hence Zimbabwe, with its agricultural strength and food exports presumed, was responsible for coordination of agricultural development in the region. Robert Mugabe was awarded the Hunger Prize for Africa in 1988, on account of his country's contribution.[39]

Zimbabwe practised solidarity with its neighbours, notably with Mozambique's FRELIMO, which had fought alongside ZANLA in the Rhodesian war. At one point as many as 15,000 Zimbabwean troops were inside Mozambique, guarding the rail and road corridor from MNR attacks, and fighting in joint operations with FRELIMO. Obviously this was for the benefit of Zimbabwe as well as the Mozambican government. But Zimbabwe also set up a Beira corridor group, chaired by Denis Norman, to invest in rehabilitation of the roads, rail links and the port.

But the world's eyes were focused on South Africa. In 1986 a Commonwealth mission, led by General Obasanjo and Malcolm Fraser, sought unsuccessfully to find a negotiating formula which could lead to the unbanning of the ANC and an end to apartheid. By 1989, with the collapse of East European communism and the growing unrest inside South Africa, the ideological and economic foundations of apartheid were crumbling. President de Klerk released Nelson Mandela from Victor Verster Prison in February 1990. This was the beginning of the end of a glory period for

Robert Mugabe and ZANU–PF, in which they had unique status as a beachhead of liberation in southern Africa.

Looking back on the 1980s, from a vantage point at the end of the first decade of the twenty-first century, it is clear that there were important shadows over independent Zimbabwe. Reconciliation was superficial. The economy could not match the progress in education and health care. The land issue festered. Violence and impunity had continued after the end of the war. Democratic values had not transformed a ruling party nurtured on Marxism, a militarist ethic and centralised control. Public expectations, in a country which was the envy of neighbours, were not being satisfied. The socio-political situation looked better, and institutions more secure, than was really the case. The 1990s led to breakdown.

FIVE

WHEN THE WHEELS BEGAN
TO FALL OFF: THE 1990s

Zimbabwe's survival as an apparently progressive country in the 1980s, after the brutalities of the civil war and with an unrepentant apartheid regime to its south, seemed to many to be an achievement in itself. To outsiders, the southern African situation in the early 1990s looked as if it was becoming steadily more benign. Following Nelson Mandela's release in 1990 a lengthy process of negotiation, punctuated by violence in the townships and countryside, saw South Africa on its way to the democratic elections of 1994. Namibia achieved independence with UN support in March 1990. Mozambique's bitter enemies, FRELIMO and the MNR, reached a general political agreement to end their civil war, in August 1992, in Rome; the MNR was rebranded as a political party, RENAMO. Only in Angola and the Congo were wars continuing, but the general direction of the region was towards peace.

Yet the 1990s, when Zimbabwe hosted the successful Commonwealth summit in Harare in 1991 and Robert Mugabe was given an honorary knighthood on a state visit to the UK in 1994, was a decade in which many things began to go seriously wrong. A structural adjustment programme, part of the Washington neoliberal economic consensus then fashionable among donors, stripped social services and welfare and sought cost recovery from poor and middle-income Zimbabweans. ESAP was nicknamed 'Extreme Suffering for African People' and gave a fillip to strikes by organised labour. A serious drought early in the decade brought hardship. There were more obvious disparities between rich and poor, with more tall buildings in Harare and more beggars on city streets.

Corruption became more obvious. There was a series of scandals in parastatals, ranging from the Grain Marketing Board to Air Zimbabwe, where ZANU–PF nominees diverted funds. In addition to filching by ministers, officials and businessmen close to the party, it became clear that the president's family was dubiously enriching itself. Leo Mugabe, the president's nephew, managed to upset the Tender Board's award of the bid for a new airport terminal at Harare in favour of a small Cyprus company; it was subsequently shown that bribes were paid to four government ministers, including US$190,000 to Leo. Leo's companies won other government contracts, and Zidco, the ZANU–PF trading company, also got preferential treatment.[1] Privatisation policies, as in eastern Europe, allowed insider dealers to make off with some state and parastatal assets.

Crucially, Margaret Dongo, a feisty former ZANU member, exposed the scandal of theft from the war veterans' compensation fund. This led to her election, after a court battle, as an independent MP in Harare in 1995. She had crossed into Mozambique in 1975 for ZANU at the age of 15 and been a founder of the War Veterans Association; when in 1995 the official results showed that she had lost in the Harare South constituency by 1,097 votes she managed to get the result nullified by the High Court, on the ground of rigging, and subsequently won a by-election in spite of ZANU thuggery.

ZANU managed to shrug off other types of political opposition with ease. When a respected former chief justice, Enoch

Dumbutshena, set up the Forum Party of Zimbabwe in March 1993, it could only win 5.9 per cent of the vote in the 1995 elections, and no seats.[2] Forum's economic programme was conservative, calling for a reduction in the cabinet from forty-three to fourteen ministers, and devolution of powers to the provinces. It faded, beset by internal divisions.

But militancy by the war vets led Mugabe to try and buy them off, allocating an unaffordable compensation of $Z50,000 each. It was the start of the inflation, and a resort to the printing press, which led to the destruction of the Zimbabwean currency and individuals' savings in the following decade.

War vets – people who had carried arms and knew how to use them – were not to be dismissed lightly. Mugabe, who was married to a Ghanaian, could recall that it was the shooting by the British of demonstrating ex-servicemen in Accra in 1948 which had expedited Kwame Nkrumah's campaign for 'positive action', and Ghana's independence. Zimbabwe's war vets united irreconcilables from both ZANLA and ZIPRA, who after fifteen years still felt cheated of the fruits of victory. Having got a lot in financial compensation once, they would want to come back for more. For Mugabe the easiest target to divert them were the white commercial farms.

The biggest disaster for Zimbabwe, unrecognised at the time, was the end of apartheid in South Africa. Nelson Mandela had come as a guest to the Commonwealth summit in Harare in 1991; the negotiations between the ANC, Nationalists and other parties in CODESA, the Conference for a Democratic South Africa, were convoluted and conducted to the background music of war in the townships and Kwa-Zulu Natal, a war promoted by the apartheid security services. But, through remarkable statesmanship and compromise, South Africa emerged from elections in 1994 with an ANC-led government of national unity. Where Mugabe had played up divisions, between white and black, Shona and Ndebele, Mandela was enacting conciliation, between black, Indian and white, between Xhosa and Zulu.

At once, Zimbabwe ceased to count for so much on the geopolitical chessboard. Zimbabwean industries such as textiles, protected from South African competition by the boycotts affecting their southern neighbour, were exposed to the full force of a much more powerful competitor. The textile centre of Kadoma, for example, became almost a ghost town. By 2010 it was said that the whole Zimbabwean economy, in its weakened state, amounted to only 2 per cent of the value of South Africa's.[3]

More troubling, for the ZANU–PF leadership, was the rapid diminution in status of a government which had worked hard to end racism in southern Africa. Mugabe had, for example, played a creative role in the peacemaking which brought an end to the Mozambican civil war; he broke one deadlock when he talked to Afonso Dhlakama, the MNR leader, in Shona in Malawi in January 1992. At the signing of the agreement between FRELIMO and the MNR in Rome, in October of that year, he made a speech which oddly echoed his speech of reconciliation in Harare in 1980. He said, 'Today is not the day of judgment. It is the day of reconciliation. Today is not the day when we should examine who was right and who was wrong. Today is the day when we must say we are all right. Both are right in being party to the process of peace.'[4]

But even before the ANC won the first democratic election in 1994, Mandela and South Africa had the voices the world wanted to hear. Mandela spent much of his single term of office on international travel, in part to thank supporters, in part to drum up investment. His long record of twenty-seven years in prison, his imaginative efforts at reconciliation, his outgoing nature and crazy shirts – all of this took the limelight away from the introverted Robert Mugabe and his government. A sense that the history of Rhodesia and then Zimbabwe was simply a footnote to the larger, more exciting story of South Africa was real, and immensely galling.

The worst moment for Mugabe personally was in 1996, when he married his former secretary, Grace Marufu, in a big ceremony in his home area of Kutama. His best man was Joaquim Chissano, president of Mozambique. But the man who stole the show, simply by his presence in a big gathering of African leaders, was Nelson Mandela. To be overshadowed at your own wedding was to rub salt into his humiliation. In fact the premature death of his first wife, Sally – whom he had met when they were both teaching at the Takoradi Teacher Training College in Ghana – was both a political and personal milestone.[5]

Sally was a political partner, granted the honorific title of *Amai*, or 'mother' in Shona, and buried after her death in 1992 in the National Heroes Acre in Harare. She had supported Mugabe through all his vicissitudes and imprisonments, and had given up a comfortable life in Ghana to be with him. After the death of her son, she had never had another child. She won credit for her charitable work. She was a feminist in a patriarchal society, and built up the ZANU Women's League after independence.

But she developed kidney problems, and was on dialysis for the last twenty years of her life. Ironically she was elected first secretary of the ZANU–PF Women's League and secretary for women's affairs in the ZANU–PF politburo in 1989, the year after Mugabe began his affair with Grace. In 1990, when she came second in elections to chair the Women's League, Mugabe overruled the result to give her the position. Grace, with whom Mugabe had two children, was a completely different character, from a poor Zimbabwean background, without political antennae, and keen on shopping and the spoils available to the mistress and wife of a 'Big Man'. Observers thought that Mugabe had lost some of his grounding, in the purposes for which Zimbabwe had won independence, with Sally's death. He lost good, affectionate political advice, domestic anger management, and a pan-African perspective.

The 1990s also saw the growth of Zimbabwe's trade-union movement into an alternative source of political power, army intervention in the Congo's civil war on the side of the Kabilas, and a more hostile relationship with the former colonial power, the United Kingdom. The arrival of Tony Blair's 'new' Labour government in May 1997 brought different, less friendly attitudes from London. In essence Blair, like Henry Ford, the autocratic pioneer of motoring, acted as if 'history is bunk'. The first international conference in the UK happened to be a Commonwealth heads' meeting in Edinburgh, at which the new British government sought to promote an image of 'Cool Britannia'; the archaic Britain of pageantry and hangovers of Empire was dead, washed away in a dawn of Labour renewal, focusing instead on the digital, the modern, the pragmatic. Extraordinarily Blair himself, though educated in Edinburgh, decreed that there should be no bagpipes playing at the 1997 summit.

The Commonwealth had been invited to the UK in 1995 by the then Conservative prime minister, John Major, who had worked as a young banker in Nigeria and had an affinity with the association.[6] The last time the Commonwealth had come to the UK had been in 1977, when James Callaghan had been a Labour prime minister with warm ties to newly independent states. But although Robin Cook, the new foreign and commonwealth secretary under Blair, proclaimed that the Commonwealth was one of the four pillars of British diplomacy, officials thought that in reality Labour was sceptical, and saw the summit chiefly as an opportunity for public relations. Many of the young policy wonks arriving in Whitehall were not born when the Commonwealth was created, and did not want to know about the struggles of independence. But Mugabe and senior henchmen in ZANU–PF

– some like Emmerson Mnangagwa had been severely tortured by the Rhodesians – had not so conveniently forgotten.

The cataclysm which engulfed Zimbabwe in the first decade of the twenty-first century had one of its roots in poor economic performance, and the neoliberal economic policies, of the first years of the 1990s. In 1991 the government adopted an Economic Structural Adjustment Policy. Bernard Chidzero, who had good struggle credentials going back to the 1960s, had worked his way up from 1968 to 1980 in UNCTAD, the UN's trade and development arm in Geneva, becoming the deputy secretary general. He was a dominant figure in Zimbabwean policymaking. He had been at the same Jesuit school as Mugabe, Kutama College, and came back after independence; he was successively the minister for economic planning and senior minister of finance, and his international prestige was such that he was a serious contender to be UN secretary general in the 1990s.

In a politburo and government that was light on economic expertise Chidzero persuaded Mugabe and colleagues to adopt ESAP (Economic Structural Adjustment Programme), the policy then in vogue with the Washington lending institutions, the International Monetary Fund and the World Bank. The collapse of East European communism seemed to justify a drastic reduction in the role of the state. ESAP was designed to strip overblown public-sector and parastatal payrolls, introduce 'cost recovery' in social service fields such as schooling and health, and promote private-sector growth. But this approach was never well adapted to African reality, and in Zimbabwe, where a small white minority was disproportionately powerful on the boards of companies, it was profoundly destructive.[7]

In 1991, the first year of the policy, average economic growth fell from 4 per cent to 0.9 per cent, and, with droughts and poor exports – now suffering from South African competition – it only reached 2.9 per cent in 1998/9.[8] Many of those workers lucky enough to have jobs in the formal economy lost them, and unemployment reached 44 per cent in 1993. Families were sent back into the rural areas, in hopes of subsistence. The real value of wages declined. There were complaints that, despite government propaganda, it was difficult for small black-owned firms to get credit. In the countryside, in the communal areas, many lived outside the cash economy.

Social gains of the 1980s were lost, with a 1993 UNICEF study suggesting that twice as many women were dying in childbirth as in 1990, and that fewer people were attending clinics and hospitals because they could not afford it under the 'cost recovery' policy. While these setbacks were to be dwarfed by the collapse in the following decade, they seemed serious at the time, in the context of the recent hopes of independence.

Throughout the 1990s there were a series of strikes by under-paid health professionals, led by nurses and junior doctors. The sight of Mugabe's lavish wedding to Grace Marufu near Chinhoyi, linked to the absence of promised increments in their payslips, led to a walkout by nurses at Chinhoyi in August 1996. This sparked a two-week strike by 70,000 civil servants, which showed the growing strength of the increasingly aggressive and independent Zimbabwe Confederation of Trade Unions (ZCTU). The strikers wanted a 100 per cent cost-of-living adjustment, housing and transport allowances and a forty-hour week.[9] The government made a few concessions. The ZCTU started to build links between public- and private-sector unions and, while the government blamed the unions for 'political' action, the union movement began to diagnose the bad state of labour relations and impoverished living standards as the product of bad governance.

In a 2000 report summarising the breakdown of relations with the government over the previous decade, the ZCTU stated:

> The relationship that had developed between the government and ZCTU from the time when ESAP was first introduced in Zimbabwe (1990–91) onwards has been that of serious communication

breakdown resulting in contradictions, counter-accusations, suspicion and animosity. This was expressed in direct attacks by government through the mass media accusing ZCTU for ineffectiveness, and harbouring a hidden political agenda.[10]

The increasing autonomy and willingness of the ZCTU to take on the government frontally had parallels elsewhere in the developing world. In Brazil, for example, a somewhat corporatist union movement had broken free of government control in the 1970s, responding to a dictatorship's compression of wages with increasingly large-scale and successful strikes. Significantly, by the early 1980s, this new confidence had erupted in the creation of a new workers' party, the Partido dos Trabalhadores (PT). In Zambia, across the Zambezi, it was the leader of the Zambian Congress of Trade Unions, Frederick Chiluba, who was elected president of the country in 1991.

In Zimbabwe a government crackdown vilifying Morgan Tsvangirai, the general secretary of the ZCTU, was matched in the second half of the 1990s by increasingly successful mass action by the unions. An attempt by the government to split the union movement, by setting up a Federation of Labour under Joseph Chinotimba, was a failure. Although the economic and social situation had deteriorated, the unions, and those they represented, had benefited from the rising educational standards of the post-independence years. There was a contrast between increasingly corrupt political elites, unwilling to negotiate with the more sophisticated social forces, and those, particularly in the urban areas, whom they governed. The unions were only part of a wider scene beyond the government's control, including a range of civic organisations built around varied interests and causes.

A crucial year was 1997, when Mugabe and the government first caved in to the war veterans, who had complained that their compensation fund had been raided. They were awarded Z$50,000 each (then around US$2,500), plus a pension of Z$2,000. Blackmailing the regime, they then persuaded the government to pay a monthly salary of Z$4,000.[11] The whole package involved more than Z$4 billion in new expenditure. It was unbudgeted, and the government did not have the money to pay. Late that year the government announced a 5 per cent 'war veterans' levy', plus an increase in sales tax and petrol duty, to try to pay for the concession. Lashing out too at the commercial farmers, the government announced that it would designate and seize 800 white-owned farms, which led to a run on the country's foreign currency reserves and a crash in the value of the Zimbabwe dollar on 'black Friday', 14 November. In the background lay a breakdown in diplomatic relations with the United Kingdom, and the knowledge that the new Blair government was unlikely to come to the financial rescue.

The ZCTU planned a one-day strike for 9 December 1997. Although the government offered to scrap the 5 per cent levy and the petrol tax, this seemed too little, too late. The union movement had coordinated its protest with civic groups and business, and the one-day strike was an unprecedented success, with street demonstrations and rallies. In Mutare at least 30,000 people marched against the new taxes. But in Harare, in spite of a court ruling, police stopped protesters from coming in from the high-density suburbs, and beat up the marchers. The day after the strike, Tsvangirai himself was brutally beaten and knocked unconscious in his office by thugs assumed to be hired by the ruling party;[12] the police were slow to investigate, in a sign of their increased politicisation. This was the first of a series of personal assaults over the next decade which led to recognition of his personal heroism and dedication.

How was it that the issue of the compensation fund for war veterans had become so toxic? Their demonstrations had threatened the government, surrounding ministry buildings in Harare such as the Ministry of Local Government, so that a visitor had to be

led out of the back door. Thanks to Margaret Dongo and even
the media, they were aware that monies from the fund had been
paid over to functionaries who could not possibly have fought in
the guerrilla war. Dr Chenjerai Hunzvi, a rabble-rousing medical
doctor trained in Poland, and who himself was accused of helping
himself to the fund, became head of the war veterans' association,
orchestrating the demonstrations against the government. He met
Tsvangirai, raising the danger for ZANU–PF of a coordinated
opposition involving both workers and war vets. The role of the
war vets in the government's propaganda story of national liberation was iconic. They were not a group – like the students, who
were stopped with tear gas when they demonstrated at the time
of the Commonwealth summit in 1991 – who could be squashed
without cost. They threatened the survival of the regime. They
had to be bought off, with cash or with land.

Furthermore, war vets could have been treated much better,
and knew it. In neighbouring Mozambique, so familiar to ZANLA
and Zimbabwean soldiers in the 1970s and 1980s, an exemplary
support scheme had been introduced after the Rome peace agreement in 1992. Backed by UNDP, donors and the Mozambican
government, a US$35.4 million trust fund administered by UNDP
was set up to help former troops and guerrillas reintegrate into
civilian life. It gave each of them cash grants of roughly US$2
a week, for over two years. Nearly 93,000 veterans, from both
FRELIMO and the MNR, benefited. They were given photo ID
cards, cheques and vouchers, and could collect the money at post
offices or branches of the Banco Popular de Desenvolvimento.
Although a third of the demobilised fighters had had no formal
education, and another third only primary schooling, there were
few problems.

The Mozambican war vets used the money to help their families, to pay school fees and to give themselves a fresh start. Their
spending helped to pump-prime activity in the rural areas most

damaged in the civil war. The administration costs were tiny, at only 0.5 per cent for the UNDP and 2.5 per cent for the bank. Most miraculously, by comparison with Zimbabwe, there was enough money over at the end of the scheme – because of a decline in the value of the metical, the Mozambican currency – to give each ex-fighter a bonus equivalent to US$52.[13]

In Zimbabwe the government managed to split the potential alliance of the war vets and the unions, and the unions continued their campaign. Yet popular discontent outran the union movement. Food prices had risen by 26.7 per cent in 1997 and in January 1998 there was a further sharp rise of 21 per cent in the price of mealie meal, made from maize, which is the staple food for most Zimbabweans. This set off several days of spontaneous food riots, starting in Harare, and affecting even small towns throughout the country. Again the government cracked down hard; ten people were killed, and hundreds arrested and attacked by the police and security services. Concern for the victims led to the birth of the Zimbabwe Human Rights NGO Forum, a coalition of human rights bodies whose protests and testimony were to be constant over the years ahead.

Mark Rule, a Zimbabwean Rhodes Scholar who provided a regular commentary on economic affairs, wrote to friends after the food riots:

> Eighteen years of mismanagement have led to low growth, steadily rising unemployment and falling real incomes, with no hope of improvement in sight. This has taken place against a background of growing affluence of political leaders and their retinues. Resentment, long simmering, has risen as much as incomes have fallen and any spark could have caused the explosion.[14]

The government combined its opposition to the union movement with an attempt to co-opt it, through a National Economic Consultative Forum. Originally an idea suggested by the unions, this was to be a tripartite forum involving government, labour, business (both 'indigenous' and white-owned) and other social sectors. But the ZCTU was suspicious, worried by Presidential Powers (Temporary Measures) Regulations promulgated in August 1998, which could make strikes illegal in the private sector, and it continued its programme of rallies and stay-aways. The tripartite national forum was not tackling the real depreciation in wages, or the cases of corruption in the war vets' fund, in Harare city council, or NOCZIM, the state oil company. Increasingly the ZCTU was building connections with civil society and other critics of ZANU–PF.

At the same time the authoritarian tendencies in ZANU did not fit well with the changing international landscape in the 1990s. The better-educated society, which had emerged at home from the first decade of independence, was asking more questions. A key moment had been the Commonwealth summit in Harare in 1991, which adopted principles which came to play a defining role in that body: just and accountable government, the rule of law and fundamental human rights. On its eve there had been a three-day conference on human rights in Commonwealth Africa, sponsored in Harare by the Legal Resources Foundation, the Southern African Nongovernmental Development Organisations Network, the Catholic Commission for Justice and Peace, and the Commonwealth Human Rights Initiative (CHRI).

The summit saw a stand-up row between Brian Mulroney, prime minister of Canada, and President Moi of Kenya. Mulroney asked why Canadian taxpayers should pay for Kenyan government corruption. In an executive session of the leaders, chaired by Mugabe, Prime Minister Hawke of Australia flashed around *Put Our World to Rights*, the CHRI report calling for a human rights declaration by the Commonwealth, and asked colleagues what they proposed to do about it. Several African countries, including Zambia and Malawi, switched to multiparty democracy.

In South Africa, a public process of consultation led to a new constitution, with a strong Bill of Rights, and a constitutional court to adjudicate it. This constitution sought to entrench certain economic rights, such as a right to housing, and gay rights, which were anathema to the authorities in Zimbabwe.

There was a momentum here, to which Zimbabwe was not immune, even with a controlled media. In 1995, following the execution of Ken Saro-Wiwa and other Ogoni activists in Nigeria, a Commonwealth summit in New Zealand set up a Ministerial Action Group – a rules committee to give teeth to the Harare Declaration. At once it suspended three governments that had come to power by military coup.[15] Dr Stan Mudenge, Zimbabwe's foreign minister and a historian of the pre-colonial era, was first chairman of this group. Mugabe was not keen on military coups; he gave Captain Valentine Strasser of Sierra Leone a dressing down at the Cyprus Commonwealth summit in 1993, and lectured President Yahya Jammeh of the Gambia, described as 'colonel, retired' at a Commonwealth meeting in Botswana four years later.

In 1997 the veil was lifted on the Matabeleland massacres of the 1980s, with the publication in Zimbabwe of a careful but horrendous report entitled *Breaking the Silence: Building True Peace*, by the Catholic Commission for Justice and Peace and the Legal Resources Foundation. Both were respected Zimbabwean NGOs, and they had carried out interviews with around a thousand survivors and witnesses of the Gukurahundi. The authors provided a context, which underlined the extent of abuse over some thirty years. They suggested that at least 30,000 had died during the Rhodesian war; that the 'protected villages', crop destruction and displacements of Smith's security forces had led to widespread malnutrition; that the attacks by the South African-backed MNR in the Mount Darwin area of north-east Zimbabwe, and the Chipinge area of south-east Zimbabwe, after independence, were responsible for 'serious human rights abuses'.[16]

But none of this could take away from the scale of the repression of the Ndebele, with around 20,000 deaths and torture in North and South Matabeleland and the Midlands provinces in the 1980s; it was a repression which had caught ZAPU MPs as well as obscure and innocent villagers. As Elinor Sisulu, writing an introduction to a new 2007 edition of the report, said, 'I was taken aback by the account of the mass shooting of 62 young men and women on the banks of the Cewale River in Lupane on 5 March 1983. The silence that greeted this massacre is in direct contrast to the 1960 Sharpeville Massacre, news of which reverberated around the world.'[17] *The Chronicle* of Bulawayo, the state-owned paper printed in the region where the abuses were taking place, had periodically covered the deaths or arrests of 'dissidents', but not the revenge by security forces.

The publication of this report in 1997 testified to a moment of optimism, about to be dashed. The authors in their preface wrote

> the current report has been possible only because Zimbabwe is currently enjoying a period of stability and national unity that did not exist ten years ago. The country now known as Zimbabwe has, in the last hundred years, had a history marred by internal conflicts: the current state of peace in the nation is unprecedented.

They added that true independence for South Africa not only closed the colonial history of Africa, but began 'a new process of accountability, and highlighted the realisation that true reconciliation between people who have traditionally been opposed is often facilitated by honest public acknowledgment of the past'. This hint that a South African-style Truth and Reconciliation Commission might be appropriate for Zimbabwe, along with specific recommendations for legal compensation, the removal of violators from positions of authority, and the recovery of human remains, was too embarrassing for the ZANU–PF hierarchy to follow up.

The unfolding efforts at reconciliation in the 'rainbow nation' south of the Limpopo had an impact on the Zimbabwean public, especially the politically aware. Though many civil servants and teachers had had to hold a ZANU party card for career reasons, their party loyalty diminished. At the upper end of the party there were also external pressures for greater democracy, from varying international sources.

One of the more interesting exercises took place on 24–27 February 1997, in Kasane, a riverside town inside Botswana but close to the borders with Zimbabwe and Zambia. This 'round table on democracy and good governance in Africa' was promoted by Chief Emeka Anyaoku, the Nigerian secretary general of the Commonwealth. As secretary general from a country which had endured a civil war and had narrowly avoided being expelled from the Commonwealth two years earlier, he was keen to push the Harare Declaration and help make Africa more democratic.

Anyaoku knew that multiparty politics faced serious diffi- culties on the continent. Traditions of authoritarian leadership, combined with the patrimonial obligations of extended families, made the concept of a 'loyal opposition' very alien. Competitive elections, where they had taken place, had a winner-takes-all quality; opponents would be trashed as national traitors, and excluded from posts; friends and family would be rewarded. He had been involved in a successful Commonwealth effort to assist Kenneth Kaunda, defeated in multiparty elections in 1991 but still regarded as father of the Zambian nation, who was suddenly made homeless and impoverished when electors ejected him from State House, Lusaka.

Anyaoku thought that African leaders needed to be encouraged to see that oppositions are both legitimate and useful. Cooperating with the president of Botswana, Quett Masire, the Commonwealth Secretariat organised a seminar at Kasane on the differing roles of governments and oppositions, and how they can work together in the national interest. Mugabe came from Zimbabwe. The occasion provided a vignette of the frosty relations that had developed between Mugabe and Mandela. Mandela, ever a stickler for punctuality, arrived for the group photo on time. Mugabe turned up late, keeping the other leaders waiting. Mandela gave his fellow president a public dressing-down. Following the meeting of leaders there was a gathering in Gaborone, involving opposition figures also; Margaret Dongo came from Harare.

The Kasane initiative demonstrated the limitations of the 'soft power' influence of the Commonwealth, one of Zimbabwe's greatest champions, in persuading that government to change direction. Nor was ZANU–PF necessarily impressed by Mandela's ANC, and South Africa's commitment to multiparty democracy.

The sense of economic and social crisis in Zimbabwe, developing in the mid-1990s, led the ZANU–PF government to strike out in two new directions – to join a war in the Democratic Republic of the Congo, and to rev up the rhetoric against the white-owned commercial farms, and the British government. Both were in a sense diversionary tactics, but both had potential to ease the economic and inflationary pressures the country was facing.

Zimbabwe joined the war in the Congo in 1998, supporting the government of Laurent Kabila with between 11,000 and 20,000 troops before their withdrawal as part of a series of peace agreements four years later. It was generally thought that the Zimbabwean forces were more professional than those of, for example, Angola and Rwanda. As many as eight nations and twenty-five armed groups were involved in a war over a vast territory, and there were strong links to the genocide in Rwanda and its aftermath. Kabila was a slippery individual and Mugabe became his strongest international backer. When Kabila died two days after an assassination attempt in Zimbabwe in January 2001, Mugabe was largely responsible for ensuring that his son Joseph succeeded him.

Why did Mugabe join this war, along with his liberation and SADC allies, Angola and Namibia? The theory was that it would pay for itself. The Congo is extraordinarily rich in many minerals, including diamonds, gold, cobalt and coltan. Businesses associated with ZANU and the Zimbabwe military could help themselves to these resources, with the Kabilas' agreement. At a time when the treasury in Harare was finding more difficulty in paying for public servants, the defence budget could be self-sufficient. Zimbabwe had surplus refining capacity for some of these minerals, and they could be shipped out from Beira.

Accounting for the war was opaque, but critics suggested that it was costing US$1.3 million a day and there was no way that government revenue was benefiting to the same extent.[18] In September 1999 an IMF spokesman said it had a document which showed the cost of the Congo expedition to be US$166 million in the first six months of the year; Dr Herbert Murerwa, the finance minister, had told the IMF that it was only costing US$3 million a month. Later still it was suggested that it could be costing US$3 million day. What was certain was that, like the payments to the war vets, Congo costs had not been budgeted for in advance. The war had been launched by Mugabe without parliamentary, and probably without cabinet, approval. Opinion polls showed that it was unpopular. It was unconstitutional, because the Zimbabwe defence forces were not supposed to invade other countries. It was another reason why, in the late 1990s, multilateral agencies lost faith in the economic policy of the ZANU government.

But there were other aspects to the Congo war, apart from its expense. It confirmed the alliance between ZANU and the military at the highest levels. Ever since 1980 the former ZANLA leaders had been significant, leading factions in the party; the liberation story, the guarding of the Beira corridor in conjunction with FRELIMO in the 1980s and the smashing of the alleged 'super-ZAPU', was now given a financial coda in the Congo.

Furthermore, the Congo war was brutal. Altogether it is estimated that 5.4 million people died, many were displaced, and rape was commonplace. Life was cheap; cruelty unpunished. This was an environment inclined to corrupt the most professional of soldiers, and prepare them and their commanders for repression, or the toleration of repression, of those deemed to be opponents at home.

Mugabe's policy did something else. It gave him enhanced regional standing, which would be important as the West started attacking him after the farm invasions began in 2000. Post-apartheid South Africa, reacting against the interventionist strategy of the former white rulers, was extremely cautious about using its military muscle in Africa. It sought instead to be a mediator and peacemaker. Zimbabwe and ZANU had no such compunction about using military force. It was good to be recognised as a loyal ally, and for the Kabilas to see Zimbabwe as their protector. Indeed President Joseph Kabila had Zimbabwean bodyguards in Kinshasa.

It was in 1997, the year that war vets were bought off with Z$50,000 each and the ZCTU organised national strikes, that the British government and the issue of white-owned commercial farms stoked national controversy again. Initially it seems as if Mugabe had some hopes from the change of government in the UK, when Labour overturned the Conservatives in May elections. Tony Blair, the new prime minister, congratulated him that month on his appointment as chairman of the Organisation of African Unity. Keen on shopping visits to London with his younger wife he asked to meet Blair on his return through London from an environmental summit in New York, but Downing Street said Blair's programme made this impossible. Mugabe thought he had been snubbed.[19] Again he felt snubbed in October, at the Edinburgh Commonwealth summit, when he tried to get Blair to pay for land acquisition. Blair's line was that this was ancient history, that there was insufficient transparency in Zimbabwe's programme, and the poorest Zimbabweans were not the main beneficiaries of the government's land policy.[20]

This breakdown was exacerbated when, on the one side, Mugabe ordered officials to draw up a list of 1,500 commercial farms for rapid takeover, and, on the other, Clare Short, the new international development secretary, wrote to the Zimbabwe government to say,

> I should make it clear that we do not accept that Britain has
> a special responsibility to meet the costs of land purchase in
> Zimbabwe... We are a new government from diverse backgrounds
> without links to former colonial interests. My own origins are
> Irish, and as you know, we were colonised not colonisers.[21]

This airy dismissal, with an Irish reference which she wrote in to strengthen a draft from her officials, infuriated Mugabe and his agriculture minister Kumbirai Kangai.[22]

Some of those involved in preparing the Short letter considered that it did not in practice involve much change in the policy of the British government. In the early 1990s the British High Commission in Harare had hoped the land question would go away. The commercial land market, with purchases and sales going through on the basis of certificates of 'no government interest', was taking land ownership not only further from the situation at independence, but very far from the original land grab by Cecil Rhodes and his friends. Only awkward lawyers, who argued that the original Privy Council ruling against the Chartered Company in the 1920s meant that there was a historic responsibility for the British government for land, kept troubling questions alive.

But there had been friction even before the change of government in the UK. Mugabe had come on a state visit in 1994, which he greatly enjoyed, at a time when Lynda Chalker, the Conservative minister responsible both for overseas aid and for

Africa, was saying in public that Zimbabwe was well governed. Nonetheless, at a meeting in Buckingham Palace during this visit, she expressed certain criticisms, including of cronyism and lack of transparency in the allocation of land. Chalker was a popular figure with many African leaders, in part because it was known that she had opposed Mrs Thatcher's 'softly, softly' approach to South African apartheid. She was tired when she saw the president at the palace, and was reading from briefing notes. Mugabe reacted violently to the criticism, accusing Chalker of being a new Cecil Rhodes.

In 1992 the Zimbabwe government had passed a Land Acquisition Act which abandoned the 'willing seller, willing buyer' principle of Lancaster House, and opened the way to compulsory purchase of commercial farms. In 1992/3 the government designated eighty-three commercial farms for compulsory acquisition, involving over half a million acres. In addition to whites, political opponents of Mugabe, including Ndabaningi Sithole and James Chikerema, were targeted. But the government, challenged in the courts on modalities and compensation, was severely embarrassed when it turned out that key members of the regime, rather than land-hungry peasants, were getting the land. Beneficiaries included Witness Mangwende, the former agriculture minister who had promoted the Act, Perence Shiri, now commanding the air force, and Augustine Chihuri, the police commissioner. Although Mugabe fulminated against 'a greedy bunch of racist usurpers', the scandal forced him to back down from these takeovers.

In 1992 also a review of agriculture in the communal areas, carried out jointly by the party and the government, pointed out that communal ownership made it hard for farmers to get the loans they needed to upgrade their incomes. The tenure system obstructed investment, because lenders wanted identified collateral and responsibility for repayment. But neither the act nor the report had an immediate impact. Observers thought that

ZANU found communal tenure politically convenient. After the crisis of land invasions broke, at the start of the new century, the party reverted to a strategy of Smith and the colonial era, providing privileges for chiefs and elders in the rural areas to ensure their backing.

In 1996, by agreement with the Zimbabwe government, the British sent an expert group under Mark Lowcock to take stock of land reform and the progress of resettlement. At this point there were still unspent funds in the original £44 million allocated by the Thatcher government for land purchase.[23] In the run-up to the presidential election of that year, comfortably won by Mugabe, he sent two ministers – Kumbirai Kangai of agriculture and John Nkomo of local government – to see Chalker in London. He himself was staying in a London hotel, to which they had to report every night. He wanted to see a new phase of the resettlement programme.

As with a previous review, eight years earlier, the new report was broadly positive about the resettlement programme. This had provided new homes and agricultural land for around half a million Zimbabweans. Although some land in Matabeleland was better suited to extensive cattle ranching, most of the land handed over under the scheme was appropriate for small-scale intensive agriculture and, even if it was not always of the highest quality, the new farmers were doing well on it. But, in looking forward, the British officials were more concerned with who would be getting the land and what support they could expect. While they argued for compensation, their main concern was with the future of agriculture in Zimbabwe, still a mainstay of the commercial economy and rural livelihoods. Indeed, when 4,000 white farmers had met Minister Mangwende in 1990 to complain of threats of confiscation, they argued that the commercial farms provided a quarter of all the formal jobs in Zimbabwe, and 40 per cent of export earnings.

Although the Zimbabwe government handed over a bound copy of their response to the Lowcock team's report, it did not offer a negotiated solution, and the two governments did not agree a new land settlement programme prior to the 1997 election in the UK. In retrospect this may have been a missed opportunity, although it is possible that the Zimbabwe government was hoping for more financial help than was feasible for Britain at the time.

The arrival of the Labour government put a new spin on relations, going beyond personal snubs and ill-judged correspondence. A senior diplomat at the Foreign and Commonwealth Office had forecast a 'car crash' immediately after the election, because the gulf of misunderstanding between Harare and 'new' Labour was so wide. It was not only that history loomed large in Harare, and was being written off in London. The new government had a more serious interest in the relief of poverty and in international development, which was to distinguish it from its predecessor.

Labour, which had created a Ministry of Overseas Development in the 1960s, had watched as the Conservatives, who came into office in 1979, downgraded this ministry into an Overseas Development Administration (ODA) within the Foreign and Commonwealth Office. The message was clear: overseas aid was to be a branch and tool of British foreign policy. Furthermore, as scandals in Malaysia and Tanzania were to show, a key purpose of the ODA was the promotion of UK business overseas.

For Labour the continuance of poverty, in a world which appeared to be getting richer thanks to globalisation – a phenomenon embraced by 'new' Labour – was a horrific stain. Tony Blair, who had been apolitical as a student, told Joan Lestor once that it was the development issue which had brought him into the Labour Party in the 1970s.[24] Hence the new government not only re-created the Ministry of Overseas Development with higher status as a Department for International Development (DFID) – which meant that Clare Short and her successors were cabinet ministers – but gave top priority to 'pro-poor development'. This meant that the difficult aim of poverty eradication throughout the world became UK government policy. While DFID did not abandon Conservative concerns with governance, and the role of the private sector in promoting development, it was looking at all sectors and developing countries through the prism of the poorest. Short was totally dedicated in wanting to help them, and angry that elites had in the past diverted precious aid funds for their own benefit.

But what seemed like common sense and solidarity in London looked like neo-colonial interference in Harare. The row between Mugabe and Chalker at Buckingham Palace in 1994 took on an ideological intensity three years later. Marxist critiques of the role of international business in developing countries merged with national sovereignty concerns with donor countries that wanted to intervene in sensitive domestic policies. If the Harare government wished to give land to its richer as well as its poorer friends, so ZANU would argue, then it was nobody's business but theirs. If this had the effect of reducing agricultural output initially, for an overriding political purpose, then so be it. Zimbabwe had only enjoyed its hard-won independence for a brief time, and would use it as it saw fit. Chief Anyaoku, who had good relations with Foreign Minister Mudenge, was told that the ZANU leadership thought that agricultural chaos was a price worth paying for restitution of the land.

Following the Edinburgh Commonwealth summit, and with the war veterans and strikers threatening his position, Mugabe ordered his ministers to draw up a list of 1,500 commercial farms, covering 4 million hectares, which could be taken over rapidly. The UK government, realising by the end of 1997 that the land question had become toxic and could not be avoided, lobbied hard to get the United Nations Development Programme (UNDP) involved, both for its money and for its technical expertise. There were several agreements involving the UNDP and Zimbabwe between 1997 and 2000, which had little effect. Mugabe kept repeating that the commercial farmers were Britain's responsibility, that the original occupiers under Rhodes had paid nothing for the land, and his government would pay nothing to regain it. He did not want aid money, but compensation. Out on the farms, where some had had squatters since independence, big farmers became more anxious about their long-term future.

Apart from the fact that most commercial farmers had only a tenuous connection with Britain, already an issue at Lancaster House, an acknowledgment of responsibility to buy them out en masse raised difficult questions. Britain's former empire, on which it was claimed that the sun never set, had seen plenty of land seizures by what was then understood as a right of conquest. Was a post-colonial British government, merely a middle power on the edge of the twenty-first century, suddenly to be held liable in compensation for historic land grabs all over the world? Further, as high commissioners in Harare like Peter Longworth pointed out to officials there, was it really sensible or acceptable to transfer a lot of money to a bunch of white farmers when black Zimbabweans had more pressing needs?[25]

What became a huge and chaotic land occupation from 2000 onwards, described in the next chapter, had started soon after independence, when around 200 farms were occupied, nearly all vacant; this number reached a peak of around 800 occupied farms in the mid-1980s.[26] Such occupations were varied in nature, and often stimulated by frustration with the government's slowness to honour its promises, at independence, to reallocate land. Some of the settlements were by former farm workers on the big farms, who had had no rights in the communal areas; some were by people from adjoining communal areas, who might have started by looking for more grazing land for their animals.

These peasant land invasions were by no means unique to Zimbabwe. In neighbouring Mozambique, abandoned Portuguese farms were being allocated on the basis of fifty-year leases, and those taking them up were required to negotiate with local communities. In Brazil a radical landless movement got going in the 1980s, occupying empty and underexploited lands, and providing part of the political constituency for the Workers' Party (the PT) and its charismatic trade unionist leader Lula.

But the heightened rhetoric about Zimbabwe's land in the later 1990s, and confusion in the government about listings for takeover, led to a complicated scene in which peasant takeovers were sometimes undertaken with the support of ZANU or the government, and sometimes in opposition to them. For instance 625 of the nearly 1,500 farms which had been listed for takeover, by local provincial committees dominated by ZANU–PF, were then delisted because they did not meet the government's own criteria. Many acquisition orders were successfully challenged in court by the commercial farmers. Peasant frustration led to around thirty occupations in 1997, mostly on farms scheduled for compulsory acquisition.

The complications were illustrated by the hostility of a group of occupiers to their MP, Minister Herbert Murerwa, when they moved out of the Dende Communal Area north-east of Harare into Munenga Farm, where they said their ancestors were buried. They were angry that the farm had been delisted. Although Murerwa told them they would get the land, they would not move without a written government assurance. In Matabeleland North, 500 people moved into four farms in Umguza district; although they were encouraged by some politicians, Joseph Msika, ZANU's national chairman and chair of the national land acquisition committee, sought to get them out.

Describing these occupations, Jocelyn Alexander wrote:

> These ... were dominated by people from communal areas and
> resettlement schemes, but also included unemployed workers
> and war veterans. Most of the land occupied was white-owned
> commercial land, but state, church and black-owned farms were
> also targeted. Occupiers generally justified their actions in terms
> of their exclusion from resettlement, and their historical claims to
> land, i.e. in terms of restitution and broken nationalist promises.[27]

These occupations, and the ambiguous response of the authorities, led to increasing questions about the security of property rights everywhere.

Mugabe's own position was equivocal. At different stages he was sympathising with the occupations. At others he was seeing them as a threat to the government and issuing stern warnings. In a few cases, the police burnt the squatters' camps, and moved the occupiers away by force. But Mugabe was also using them to pressurise donors and the UK. When a donors' conference took place in Harare in September 1998, when the government was talking of a new land policy with 5 million hectares for smallholders, donors were taken to meet occupiers in Svosve so that they could see the land hunger at first hand.

The donors' conference in September 1998 was organised by the UNDP, which had been involved in Zimbabwe since independence, and which the UK saw as an institution that could internationalise the problem; this initiative recalled the pre-independence discussions of Cyrus Vance and David Owen, with their hopes for a large-scale aid programme under UN auspices. It was financially ambitious. There would be a fund of US $2,000 million for land resettlement, with donors providing 60.7 per cent, the government 35.8 per cent, and the settlers themselves 3.5 per cent.

The conference also proposed a two-year inception phase in which the Zimbabwe government's new resettlement schemes could be tested alongside ideas from the private sector and civil society. The Commercial Farmers Union proposed a 65,000 hectare pilot project, for example.[28] However, the donors continued to make clear that there had to be transparency in land transfer, which should follow the rule of law.

Meanwhile the ZCTU was keeping up the pressure on wages and the economy. Writing at the end of the year, Mark Rule commented that 1998 had been the year of the unions.

> What specific event was the most important and most likely to affect the future of the country? Almost certainly the growing militancy – and success – of the trade unions. The ZCTU has established itself as virtually the only body since independence able to confront the Government on general policy and to force it off its chosen path.[29]

The Zimbabwe dollar more than halved in value in the course of 1998.[30]

By 1999 it was obvious that the Zimbabwe government was not terribly interested in transparency, or donor requirements. The IMF slowed down its negotiations to provide aid, in protest at the kidnapping and maltreatment of the two Zimbabwean journalists Ray Choto and Mark Chavanduka, which had led to widespread diplomatic protest. In April 1999 Mugabe attacked the IMF: 'Let that monstrous creature get out of our way... Why should we continue to plead? Let us look elsewhere for resources.' In fact the previous year President Gaddafi of Libya had awarded US$100 million lines of credit to NOCZIM, the near-bankrupt oil parastatal. This was the start of a policy designed to escape the Western-dominated donors, and to look for finance and investment from countries such as China, Malaysia and Libya, which shared more authoritarian governance.

In the 1990s the resettlement project had petered out, with ESAP encouragement for agrarian capitalism and continuing peasant frustration. Between 1990 and 1996 only 20,000 households had been resettled.[31] The government's motivation now was wholly political, and concerned with retaining power for ZANU–PF. Manipulation of the land issue as a nationalist campaign, which could reinvigorate the faltering party base and bring in the war vets as shock troops, coincided conveniently with a downturn in relations with the United Kingdom. The former colonial power was characterised as the enemy that lay behind the white farmers.

In July 1999 Tony Blair appointed Peter Hain as Africa minister in the Foreign and Commonwealth Office. For Blair, busy with a bombing campaign designed to get the Serbs out of Kosovo, Zimbabwe was not high up the agenda. Later that year, in a radio interview prior to attending a Commonwealth summit in Durban, he would say that he would have preferred to stay at home, watching an England versus Scotland soccer match. Seen from Harare, however, Blair's emerging and gung-ho doctrine of 'liberal interventionism' – which would see British military involvement in former Yugoslavia, Sierra Leone, Afghanistan and Iraq – looked dangerously like support for regime change in central Africa too.

The appointment of Peter Hain harked back to a time when the political left in the United Kingdom had been keenly engaged in the anti-racism struggle in southern Africa. Then a Young Liberal, Hain had led the successful campaign against a white-only Springbok rugby tour in 1970, and was exposed to a number of dirty tricks by BOSS, the South African intelligence service. He knew what he was up against. Born in Kenya, he had moved to South Africa as a child, where his father was victimised under the Suppression of Communism Act, and then came to England. Hain said he was among those who celebrated when Robert Mugabe and ZANU won the elections in 1980.[32] Hain's predecessor, Tony Lloyd, had not got on well with the Zimbabwe government and Foreign Office officials hoped that

Hain's anti-apartheid credentials would allow for an improved atmosphere.

In November 1999, Robert Mugabe and Peter Hain met in a hotel in London's Victoria district. The meeting was amicable, with Mugabe patting him on the knee, describing him as 'my friend'. However, the following day, gay rights campaigner Peter Tatchell attempted a citizen's arrest of the Zimbabwean president; this was in response to the arrest and torture of the two journalists in Harare, Ray Choto and Mark Chavunduka.[33] In Hain's words, Mugabe 'went ballistic', assuming that the minister or the British government had set up Tatchell to do it, which was not the case. Mugabe's homophobia was legendary. He had insisted that the organisation called Gays and Lesbians of Zimbabwe (GALZ) be evicted from the Harare international book fair in 1995. As relations with the UK collapsed he enjoyed describing the Blair government as a bunch of 'gay gangsters'.

In fact Hain felt that Zimbabwe, and its anti-apartheid supporters in the UK, had been betrayed by the corruption and cronyism of ZANU–PF. He thought Clare Short was right in her attitude to pro-poor development, and there was nothing to be gained by pussyfooting with Mugabe. With the approval of Tony Blair and his spin doctor Alastair Campbell, he embarked on a war of words with the Zimbabwe regime, confident in his own struggle credentials. He was deeply disappointed that the ANC government in South Africa, led since 1999 by President Thabo Mbeki, was using the same arguments for 'quiet diplomacy' and 'constructive engagement' with Zimbabwe, which he and other campaigners had criticised in the 1980s, when used by Reagan and Thatcher to avoid confronting apartheid South Africa.

But if relations were going downhill with Britain, Mugabe's relations with South Africa were into an upswing. Thabo Mbeki was elected unopposed as ANC president in 1997 and in 1999 he was elected president of South Africa with an ANC landslide; his share of the poll at 66.4 per cent was higher than Mandela's of 62.6 per cent. Although the contacts of the new South African president with Mugabe would not always be friendly, they represented a vast improvement for the Zimbabwean over the testy and moralistic attitudes of Nelson Mandela. At a personal level Mbeki and Mugabe had much in common. Both were introverted, intolerant of dissent, and feeling that the world did not fully recognise their worth.

It was the political affinities between Mugabe and Mbeki that were more important. Both were facing a crisis of unmet expectations in their peoples, attacks from trade unions, criticism over unreformed land ownership and that a narrow band had benefited from black empowerment; they confronted remnants of racism and the challenge of youth unemployment. Mbeki was profoundly suspicious of white racism and neo-colonial meddling and was happy to endorse many of Mugabe's favourite lines – that the UK had failed to deliver on promises at Lancaster House to fund land redistribution, and that Zimbabwe's economic problems were not due to mismanagement and corruption but to the damage inflicted by the structural adjustment programme.

Mbeki was also less wholehearted than Mandela on issues of human rights and corruption. Human rights had divided the two men in late 1998, when Archbishop Desmond Tutu presented his Truth and Reconciliation Commission report. Mandela, as president, accepted it. Mbeki, as head of the ANC, tried to challenge it legally because it was 'scurrilous' that the ANC had been found guilty of gross violations in the treatment of its detainees in Angola.[34] In charge of a defence subcommittee, before he became president, Mbeki pushed for expensive arms procurement deals, which led to major corruption scandals later.

Hence, as new political struggles in Zimbabwe developed in 1999, with the growth of a movement for constitutional reform and

continuing economic problems, Mugabe could take comfort from
the arrival of a more sympathetic leader south of the Limpopo.

In the background, however, lay a coarsening of the human
rights situation, where the bread riots of 1998 had led to beatings and tortures by the police and security services; use of
the *falanga*, or beatings on the soles of the feet, became more
common where police sought information in criminal cases.
The newly formed Zimbabwe Human Rights NGO Forum, an
umbrella group which came to have nineteen member bodies in
Zimbabwe, had investigated the aftermath of the food riots, when
government helicopters had fired tear gas into angry crowds; the
UN Human Rights Committee had called for an independent
commission of inquiry but this request, like the report from the
Forum, was ignored by the government. Zimbabwe had never
signed the UN Convention against Torture, and it was significant
that in 1991, the year of the Commonwealth summit in Harare,
Mugabe had offered asylum to the former Ethiopian leader
Mengistu Haile Miriam, alleged to have killed half a million
'counter-revolutionaries'.[35]

The Forum was worried that, as in countries like Rwanda,
political and economic instability could lead to a rapid and disastrous decline in human rights. Looking back on events in 1999
it stated:

> The situation in Zimbabwe is undoubtedly a cause for major
> concern. Since the formation of the Human Rights Forum, in the
> midst of riots and civil disobedience, the socio-political situation
> has been deteriorating at an alarming rate. The near-demolition
> of the Zimbabwe economy has resulted in a huge increase in the
> number of very poor people and rampant inflation, with massive
> and constant price rises.[36]

The Forum, quoting the minimalist poverty datum line statistics,
stated that the proportion of 'very poor people' in the country had

risen from 67 per cent to 76 per cent in one year, 1998/9. Those who could, began to leave. Ironically, the United Kingdom was recruiting trained teachers and health workers.

It had been clear since the 1980s, and the Matabeleland massacres, that Mugabe cared little for human rights at home when he saw political survival as at stake. Some observers believed that his anxiety about the capacity of the International Criminal Court to hold rulers to account was a reason why he postponed any thoughts he might have had about retirement. In November 1999, still angry at Peter Tatchell's ambush in London, he let off homophobic steam to British journalists at the Commonwealth summit in Durban. He said he had not been satisfied by the official apology, and that Blair was heading a 'gay government' in the 'United Gay Kingdom'. Unlike the majority of Commonwealth leaders, he also did not attend a Remembrance Day parade on 11 November.

But there was a curious episode at Durban. Following the establishment of the pioneering rules committee for the Commonwealth in 1995, the Ministerial Action Group (CMAG), there had been continuing pressure from NGOs and some governments to give it more teeth. It was supposed to enforce the Harare declaration on just and accountable government, the rule of law and fundamental human rights. But in practice its remit – unpopular with governments put on its list, which were suspended from the councils of the Commonwealth – had been limited to countries subject to military coups.

Working with this group of foreign ministers, Chief Anyaoku, in his last year as secretary general, proposed a toughening up of its terms of reference. It recommended to Commonwealth leaders that it should get involved: when a government postponed an election; when a government intervened in the judiciary; or when a government clamped down on the media. Anyaoku and CMAG believed that it would be possible to define these violations objectively, and he thought that he had taken political precautions to ensure that the proposals would go through at Durban. Specifically, he had contacted the two leaders most likely to torpedo them, Robert Mugabe and Prime Minister Mahathir Mohamed of Malaysia, and got their agreement in advance.[37]

But when the proposals were put to leaders in an executive session they were rejected by, of all people, the prime minister of Barbados. When a couple of other leaders chipped in with hostility, the scheme was lost. Barbados, with one of the oldest parliaments in the world and an estimable human rights record, was least likely ever to feature on a CMAG agenda. The argument presented by Owen Arthur, the Barbados prime minister, was the one of infringement on national sovereignty, which had been overtaken when CMAG had been set up in 1995.

For Zimbabwe, on the edge of a full-blown crisis, this outcome was to lead to confusion in its relations with the Commonwealth, until in 2003 the Mugabe regime walked out of the association. The Commonwealth had been a godfather at the birth of independent Zimbabwe. It was not the United Kingdom in disguise. With its majority of developing nations, which still belonged to the Non-Aligned Movement, it was not 'the West'. The coming breakdown with the Commonwealth would point to the growing isolation of ZANU-PF at the start of the twenty-first century.

SIX

DISASTER YEARS
AND THE THIRD CHIMURENGA

It was around the start of the new millennium, boasted of by President Thabo Mbeki of South Africa as an era of African renaissance, that Zimbabwe became a failed state.[1] Not all state institutions collapsed, and instruments of coercion remained strong. But the state could no longer provide many of its citizens with food, basic services, a guaranteed rule of law, and socio-economic as well as civil and political rights. Adverse signs had been building up in the last decade of the twentieth century. Ironically, it was a democratic gesture by Zimbabwean voters, who rejected a new constitution in the referendum of March 2000, that precipitated collapse. A vengeful reaction to defeat by Mugabe, and the coterie round him, unleashed a chaotic period of land invasion, inflation and impoverishment.

The campaign for a new constitution, to replace the shop-worn and amended one inherited from Lancaster House, began in late 1997. The official launch of a non-governmental National Constitutional Assembly (NCA) took place at the University of Zimbabwe on January 1998. The initiative came from the Zimbabwe Council of Churches, with seed money from the institute associated with Germany's Social Democrats, the Friedrich Ebert Stiftung. The involvement of a wide range of civic groups, as well as church bodies, human rights activists, lawyers and journalists, testified to the growth of a vigorous culture of debate and participation in Zimbabwe, in spite of government controls on the media, and the narrowness of officially permitted political space. Women's groups and residents' associations also formed part of the NCA coalition, which had diverse ideological factions.

But the most important element was the involvement of the trade unions, and the election of Morgan Tsvangirai of the ZCTU as president of the NCA. Tsvangirai, a Shona speaker born in rural Manicaland in 1952, had grown up poor and left school early to work in a textile mill and then a nickel mine. Like Mugabe, he came from a family whose father had deserted it. He had become nationally known when he was arrested supporting student protests in 1989, and, in spite of physical assault and constant attempts at intimidation, his reputation had grown steadily. He maintained a simple lifestyle while excoriating the corruption and riches of the ZANU elite.[2] He had built ZCTU into an organisation of 400,000, about a third of the formal labour force, and with street protests and stay-aways they had become hardened against state repression. When Mugabe used the Presidential Powers (Temporary Measures) Act to ban national strikes for six months, it did not make a great deal of difference.

To begin with, ZANU–PF dismissed the NCA as not worth worrying about. The party's legal secretary Eddison Zvogbo remarked: 'How can a few people sit under a tree and claim to be a National Constitutional Assembly. They are neither constitutional nor an assembly.'[3] The NCA had difficulty in spreading its message into rural areas, and was ignored by the official media. But the NCA found ways of getting through by means of community outreach, and in March 1999 the government tried to co-opt the movement by launching a well-funded Constitutional Commission of its own. This had the effect of permitting ZANU–PF members to join the debate; some of them were also fed up with economic decline and an increasingly geriatric leadership. Rather as the ZCTU had found itself drawn into wider issues of national governance, the women's movement saw the constitutional issue as an opportunity to engage with the state and civic allies; an influential Women's Coalition on the Constitution was launched in June 1999.

The government's Constitutional Commission was dominated by ZANU nominees. The NCA boycotted it, because the Assembly wanted a people-driven process, which would stress government accountability. In the course of 1999 the debate over a new constitution was interwoven with something much more threatening to the Mugabe regime – a serious attempt to change the government at an election. The crucial initiative took place in September when, after six months of discussion, the ZCTU and some thirty civic groups met to establish a Movement for Democratic Change to compete in the elections scheduled for 2000. Initially this was rather more of a movement than a party, and there was a certain vagueness in policy. But Tsvangirai was chosen as its leader and the motivation was plain. The MDC's Shona slogan was *Chinja maitiro* – 'Change the way you are doing things.'

The Constitutional Commission's proposals recommended independent commissions on public expenditure, elections, corruption and the media; but it left huge powers and patronage in the hands of the president and, although the president would in future be limited to two further terms of five years, offered him a further ten years.[4] Attempts to restrict Mugabe further were disallowed by Judge Godfrey Chidyausiku, who was chairing the commission, and the president then gazetted an amendment of his own, which would allow the expropriation of land without consultation, stating that Britain would be responsible for the payment of any compensation. While this was a blatant attempt to shore up ZANU's rural vote, it also mobilised white farmers and their employees to come out against the new constitution.

By the violent standards of electioneering in Zimbabwe the run-up to the referendum on the constitution, in February 2000, was relatively peaceful. Many observers thought that the government would walk home easily, as it had done in previous elections. The government media were in full cry, and there was a strong anti-white animus. 'While 20 years ago we fought [the whites] using AK rifles, today we are using a pen and ballot paper. But the war is no less important than in the 1970s. The enemy is the same', said the *Sunday Mail*.[5] The notion of a ZANU–PF still at war, especially with white farmers, was to become real as the year went on.

But the result of the referendum was a surprise. With only a quarter of the electorate voting, 54 per cent of those who cast ballots voted No. Most of these No votes were from urban areas, suggesting that the involvement of the trades unions and civic organisations had been strategic. Neither ZANU's rural supporters, offered hints of land for free, nor the white farmers under threat had the same political significance. 'The president has with fair dignity accepted defeat', wrote Mark Rule in his circular.[6] Mugabe went on television to acknowledge that the result was 'unfortunate' and said, 'Let us all accept the verdict and plan the way forward.'

Behind the scenes, however, Mugabe was planning retribution: mass invasions of commercial farms, and assaults and thuggery in the campaign leading to parliamentary elections on 24 and 25 June. The unpopularity of ZANU–PF had been brutally exposed, and a few members of the central committee, meeting three days after the referendum, even dared to call on Mugabe to step down. The government's strategy was twofold, and immediate: to unleash the 'war vets' and its other supporters in a series of land invasions, and to intimidate its opponents by violence.

ZANU–PF had sensed a significant threat of regime change, and to its liberationist assumption that it should be the ruling party for ever.

The land invasions started on 26 February, as armed gangs, transported by government and army trucks, invaded white-owned commercial farms; by 8 March nearly 400 farms had been invaded. Occupiers pegged out plots, threatening the owners. The operation seemed chaotic, sometimes frenzied, as animals and trees were hacked to pieces, and unrelated to any serious plan for agricultural settlement. Police stood by. The Commercial Farmers Union got a High Court order to state that the oc-cupations were illegal, but this was ignored by the government. Mugabe and Peter Hain, the British minister he now abhorred, exchanged threats, with Hain saying that Zimbabwe could fall over the abyss, and Mugabe altering the constitution to permit expropriation of white-owned farms without compensation.

But although the invasions looked anarchic, and were some-times spontaneous, there was often purpose and organisation behind them. The 'war veterans' might have been too young to have fought in the civil war, but they and the ZANU youth militia were demonstrating the party's iron fist in rural areas. Hunzvi and the militarised group at the top of ZANU, and in the army and police, directed the gangs' movements. Hunzvi, who gloried in the nickname 'Hitler', was a deeply ambiguous figure; on trial for embezzling the war vets' fund, he managed to get elected as ZANU–PF MP for Chikomba in June. Farmers and their workers who had supported the MDC and the No vote were particular targets; Mugabe was enraged by pictures in the controlled media of wealthy farmers handing over cheques to the MDC. He attacked 'entrenched colonial attitudes' among the farmers, affecting colour, ownership and employment. The ZANU line that the white farmers, a bulwark of the Smith regime twenty years earlier, were still the enemy had just enough credence to stir up supporters in a process which acquired the colloquial Shona description *jambanja*, 'violent chaos'.

Philip Barclay, second secretary at the British embassy in Harare from 2006 to 2009, by which time the white farmers only numbered a few hundred, was not unsympathetic to them. But he wrote that they could not see black farm workers as anything but labourers, and there was an unpleasant side to white farming culture.

> Most Zimbabwean farmers I have met have attitudes that would simply not be tolerable in modern Western society. I remember standing with a group of farmers outside court in Chegutu, waiting to see whether a magistrate wanted to prosecute them. As they got used to my presence, they started to joke about farm dogs chasing black labourers. In no time they were happily talking about niggers and kaffirs. With a change of accent they would have fitted right into 1950s Mississippi.[7]

Inevitably, in the chaotic, intimidatory invasions which began after the referendum in 2000, there were deaths. The first two to be murdered were David Stevens, a farmer and MDC organiser in Macheke, killed along with his foreman, Julius Andoche. Threats to wives and children caused the Commercial Farmers Union to urge withdrawal to Bulawayo of many farmers in Matabeleland. Mugabe referred to white farmers as 'enemies'; Hunzvi said that this was 'a revolution' and no one should raise eyebrows over the deaths of four white farmers.[8] In many of the invasions the farm houses were burnt, the barns and equipment trashed. But while the white farmers lost property and in a handful of cases their lives, it was their workers who suffered the most.

Altogether it is estimated that some 200,000 workers lost their jobs in the ensuing mayhem;[9] these were around two-thirds of the original labour force, and many were punished, tortured or 're-educated'. Techniques of self-criticism and public humili-ation borrowed from China's Cultural Revolution under Mao, and developed in ZANU–PF's *pungwes* during the war against Smith, were aggressively used once more. Workers whose parents or grandparents had arrived from Malawi or Mozambique were treated by the war vets, and ZANU's youth militia who worked with them, as not quite Zimbabwean. Attempts to invoke the police were usually fruitless.

A report by the Catholic Institute for International Relations showed what an attack on workers at the Chipeza Farm Estate, near Marondera in central Mashonaland, could mean for the workers.

> On 15 September 2000, as farm workers were resting at their homes, they were attacked by more than 200 squatters. The invaders came with pick-axe handles and other weapons, and carrying torches made from grass from fields that normally would have been cleared for replanting but had remained fallow because of harassment of workers.
>
> The terrified workers, mainly women and their children, fled into the bush. The squatters broke into huts and stole personal belongings. Thirteen huts were burned down. The workers watched their belongings go up in smoke and only ventured back towards evening when everything was quiet.[10]

In June 2000, the National Employment Council for the Agricultural Industry, which brought together government, employers and unions, reported that so far that year 3,000 farm workers had lost their homes, 26 had been killed, 1,600 assaulted and 11 raped. While 47.2 per cent were supporters of the MDC, 43.6 per cent had no affiliation and 4.7 per cent were ZANU–PF supporters.[11]

How far did Mugabe and the ZANU–PF leadership actually care about the loss of agricultural production and exports caused by such disorderly takeovers? For Zimbabweans the crucial output was of maize, the source of mealie meal or *sadza*, on which most households depended. Peasant agriculture could not make up quickly for the decline in maize produced by the former commercial farms, and in 2001/2 this was 70.4 per cent less than it had been in the 1990s, and in 2004/5 it was still 45.6 per cent less.[12] Droughts in 2001 and 2002 had not helped. It seems that the government simply did not care about the consequences of the land invasions for its people's food, by comparison with the political imperative. In this respect it may have been influenced by the ruthless Maoist ideology of the early 1960s, when possibly 45 million Chinese died in the famine caused by the 'Great Leap Forward' and Mao himself said 'It is better to let half of the people die so that the other half can eat their fill.'[13] Nonetheless, in the Shona countryside, and in particular for invaders from overcrowded communal lands, the fast-track land reform was popular. The authorities attempted to rationalise the takeovers into technocratic categories developed earlier – A1 smallholder plots, and A2 commercial farms, which varied considerably in size.[14]

The Western, and particularly the British, media focused on the violence directed at the whites. Much less attention was given to the assaults and intimidation suffered by the farm workers. This played into the hands of Mugabe and ZANU–PF, whose racist, anti-white propaganda sought to link the Fast-Track Land Resettlement Programme with a revolutionary narrative of liberation. The so-called third *chimurenga* was billed as a third chapter in a story of Zimbabwe's capture of freedom and economic sovereignty. In reality it illustrated how ZANU–PF was ready to declare war on significant sections of its own population in order to retain power. For the land invasions were intimately connected with the party's strategy for the June 2000 parliamentary elections.

The speed of developments in Zimbabwe in 2000 was dramatic. The MDC had only been formed the previous year, but after the constitutional referendum it looked as though ZANU–PF had lost most of its support in the urban areas. The results of economic and social decline, and government corruption, were visible everywhere. A new independent daily, *The Daily News*, was telling of scandals. The land invasions pointed to a collapse in the rule of law, which also impacted on industrial firms, where there were sit-ins and occupations. People thought they could help themselves to anything, and that assets could be won without effort. Where possible, domestic and international capital fled the country. International sanctions were threatened; at a meeting of parliamentarians from the European Union and the African, Caribbean and Pacific countries, Glenys Kinnock proposed a motion that non-humanitarian aid be suspended. Significantly, while 39 European MPs voted in favour and only 1 against, only 6 from the ACP countries voted in favour and 43 were against.

Both the MDC and the government thought there was a serious prospect that the MDC could win a majority of the elected seats. But what did the MDC, a loose coalition, really want? It clearly wanted to remove Mugabe, a new constitution, and more transparency in government finance. It sought an end to the Congo adventure, to violence in the countryside, and to human rights abuse. It clearly had a lot of sympathy from the United Kingdom and international donors, and would hope to rebuild Zimbabwe's relationship with global financial institutions. But it seemed fuzzy on agricultural policy, torn between its support from commercial farmers and its desire for rationality in land reform, and a recognition that ZANU–PF land occupations had genuine popular appeal and might be hard to undo. Its slogan had been 'land to the people not politicians' and its founding manifesto of 1999 stated that the party would 'redistribute over five years at least 5 million hectares of agricultural land to 100,000 families'.[15]

The MDC also faced a strategic challenge, which would dog it throughout the first decade of the twenty-first century, and to which there was no easy answer. It faced a ruthless opponent, high on its own ideology, which was quite prepared to use ballot-rigging and strong-arm methods to retain power. Morgan Tsvangirai himself was an admirer of Gandhi and Nelson Mandela, and not an anti-democrat or revolutionary. His party's symbol was an open palm, contrasting with ZANU's clenched fist. When MDC activists were murdered in 2000, he forbade a response in kind. Although 'people power' could shift governments from eastern Europe to the Philippines, neither votes nor general strikes would necessarily remove ZANU–PF from power in Harare. What then?

Tsvangirai, by his courage and force of personality, was the natural leader of the MDC coalition. But he had come out of the labour unions and into national politics quite suddenly. He had real difficulty in winning support in some sectors in Zimbabwe, and from leaders and opinion formers in the Southern African region.

In Zimbabwe he was up against ingrained respect for education, and a snobbery which meant that President Mugabe, a teacher with seven university degrees,[16] was taken more seriously than someone who never had a full secondary education. Lula, the trade unionist who became president of Brazil in 2002, had faced similar objections. Though Tsvangirai was an avid reader and autodidact, was he sufficiently prepared intellectually to choose between conflicting advisers in the MDC, particularly between free marketeers and developmentalists on the economy?

Tsvangirai also had to live down the failures and corruption of Frederick Chiluba, the trade unionist who was president of Zambia from 1991 to 2001. Chiluba, who had been imprisoned by Kaunda, became authoritarian and corrupt in office. He presided over a large-scale and unpopular programme of privatisation. His Movement for Multiparty Democracy, a coalition of unions and civil society which had much in common with the MDC, as well as the similarity of title, was beginning to break up. Tsvangirai, like Chiluba, had a history that lay outside the liberation struggle which still dominated governmental attitudes in Mozambique, South Africa, Namibia and Angola. Tsvangirai seemed to be trying harder to win backing in Europe than from suspicious regional neighbours.

Launching the ZANU–PF manifesto on 3 May 2000, Mugabe denounced whites as 'sell-outs' and said that the MDC were their puppets. Violence was overt, with ministers and candidates using threatening language and presumed MDC supporters beaten up. The Amani Trust, a human rights group, recorded nineteen deaths in May, and a total of 5,070 cases of political violence – nearly all caused by ZANU–PF.[17] Three weeks before the election the MDC said that it was only possible to campaign safely in 25 constituencies; 46 were affected by intimidation; and in 49 the levels of violence were so high that the MDC could not campaign at all. Furthermore, there were serious questions about the electoral register and the management of the election. Bishop Peter Hatendi, a former chairman of the Election Supervisory Commission, resigned saying that the registrar general and electoral process had lost all credibility.

With a weighting of constituencies that favoured Shona rural areas where the ZANU–PF machine was strongest, and the president's ability to nominate thirty unelected MPs, Mugabe and the leadership could have been reasonably confident. There was a reduction in violence immediately prior to the election, even though a thousand farms remained occupied. But the result was unexpected. ZANU–PF won 62 seats, with 48 per cent of the votes; the MDC won 57 with 47 per cent. Four white MPs were elected for the MDC. Tsvangirai, who lost in his home area of Buhera North, managed like others to get elected after persuading the courts of irregularities. Seven ZANU–PF cabinet ministers lost their seats. A black Zimbabwean journalist, covering the election for a news agency based in South Africa, said she was sure that ZANU–PF had been defeated. She saw voters unable to cast their ballots due to a lack of polling stations in the towns, and police assisting disabled and partially sighted voters to cast their ballots for ZANU-PF.[18] Tsvangirai had to choose whether to accept the results, as amended by courts which still had an element of independence, or to reject them. The MDC accepted them. From 2000 onwards there would be a strong opposition presence in Zimbabwe's parliament.

The orchestrated chaos of the farm invasions and the violent June elections led to a rapid decline across most measures of national life. In fact one of the strangest aspects of Zimbabwe's tragedy, which reached its nadir in 2008, was that observers were constantly forecasting a total collapse which did not quite seem to happen. Partly this was due to the extreme toughness of ZANU-PF, its securocrats and hangers-on, with their greed, ingenuity and need to survive. But it was perhaps more that this was a real enough collapse that was partly invisible, not demonstrated by successful mass action on the streets: a silent fall in life expectancy, hidden malnutrition, and a steady migration of desperate people into South Africa and other neighbouring states. There was no 'orange revolution' of a Ukrainian kind, and there were frequent Western misperceptions of African reality. In South Africa many had forecast that apartheid would end with a bloody race war; they were wrong about a massacre of whites, but many thousands of black citizens were killed in the run-up to the 1994 elections.

After the June election Mugabe changed his finance minister. Herbert Murerwa, who had been a London high commissioner in the 1980s, was moved to higher education, to be replaced by Simba Makoni, a younger technocrat who had been secretary general of SADC, the regional body. He faced a raft of problems, including an overvalued Zimbabwe dollar, suspension of aid from the World Bank and of foreign investment, and the loss of income from commercial farms and the gold mines; about 90 per cent of the gold mines, which were reckoned to provide 30 per cent of the country's foreign exchange, were threatened with closure as a result of inflation and the shortage of raw materials. There were particular issues with the supply of petrol products and electricity, which needed foreign exchange. By the end of 2000, Makoni said that the economy had contracted by 4.2 per cent; the IMF said that real gross domestic product had fallen by 5.5 per cent.

One problem, which was exacerbated by the farm invasions and economic collapse, was HIV/AIDS. The first cases were diagnosed in Zimbabwe in the 1980s. By the later 1990s NGOs, the trade unions and lorry owners had all become active in awareness campaigns. But for a long time, as Zimbabwe became one of the worst affected states in the world, the president was in denial. In a report to the UN Millennium Summit in August 2000 the National Association of Non-Governmental Organisations (NANGO) estimated that 1.2 million would die by 2005 and that life expectancy would drop by twenty-one years by 2010 due to this disease.[19] People of working age were most affected, women far more than men, and the commercial farms and rural areas suffered worse than the towns. The number of orphans was increasing.[20]

The ZANU–PF slogan in the June 2000 elections had been 'Land is the Economy and the Economy is Land', and with a presidential election coming up in 2002 there was no let-up in farm invasions. In the first half of 2001 some classes of property which had been excluded from expropriation – coffee, tea, timber and sugar plantations – became eligible. In July of that year, notices of expropriation were given for 7,132 properties. A Supreme Court ruling in December 2000, on a case brought by the CFU, found that the rule of law had been persistently violated in commercial areas since February 2000, that the commissioner of police, the president and all ministers involved should remove unlawful invaders, and that a workable land reform scheme should be produced by 1 July 2001. But none of this happened.

Inflation had accelerated. The consumer price index was up by 64.4 per cent, year on year, in June 2001. The knock-on effect of the agricultural crisis and rejection of the rule of law were affecting the wider commercial economy. Mark Rule wrote:

> Company managers are besieged and often attacked by rowdy bands and veterans drunk with their physical power if with nothing else. Money is extorted from the companies, allegedly to pay what is due to aggrieved workers, past or present. Chinotimba [a leader of the war vets] promises to 'deal with' another 20 companies in the coming days.[21]

As well as a matter of ideology, the attack on the commercial farms, and more especially the farm workers, had a partisan purpose. They made up a substantial voting bloc; an MDC politician estimated that they amounted to 600,000 electors.[22] In addition to the violence and propaganda to which the farm workers were subject, the ZANU–PF majority in parliament passed the Citizenship Amendment Act number 12 of 2001, which stripped them of dual citizenship. Around 30 per cent of farm workers were affected, along with nearly all the 80,000 or so whites left in the country. It had been an aim of ZANU–PF to encourage all 'foreigners' to depart.

The criticisms of civil society, of trade unions and of those outside Zimbabwe were on the whole shrugged off or rebutted by ZANU–PF. Mugabe rejected suggestions that he might retire,[23] and characterised election campaigns as a struggle between his party and Tony Blair, the UK prime minister. He said that the only good Blair was the Blair toilet, widely used in Zimbabwe. But there were some critics inside the ruling party, notably Eddison Zvogbo, who said in September 2000: 'We have tainted what was a glorious revolution, reducing it to some agrarian racist enterprise.'[24]

More significant, however, was the role of Jonathan Moyo, the minister of information, who tightened the government's control of official media, promoting a relentless drumbeat against the MDC, the whites, Britain and the West. It was he who proclaimed that the land invasions were the 'third *chimurenga*' – part of a heroic history of national resistance, in a direct line from the liberation war and the uprising against Cecil Rhodes. Moyo, a former academic, was a Machiavellian figure, directing policy and also writing songs and jingles. He had been critical of Mugabe in the 1990s, opposed to a one-party state, and was to be involved in an unsuccessful ZANU–PF plot against the president in 2005. But in 2002 he was an effective apologist and strategist for the regime.

The opposition's efforts in 2001, with boycotts, stay-aways and attempted street demonstrations, had been met by violent police repression. Tsvangirai, whose supporters faced intimidation while he himself survived three potential assassination attempts in his presidential campaign, was defeated by Mugabe in the presidential election of March 2002. The figures announced were 1,685,212 for Mugabe, 1,258,401 for Tsvangirai. As before, there had been delays at the polls, and almost certain rigging; over the previous two years the MDC and civil society had lost confidence in the impartiality of the election authorities. Nonetheless Mugabe's popularity, not least because of the land issue, was real enough. The campaign saw a peak in repression: 54 murders, 945 cases of torture, 214 kidnappings, 229 cases of intimidation, 143 cases of unlawful detention, 29 disappearances, 99 cases of unlawful arrest, and 70,000 people displaced from their homes.[25] The government limited access by outside observers; the European Union was banned, protesting at restrictions, the Commonwealth fielded a team that contained no white faces.

Most seriously, Tsvangirai and other MDC leaders had been charged with treason on the eve of this election. He was secretly caught on video telling Ari Ben-Manashe, a Canadian-based former Israeli intelligence operative, now acting as an agent for the Zimbabwe government, that Mugabe should be eliminated. It was not until 2004 that Tsvangirai was acquitted, after explaining that he had never meant that the president should be physically eliminated. But although Tsvangirai had been caught in a stunt, the treason allegation was convenient for ZANU–PF, and prevented him from travelling outside the country for a vital couple of years.

Notwithstanding the dirty tricks, repression and rigging, Tsvangirai made one of his most eloquent and optimistic speeches as the presidential votes were being counted. 'Together we have travelled a very difficult road to achieve democratic change', he said.

> Your resilience to reclaim your rights, as expressed by the overwhelming turnout, has shaken the corridors of power. Rarely in the history of mankind have a people faced such brutality while retaining such gracious exuberance....
>
> The tide of change is irreversible, but we must be prepared to pay a high price for our freedom. President Mugabe and his colleagues are afraid of the people and we have heard they may do anything to kill the messenger. If they do, you must stay strong and carry on the work we began together. Among you walk heroes – heroes who waited hours and hours to vote, heroes who refused to be turned away. These are the heroes of the new Zimbabwe whose voices must be heard around the world.[26]

The government pushed through two of its most oppressive pieces of legislation, aimed at civil society and the independent media, in 2002. One was the Public Order and Security Act, used to arrest citizens trying to hold public meetings; the second was the Access to Information and Protection of Privacy Act, which gave Jonathan Moyo considerable powers to close newspapers and ban foreign correspondents from Harare. The regime had already scored an important victory the previous year, when a bomb destroyed the offices of Zimbabwe's *Daily News*, the independent daily which was outselling the government-owned *Herald*. The *Daily News* had, among other exposés, shown that the Zimbabwean and Congolese authorities had hushed up the death of Laurent Kabila on a visit to Harare. Subsequently it was forced to close, and its editors were forced into exile.

But what was the rest of the world thinking and doing about Zimbabwe? There was a sharp divide between the position of African states, especially those in the region, and countries further away – the Europeans and North Americans, on the one hand, and ZANU–PF's traditional friends in China, North Korea and Malaysia, on the other. The lack of a united front across the international community as a whole gave the Zimbabwe government substantial wriggle room, which it was able to exploit for most of the first decade of the twenty-first century.

In southern Africa, where Mugabe had retained credit as a liberation leader who had shown solidarity in the struggle for freedom and against racism, the land invasions had widespread sympathy; human rights abuses were overlooked; the economic consequences were blamed on white or Western hostility, or on sabotage. While in Mozambique and in Tanzania the government owned all the land, leasing it to farmers, the slow progress of land reform in South Africa and Namibia made it a touchy subject for their governments. There were nuances too in the official position of neighbours. Mozambique, South Africa and Namibia were ruled by liberation movements which had a kinship with ZANU–PF; Botswana and Zambia, which had had a peaceful route to independence, were more willing to cherish democratic values, in preference to permanent revolution across the Zimbabwean border. SADC, the regional grouping headquartered in Gaborone, was weak, and dominated by its largest member, South Africa.

The key player in the region, as it had been ever since Cecil Rhodes carved out a new country, was South Africa. South African pressure could have forced change on Zimbabwe, just as apartheid South Africa's pressure persuaded Smith to come to terms with the nationalists. President Mbeki, visiting Zimbabwe on 3 August 2000, offered Mugabe support on the basis that the rule of law was respected; Mugabe told him that the invading war vets would leave unwanted land within a month, but a day later he contradicted this.

Thabo Mbeki was to be the dominant international figure in the ongoing Zimbabwe crisis until, having been forced to step down as South African president in 2009 following a revolt in the ANC and a court decision that he had interfered with a case involving Jacob Zuma, he handed over his role as SADC mediator to his successor, by then President Zuma. Personally enigmatic, Mbeki had to balance several factors. He ignored public calls by Tony Blair and the media in Britain and Europe to take strong action, preferring quiet diplomacy behind the scenes. Blair was under the illusion that Mbeki was a modernising, social democratic leader like himself, and overlooked the South African's very different experience, of racism and conspiracy. Mbeki's quiet diplomacy led to accusations from the MDC that he was too partial to Mugabe, or that he would like to see a 'reformed' ZANU–PF in power, rather than an MDC which was elected by a majority.

What were the issues for Mbeki? He himself was strongly committed to building a South Africa in which the black majority had economic as well as political rights. He also wanted an 'African renaissance' in which the continent was no longer marginalised in the world. As part of this, at precisely the time Zimbabwe was entering its years of dramatic decline, he and the leaders of Nigeria, Algeria, Egypt and Senegal were promoting the New Partnership for Africa's Development (NEPAD). NEPAD combined an aim for sustainable growth with a desire to strengthen democracy, and its peer review mechanism was to be a pioneering attempt to use peer pressure to implement these objectives. The Organisation for African Unity, at a summit in July 2001, adopted NEPAD's strategic framework. The realities in Zimbabwe were a challenge to the claims for NEPAD.

For the wider impact of the problems in Zimbabwe caused a decline in the value of the South African currency, and worries for external investors about political and economic stability for the sub-Saharan region as a whole. Mbeki was also conscious of two other issues for South Africa, land ownership and the loyalty of COSATU, the ANC's trade-union allies. Soon after the land occupations in Zimbabwe, landless people in the South African provinces of Mpumalanga and the Eastern Cape marched to government buildings to demand land reform. Tensions increased between commercial farmers and farm workers. The South African government hurriedly produced a scheme for land redistribution which promised to transfer a third of commercial farming land over five years; but significantly, and differently from the Fast-Track proposals in its neighbour, it required applicants for the new land scheme to put up a deposit before they could get government grants for land.[27]

The trade-union issue was also significant. The ANC did not rule South Africa alone, but as part of a tripartite alliance with the South African Communist Party and COSATU. There had been frictions in this alliance, particularly over the ANC's embrace of a mixed economy, the slowness of black empowerment, and wage and social issues. There was periodic talk of COSATU breaking away, and setting up a labour-based party, as the ZCTU had helped establish the MDC. This was a threat to the ANC, and it was buttressed by the fact that the ZCTU had long had fraternal relations with COSATU. Although ZANU–PF attacked the MDC when it seemed to be friendly to the Democratic Alliance, the South African opposition party which had considerable support among whites, the Zimbabwe regime exposed a danger to Mbeki in 2004 when it expelled a fact-finding group from COSATU which had come to assess the situation north of the Limpopo.

Mbeki had easier personal relations with Mugabe, treating the older man with respect as a fellow president, than he did with the less educated Tsvangirai, who lacked struggle credentials; protocol among African leaders made it unusual for them to consort with opposition figures until they took power.[28] Above all the Zimbabwe crisis raised conflicting issues for the South African president, at a time when he wanted his country to get away from its apartheid-era reputation for aggression towards neighbours. Hence he opted for a quiet diplomacy, which for many seemed an ironic and bitter parallel with the Reagan/Thatcher policies of engagement with apartheid.

Further from Zimbabwe, the response in Europe and North America, the heart of the international donor community, became sharper as the excesses of the Fast-Track occupations became fully understood. Productive farmland was returning to bush, and in 2002, a drought year, the World Food Programme began providing essentials to a country which had been a breadbasket; seven years later, in another drought year, it was estimated that by then at least two-thirds of Zimbabweans depended on food aid. Workers were losing their jobs, and going hungry. As early as 16 May 2000, the World Bank suspended US$213 million of aid, because Zimbabwe had failed to repay existing loans. The European Union withdrew multilateral assistance. In 2001 the US government passed the Zimbabwe Democracy and Economic Recovery Act, which cut off multilateral support from several agencies in which the United States was a big shareholder, and targeted Mugabe and key named individuals seen as responsible for human rights abuses. Significantly the Act had bipartisan support and, going through Congress for much of the year, it largely escaped criticism from the black caucus which had fought apartheid a decade earlier.

Inevitably the United Kingdom had a central role in the international debate. It had a Labour government, promoting a war on poverty and, during Robin Cook's tenure as foreign secretary, aspirations to an ethical foreign policy. Its prime minister, Tony Blair, did not seem greatly interested in the problems of Africa until after he won re-election in 2001, when Mugabe sent him a message of congratulation. The two diplomats in the eye of the storm, successively high commissioners in Harare, were Peter Longworth, a former industrial correspondent for the *Bristol Evening News* (in Harare from 1998 to 2001), and Brian Donnelly, later knighted, who served from 2001 to 2004. Both thought that the name-calling of Mugabe in London was ill-advised, and that for too long the British position had been dominated by DFID rather than FCO considerations. Donnelly had been warned by Clare Short, before taking up his post, 'Don't forget that it's *my* money!'[29]

The British had to consider the possibility of withdrawing UK citizens at short notice, but there was never any possibility of UK military intervention, as had happened in Sierra Leone in May 2000. In late 2001, the official *Herald* newspaper and Mudenge, the foreign minister, accused Donnelly of arranging the pillage of five white farms to justify British military action. It was nonsense, but it illustrated anxiety in some parts of ZANU–PF.

The Conservative press in London attacked Labour for doing too little about the farm invasions, and stressed the hardships of white farmers rather than the wider human rights abuses affecting their workers. But there was general condemnation of the intimidation of MDC and civil society opponents of ZANU–PF, the bogus nature of many 'war vets', the danger to food supplies, and the employment in repression of youth militias, the police and army, and state terror. The problem for the British was that they had little capacity to intervene directly – the dilemma which had haunted Whitehall for so much of the history of Rhodesia and Zimbabwe. Hence they resorted to abuse of Mugabe from London, desperate pleas to Mbeki to do something, and efforts involving the UNDP and Commonwealth to internationalise the land question. Support for the MDC from the Westminster Foundation for Democracy was counterproductive, when ZANU and the state media complained at partisan interference in a country's internal affairs. The UK government was cautious about overt demands for regime change in Harare, but in its calls for respect for democracy it was fairly clear that it would like the MDC to be voted in instead of ZANU-PF. The only thing it could do itself, as demanded by Mugabe, was to pay compensation to the commercial farmers.

There were various moments when such a solution seemed possible. One, involving Robin Cook in talks in Cairo and London, saw £60 million on the table to give to these farmers; but it was stopped by the DFID, which would have had to put up the money, when officials said that this would be giving in to blackmail. Again, at a meeting of foreign ministers under Commonwealth auspices in Abuja in 2001, just prior to the attack on the World Trade Center, which changed the international climate so drastically, it looked as though a deal would be done. But Zimbabwe would have had to reinstate human rights guarantees; its foreign minister, Stan Mudenge, had gone beyond his brief, and nothing came of it. On the ground it was becoming more apparent that, while the invasions of commercial farms looked chaotic, it was ZANU-PF bigwigs rather more than the landless who were benefiting; black and Asian commercial farmers, who had paid for farms in the past, were being ejected along with whites.

One of the most relevant players in the international firmament was the Commonwealth. The Commonwealth had been important in bringing Mugabe to power, and Zimbabwe to a recognised independence. It had followed up its Harare Declaration with

CMAG, its rules committee of foreign ministers, initially chaired by Stan Mudenge. As the Zimbabwean crisis developed there was strong pressure on CMAG by human rights NGOs to suspend the Zimbabwean government from the councils of the Commonwealth. Don McKinnon, the New Zealander who was secretary general from 2000 to 2008, lacked the rapport with African leaders of his two predecessors. CMAG did suspend Zimbabwe in 2002, in spite of complaints from Mudenge that this was ultra vires, as the country had a civilian government and suspension should be a sanction reserved for military coups. A Commonwealth election observer group had been sharply critical of the 2002 elections. Other African governments said that the Commonwealth, which was allowing a doubtfully civilian regime in Pakistan to rejoin, was unfair to Zimbabwe.

A tangled debate, which involved failed mediation by the leaders of Australia, Nigeria and South Africa, was only finally resolved in 2003 when the Commonwealth summit in Abuja ended with Zimbabwe's withdrawal from the Commonwealth. It was clear by then that Zimbabwe, whose adherence to Commonwealth values was strongly attacked by the UK and Australia, had also lost support in the Caribbean. But President Mbeki attacked the Commonwealth at Zimbabwe's departure, even though South Africa had been party to attempted mediation. The precise sequence was interesting. P.J. Patterson, prime minister of Jamaica, was chairing a mediation group of leaders in Abuja. He, President Obasanjo of Nigeria and Mbeki all spoke to Mugabe by phone. Mbeki argued that within six months he would have resolved the Zimbabwe situation, and nothing should be done to upset Mugabe. The mediation group produced an anodyne statement, but Mugabe announced withdrawal from the Commonwealth anyway. As Tony Blair was departing from Abuja, at the airport, his thumbs up at the departure of Mugabe was televised. This infuriated a number of African leaders, and Mbeki broke ranks to say that he had never been committed to the agreed statement from the Patterson group.[30]

The early years of the new century saw Mugabe and other ZANU–PF leaders prevented by targeted sanctions from flying to the European Union, and their assets frozen there. This ended the regular shopping trips that Robert and Grace Mugabe had been making to London's West End and Harrods, but did not end the expeditions to shopping malls in South Africa and further afield, to Malaysia and Hong Kong.[31] For overlooked in easy talk of an 'international community', and its hostility to the Zimbabwe government, was the fact that that government had important friends. The most powerful was China, still ruled by an authoritarian Communist Party. Its Cultural Revolution, influencing ZANU–PF cadres in their brutal treatment of farm workers and opponents, might have been forty years ago; its current economic advance, investing in Africa's raw materials without bothering about the human rights conditionalities demanded by the West, was very opportune. The government launched a 'Look East' policy, in an effort to stall the economic decline by winning Chinese investment, along with a series of price controls, which were made ineffective by inflation. However, the Chinese were initially cautious. In 2005 they refused to provide the $295 million that Zimbabwe needed to pay the country's debts to the IMF.[32]

The precipitous decline in the economy had many effects. Formal-sector employment dropped from 1.4 million in 1998 to 998,000 in 2004[33] – a blow to ZCTU, which saw a decline in its membership. Six banks were in crisis that year, affected by the spiralling inflation; Chris Kuruneri, a former minister of finance and sometime jazz player, was put in prison for extensive breaches of exchange control and use of a Canadian passport; Herbert Murerwa, back as finance minister again after Makoni resigned, raised the threshold of income tax from Z$2.4 million to Z$9 million a year. Makoni told Brian Donnelly: 'The trouble is,

Brian, that half the cabinet doesn't understand economics, and the other half doesn't want to.'

The worst effects were on agricultural production, hitting not only exports but also the country's ability to feed itself. Very few of the commercial farms which were occupied, or reallocated, maintained their previous output.[34] Travellers in the countryside saw many of the invaded farms virtually abandoned, or reverting to bush. A drought in 2002–3 hurt the all-important maize crop, as well as other cereals. Whereas maize output had been running at an average of 1.7 million tonnes in the 1990s, the best year between 2001 and 2008 saw only 1.5 million, in 2005–6. In 2007–8, by which time millions of Zimbabweans were relying on food aid from the World Food Programme and NGOs, it was only 647,000 tonnes.[35] A decision in 2001 to make maize and wheat 'controlled products', which could only be sold by farmers to the official Grain Marketing Board, led to unsustainable subsidies and exacerbated shortages. The board was buying maize at Z$33,000 per tonne, but selling it at Z$6,000 per tonne. The accelerating inflation, which had begun with the war vets' compensation and Congo war in the late 1990s, was such that around Z$8,000 was needed in January 2006 to buy what Z$1,000 would have bought in January 2005.[36]

This terrifying implosion destroyed individuals' savings, and undermined the budgets of public authorities and local government, but it gave opportunities to those close to the government who could manipulate exchange rates. A small number, who had access to valued assets or could acquire them at knockdown prices, enriched themselves. Gideon Gono, governor of the Reserve Bank of Zimbabwe, was central to this process of enrichment for ZANU–PF's friends, even as he was scrambling to introduce ever larger denominations of devalued currency for the public at large. In the course of the decade, for example, cheap diesel provided for the 'new' commercial farmers was being sold on by them, at a profit, in the towns.

The ruthless application of state terror in the early years of the twenty-first century led not only to human rights abuses but to everyday heroism by the victims. A number of organisations, including the Amani Trust (which became the Research and Advocacy Unit), Women of Zimbabwe Arise, the Legal Resources Foundation, Zimrights and the Zimbabwe Association of Doctors for Human Rights, provided witness, regular reports and succour for the abused. A handful of lawyers were willing to represent ordinary victims as well as high-profile MDC and ZCTU figures, even as the Zimbabwe Republic Police had become hopelessly politicised and courtroom odds became increasingly stacked in favour of the state. Indeed it was a remarkable testimony to the courage and tenacity of Zimbabwe's civil society that it kept going, in spite of economic collapse, its own problems of funding and personal risk. The arrival of mobile phones and the Internet meant that its findings reached sympathisers around the world quickly and on a regular basis.[37]

One small and brave body which pursued a strategy of civil disobedience, holding monthly demonstrations in the big cities and ignoring official requirements for advance permission, was WOZA – Women of Zimbabwe Arise. It called for the restoration of full human rights. In a survey of 1,983 of its members, covering their activism between 2000 and 2007, 1,206 had been arrested at least once; 949 had suffered death threats and 832 had been assaulted; 1,347 had been forced to attend political re-education meetings. Further, a third of the sample – 647 – had been physically tortured; this could involve *falanga*, being kicked with boots, or 'air chairs', being made to stand for long periods with knees bent. The worst abuse took place in police cells, or in the unpleasant and underfinanced prisons.[38]

The land invasions, and aggression by 'war vets' and state agencies, led to capture of the judiciary by ZANU–PF. A key moment was in March 2001, when Anthony Gubbay, a barrister who had represented African nationalists during the Smith era and had been appointed chief justice by Mugabe in 1990, was forced out of office. Chinotimba and a gang of war vets had invaded the Supreme Court and subsequently harangued Gubbay, saying 'He is a British imperialist agent, and he must go.' He was replaced by Godfrey Chidyausuku, who had managed the constitutional review on Mugabe's behalf. Gubbay's main crime was that his court had declared the land occupations illegal.

The loss of independence of the judiciary impacted particularly on electoral challenges. After the 2000 elections, MDC petitions complained of bribery, coercion, torture, murder and hate speech as vitiating the results in particular constituencies; although the MDC was initially successful, ZANU–PF appealed, and by 2005, when the next round of parliamentary elections came round, only one case had been settled by the Supreme Court. Judges did not always rule in favour of the state, but they became skilled at dragging out proceedings where the state had an interest.

For many in civil society, and Zimbabwe's once proud education system, it was the ruling party's misuse of a youth militia that was most scandalous. A national youth training scheme, designed to provide discipline and skills for unemployed young people, was turned into the 'Green Bombers' – a strike force of thugs to beat up the government's opponents. The youngsters were exposed to *pungwes*, political education and self-criticism, and brutalised themselves. They were taught that the MDC were sell-outs, British stooges and betrayers of the country's liberation. Some were disillusioned.[39] Others, following Mugabe, who said he had 'degrees in violence', would find it difficult to escape the legacy of crimes against their communities.

Hunger and economic collapse led significant numbers to leave Zimbabwe. By the end of the first decade of the twenty-first century it was reckoned that between 3 and 4 million people had emigrated. They did not all leave at once, and South Africa, the neighbour to which most went, tried to send them back. It created a deportation holding centre at Lindela. In 2005, as many as 150,000 Zimbabweans were deported from South Africa.[40] Paul Verryn, who provided a Methodist refuge in downtown Johannesburg, estimated that only 60,000 Zimbabweans in South Africa had proper papers.[41] Those who got there found work at all levels, stimulating a xenophobia in the townships, but it was estimated that the remittances from each Zimbabwean abroad were helping five others at home to survive.[42] In addition to South Africa, there were significant Zimbabwean diasporas in other neighbouring states, as well as in the UK and Australia. Although there were CIO spies among the migrants, the great bulk were hostile to the Mugabe regime, and activists – like those who maintained a weekly vigil outside the Zimbabwe embassy in London – tried to focus public attention on its failings.

Around the middle of the decade the deepening crisis led to splits in both the MDC and ZANU–PF. In parliamentary elections in 2005, accompanied by the now standard processes of government intimidation and abuse, ZANU–PF won 78 seats to the MDC's 42; this meant that the government could now amend the constitution as it chose. The government celebrated its victory by unleashing Operation Murambatsvina, an assault on its urban working-class opposition, described in the next chapter. The Zimbabwe Human Rights NGO Forum reported a sharp rise in unlawful arrests and detentions – up from 389 in 2004 to 1,286 in 2005.[43]

As before, the government said it was fighting the British and their MDC stooges. 'Robert Mugabe duly defeated Blair', Mark Rule commented laconically after the 2005 elections. In fact the British had toned down their anti-Mugabe rhetoric. In late 2001, shortly after Brian Donnelly had arrived in Harare as high commissioner, he had been accused of using specific farm invasions as an excuse for British intervention. The so-called 'Donnelly plot' was a nonsense, and although Blair might be willing to deploy the SAS in Sierra Leone there was never a possibility of military intervention in Zimbabwe. In any case the context of international affairs changed drastically, with al-Qaeda's attack in New York in September 2001, followed up by the invasion of Iraq in 2003. Zimbabwe slipped down the Western agenda.

The replacement of Robin Cook by Jack Straw as foreign and Commonwealth secretary in 2001, prior to the attack in New York, saw a reduction in the war of words between London and Harare. Straw was a more mollifying figure, serving until 2006. The pernicious impact of the 'war on terror' on the human rights claims of the UK government became increasingly apparent, making finger-wagging at the expense of others harder. International lawyers pointed out that the 2003 invasion of Iraq, in which the UK participated alongside the USA, was not lawful; there was UK complicity in rendition of suspects who had been tortured.

The average rate of inflation in Zimbabwe was 144.4 per cent in the middle of 2005, and the consumer price index for July was 47.1 per cent higher than the previous month. The process was accelerating. Gideon Gono failed in an attempt to sell bonds for parastatals and local authorities; the government was unable to negotiate loans in South Africa; and it was by the skin of its teeth, and by paying off US$120 million of arrears to the IMF in September, that Zimbabwe escaped expulsion from the Fund.

The split in the MDC was formalised in October 2005 when a minority broke away from the party led by Morgan Tsvangirai to support a second MDC, which came to be known as the MDC–M, after Arthur Mutambara, its leader. The excuse for the break-up, which was to complicate Zimbabwean politics considerably, was that the Mutambara faction wished to compete in Senate elections set for 2006, while Tsvangirai wished to boycott them. Tsvangirai argued that the country could not afford this extra set of elections; his opponents, with most of their support in Matabeleland, were unwilling to see their political positions there given away without a fight. Apart from everything else the split was a product of frustration and exhaustion in the MDC. Its attempt to win power by peaceful demonstrations – a nationwide jobs boycott in March 2003 and a 'final push' on the streets in July – had failed; so too had three polls in five years.

But there was much more to the split. The MDC, formed quite hastily from the campaign for a new constitution, was far from homogeneous. It included the unions, a wide range of civil society organisations, intellectuals, white farmers, and farmworkers. Beyond wanting an end to Mugabe and ZANU–PF's reign of terror and corruption, these elements had quite varied ideas as to the Zimbabwe they would like to see. There were free marketeers and welfarist social democrats. There were frictions between 'intellectuals' and 'workers'. There were those who formed part of a kitchen cabinet round Tsvangirai, and those who wanted to see a more grassroots democracy. Worryingly, there were those who were willing to use violence in intra-party disputes, or to challenge ZANU–PF's grip, using some of the unemployed youngsters who could be hired. Tsvangirai himself was accused of tolerating violence. There were also those who feared that MDC was getting to be too like ZANU – with a leadership that was too authoritarian.

Inevitably, there were personality conflicts. One of the sharpest was between Welshman Ncube, the MDC secretary general and an academic married to one of Jacob Zuma's daughters, and Tsvangirai, who he complained was becoming dictatorial. In October 2005 a majority on the MDC's national executive voted to remove Tsvangirai. It is alleged that this was unconstitutional, in that not all the executive voted, and that the party at large should have been involved.[44]

However, Tsvangirai fought back, appealing to the wider party membership. In March 2006, he advertised a national congress on the Voice of America, which had built a significant listener base in Zimbabwe as an alternative to the propagandist state broadcaster.

The call brought 23,000 MDC supporters to the national sports stadium. This was an amazing testimony to the resilience of the party, given the intimidation it had faced, as well as to the popularity of Tsvangirai. Verification by a non-governmental umbrella organisation, NANGO, accepted that 18,500 were legitimate MDC representatives from all the country's provinces. A month before, in Bulawayo, a mere 900 had turned up to the launch of the Mutambara MDC. The Tsvangirai congress reinstated him as president, elected a rising star, Tendai Biti, as secretary general, and also backed Roy Bennett, a tough Shona-speaking white MP who had served eight months in prison after fighting the justice minister in parliament, and who was a bête noire for Mugabe and ZANU–PF because he had switched to the MDC in the 2000 election, taking the Chimanimani constituency with him.

People in the mainstream MDC suspected the hand of Thabo Mbeki in the attempted coup against Tsvangirai. Mbeki and Tsvangirai did not hit it off and it was thought that the South African president, in his tortuous negotiations in Zimbabwe, had come to the conclusion that both ZANU–PF and the MDC needed new leadership. Mutambara had led student protests against ZANU–PF in 1988, but had been out of Zimbabwe for fifteen years when he was approached by Ncube to lead the MDC breakaway. He had been a Rhodes Scholar, taught robotics at Massachusetts Institute of Technology, and seemed to exemplify the high-achieving Zimbabweans of post-independence.

Mutambara's advantage for Ncube, and the others behind the new party, was that he was Shona in a party that rapidly came to seem a sectarian Ndebele group. One of those elected to the Senate in 2006 on this ticket was David Coltart, a Bulawayo human rights lawyer, who had been part of the team which arduously amassed evidence of the Gukurahundi against the Ndebele. But from the start the political judgement of Mutambara had been questioned, and Ncube seemed to be the brains behind the new party. The issue of boycott of the Senate elections was not trivial, given that boycott had been an issue for the MDC at each election in the new century where rigging was anticipated. But the split in the opposition was good news only for ZANU–PF.

For ZANU–PF had been having its own travails. These were brought to a head in a Tsholotsho Declaration of November 2004, which aimed to provide an ethnic and Shona clan balance at the top of the party, instead of the near monopoly of the Zezuru group to which Mugabe belonged. Mugabe denounced it as a 'Tsholotsho plot'. In a lengthy apologia afterwards, Jonathan Moyo, who was centrally involved and who was to be elected as an independent MP for Tsholotsho after falling foul of ZANU–PF, argued that the party had known about the plans all along.[45] In addition to providing ethnic balance, the scheme would allow for a secret ballot for the top jobs by the provincial executives.

This crisis inside the ruling party reflected several factors: a response to the disastrous state of the economy and its own unpopularity, a desire for renewal among its younger members, and the struggle for succession to Mugabe. By 2004 inflation stood at 622.8 per cent, exports were only a third of the level of 1977, when the ostracised Smith regime was constrained by sanctions, and the currency had lost 99 per cent of its value since 2001.[46] The impatience of younger members coincided with an appreciation that mortality was eroding the gerontocracy at the top of ZANU–PF. Mugabe himself was 80 in 2004. When Simon Muzenda died in September 2003, also aged 80, it stimulated a battle for the Mugabe succession. Muzenda had become vice president in 1987, when Mugabe became executive president, and it was generally supposed that whoever succeeded him in the ZANU slot – for there was also an ex-ZAPU vice president following the unity accord – would be the next president.

Two factions were in contention. Both had credentials dating from the armed struggle in the 1970s. One was built round

Emmerson Mnangagwa, who blew up a train at Victoria Falls
when he was under 21 and went on to build a business empire;
as parliamentary Speaker after 2000 he was investigated by the
UN for illegal exploitation of the Congo's minerals. The other
was General Solomon Mujuru, whose *nom de guerre* had been
'Rex Nhongo' during the war, married to Joice Mujuru, also an
ex-guerrilla. He had commanded the unified Zimbabwe Army
after independence. Both Mnangagwa and Mujuru were tough,
and heavily involved in farm invasions and the brutal aspects
of ZANU–PF rule. Both had become rich, and were part of the
security-sector clique which became increasingly powerful as
the economy plummeted. In the run-up to the denouement at
Tsholotsho it appeared as if Mnangagwa was more popular in
the party, with a majority of the provincial executives behind
him. Mbeki, involved in his endless conversations with the Zimbabwean politicians, was thought to back him.

But a crucial difference was that the Mujurus were Zezurus,
like Mugabe and the inner group at the top of the party. Mnangagwa was a Karanga, another of the Shona clans. To choose
Mnangagwa would break the grip of the Zezurus, which was one
reason why he had more backing. But Mugabe was not having this.
At the ZANU–PF women's congress he and his wife promoted
the idea that one of the vice presidents should be a woman. He
called an emergency politburo meeting to coincide with a speech
by Mnangagwa at Tsholotsho, a town west of Bulawayo. Joice
Mujuru became vice president. A party congress in December
reaffirmed Mugabe's authority. Six provincial chairpersons who
had been party to the 'plot' were suspended from ZANU–PF,
along with a leader of the war vets, Jabulani Sibanda. Mnagagwa
lost his party post as secretary for administration, and was made
secretary for legal affairs, where he had less scope for appointing
his protégés. In government he was shifted sideways, to become
minister for rural affairs.

Jonathan Moyo was left complaining about the undemocratic and unconstitutional ways of the ZANU–PF leadership as though this was news to him, and was out in the cold for four years. He wrote:

> The current political and economic problems facing Zimbabwe are due to the fact that the country is being ruled by a hopelessly clueless, tired and terrified undemocratic clique which desperately wants to cling to power by fair means or foul at the clear expense of the national interest.[47]

Between the Tsholotsho episode and the division in the MDC there was one intriguing development. Behind the scenes, sometimes with South African involvement and sometimes without, there had always been exchanges between the Zimbabwean actors caught up in the national disaster. In 2005 Mbeki was working with Mujuru; Mujuru argued that it was essential to do a deal with Tsvangirai and the MDC. Mbeki's preference was probably still the reform of ZANU–PF, and a government of national unity of the kind that emerged from South Africa's first multiracial election in 1994.

One day in 2005, Tsvangirai was picked up by the Central Intelligence Organisation and taken to see the Joint Operations Command, the heart of the government's security apparatus. The military leaders told Tsvangirai that they would never allow him to win. But they offered him a deal under which Joice Mujuru would become president, Simba Makoni prime minister and Tsvangirai deputy prime minister. They sought to bully him into acceptance, but Tsvangirai rejected the proposal.[48]

By the middle of the first decade of the twenty-first century, therefore, the socio-political situation in Zimbabwe was dire. A large chunk of the population wanted a change of government. ZANU–PF was using all of the tools at its disposal to hang on to power, ignoring falling living standards, life expectancy and a haemorrhaging of people through emigration. External concern

FROM OPERATION MURAMBATSVINA
TO AN INCLUSIVE GOVERNMENT

One view of Zimbabwe in the first decade of the twenty-first century was that it was undergoing a lengthy civil war, not precisely a shooting war of the kind that had caused havoc in the countryside in the 1970s, but a struggle for power, land and survival that involved brutal displacement for hundreds of thousands of people and premature deaths. It saw ZANU–PF lose support in rural areas, and it reached a kind of peak with Operation Murambatsvina, 'a clearing out of rubbish' in urban areas, in 2005. Whereas it is estimated that some 200,000 farm workers lost out in the commercial farm invasions, the Murambatsvina removals are thought to have destroyed 650,000 to 700,000 homes and livelihoods, with 2.4 million people directly and indirectly affected.[1]

The operation, chiefly but not exclusively directed at urban areas which had supported the MDC, involved the forced eviction of families living in shacks not deemed to meet planning requirements, or carrying on as vendors and currency traders on the edge of conventional commerce. Their homes were bulldozed. They were physically transported into the bush if they had no relations they could go to. Police as well as municipal authorities took part in the expulsions. In a parody of Maoist self-criticism, home-owners could be required to knock down their own premises. For the victims, it was a horror story.

The authorities justified this campaign as one of slum clear-ance, and a cleaning up of the towns, but the trigger was the March 2005 parliamentary elections in which the MDC again made a strong showing, although ZANU–PF was declared the victor; once again there was a clash between the European Union, which said that the election had not been free and fair, and the SADC and African Union observers, who could see nothing wrong with it. The urban context was similar to that of other developing countries: there was a migration from country to town, where people had built their own shacks with whatever material they could get, and were trying to make a living in a depressed economy where conventional paid employment was rare. Indeed there were significant slum clearances in the Nigerian cities of Lagos and Port Harcourt in the same year. The campaign in Zimbabwe, subtitled 'operation restore order', began in May 2005, and was supposedly a joint initiative of the Zimbabwe Republic Police and the Harare city municipal force.

As with the farm invasions, the operation was an odd mixture of chaos and planned aggression. Petrol was used for bulldozers in a country suffering an acute shortage of fuel; traders who had a business relationship accepted by their local authorities were pushed aside, along with those described as 'human dirt' or thieves. The scale and cruelty of the dispersals, not preceded by any dialogue with those likely to be affected, raised huge human rights concerns inside and outside Zimbabwe. But it was also a sign that ZANU–PF, worried by the economic decline and divisions in its own ranks, was willing to crack down harder to show the population who was in control.

Police and municipalities had had run-ins in the past with pave-ment traders on a regular basis, and the state media characterised some of them as migrants from neighbouring countries. But the official campaign, spreading from Harare to the rest of the country in the middle of the year, was something quite different. Opinion inside Zimbabwe polarised on political lines, with pro-government media accepting that a clean-up was necessary, while opposition papers like the *Standard* pointed to its ruthlessness and family tragedies; some NGOs offered humanitarian help.[2] Reports in the international press, backed up by television and video, caused Kofi Annan, the UN secretary general, to send a special envoy, Anna Tibaijuka, to assess the situation. Annan was Ghanaian; Tibaijuka, who was heading UN–Habitat, the human settlements programme, was Tanzanian. Neither could be described as necessarily unfriendly to Zimbabwe. The involvement of the UN was a sign that human rights concerns about the ZANU–PF government could no longer be dismissed as a Western plot.

The Tibaijuka report was damning. She wrote that 'while purporting to target illegal dwellings and structures and to clamp down on alleged illicit activities [the operation] was carried out in an indiscriminate manner, with indifference to human suffering.' She pointed to a governance crisis which made it unclear where the operation had originated, the weakness of Operation Garikai, which was supposed to provide new plots and support for the evicted, and the fact that the authorities would not allow the World Food Programme to provide direct relief to the hungry homeless. She argued that Zimbabwe citizenship should be granted to those who had been born abroad. But she did show sympathy to the government on the land issue which had precipitated decline at the start of the decade.[3]

Robert Mugabe tried to dismiss concerns, saying 'There is no demolition campaign. It's a clean-up operation, and that's what all countries do.' His government released a 45-page rebuttal of the Tibaijuka report, and ministers claimed that it had been carried out within the law, and that the High Court had ruled against some displaced persons. However, Pearson Mbalekwa, a member of ZANU–PF's central committee and an MP, resigned in protest, describing the operation as callous.[4] Tibaijuka forecast that it would take many years before Zimbabwe and the families concerned would recover.

Tibaijuka's critique of governance in Zimbabwe struck a chord with many, although the operation was probably coordinated by a group including Didymus Mutasa, in charge of the Central Intelligence Organisation, and Ignatius Chombo, a local government minister. By the middle of the decade, parliamentary oversight in the country was marginal. Senior civil servants were required to be ZANU loyalists. The actual authority of ministers was unclear in a regime where Robert Mugabe was 'the Big Man' and there was a creeping militarisation, as former officers took senior jobs in parastatals and government. Behind the politburo and central committee, and apparatus of government, real power seemed to be moving to the Joint Operations Command (JOC), which brought together senior military, like Perence Shiri, and the police commissioner, Augustine Chihuri, who had dismissed the victims of Marambatsvina as 'worms'. The JOC had originally been a device of the Smith government, in its total war against the nationalists. It had been taken over by ZANU as a coordinating mechanism to defeat what these ultimate loyalists saw as a counter-revolution; although they were ageing, the JOC members had close bonds with Mugabe dating back to ZANLA days, and were steeped in blood.[5]

The period from Murambatsvina to the beating up of Morgan Tsvangirai and MDC and civil society leaders in the 'Day of Prayer' in 2007 was one of continuing economic decline and political stasis. The maize output in 2006 was only half what the country required, and dependence on international food aid increased. The accelerating inflation meant that the Reserve Bank introduced a Z$100,000 note. Just before Christmas in 2006, the government nearly trebled the official price of bread from Z$295 to Z$825 a loaf, but price controls, inflation and actual shortages made nonsense of economic policy. Although there had been a moment of optimism in 2005, gross domestic product was in a relatively steady decline from US$10 billion in 1997 to US$2 billion in 2008. Tragically, average life expectancy was falling from 60, a respectable figure in Africa, to 34. Repressive legislation – POSA, AIPPA and allegations of treason – were used to hammer dissent.

The MDC was accommodating itself to a split, which was highly convenient to ZANU-PF, and may have been actively nurtured by the CIO and Thabo Mbeki. Welshman Ncube, a key strategist for the small Mutambara faction of the MDC, accepted one of the white commercial farms that had been taken over. The Mutambara group did not want to abandon the MDC brand, and was henceforth known as MDC-M, in contrast to Tsvangirai's MDC-T. Mark Rule, critical of the government but not enamoured of the MDC, wrote after it split: 'Its future is uncertain and should it, by some unforeseeable miracle, achieve any element of power, there is no reason to expect it to yield any marked or lasting improvement on what there is today.'[6]

The role of Thabo Mbeki, initially as president of South Africa but then as mediator for SADC after he lost the presidency of the ANC to Jacob Zuma at the ANC's Polokwane conference in December 2007, was one of the great puzzles in the continuing Zimbabwe crisis. For those opposed to Mbeki he was merely an appeaser of Robert Mugabe and the ZANU-PF hardliners. He could, like the white South Africans pressuring Ian Smith, have threatened the power and fuel supplies for Zimbabwe – huge debts were building up for electricity alone. But it was clear that, apart from any personal obligations going back to at least the 1980s, his foreign policy was to prioritise an anti-racist, anti-imperialist line which would make it impossible for him to jump to support the kind of Western attacks on Mugabe espoused by Tony Blair.[7] It was also uninterested in human rights issues, which Nelson Mandela had championed as president; Mandela and Archbishop Tutu spoke out about the violations in Zimbabwe, but the non-governmental Human Rights Watch in 2009 pointed out that, in its recent two-year stint on the UN Security Council, South Africa had opposed or refused to back resolutions on behalf of victims in Sudan, Myanmar, Uzbekistan, Belarus, North Korea as well as Zimbabwe.[8]

But the fact that Mbeki was a believer in quiet diplomacy did not mean he was doing nothing. He had been intervening in both ZANU–PF and the MDC, apparently seeking a post-Mugabe outcome which could bring together a 'reformed' ZANU with a weakened or non-Tsvangirai MDC in a 'government of national unity'. He was forced to up his game after a catastrophic ZANU public relations disaster on 7 March 2007 when a civil society group, the Save Zimbabwe Campaign, organised a Sunday prayer march in Harare.

The context was that the main MDC formation, unbowed by terror and a series of cheated elections – let alone the haemorrhage of support through emigration – was gearing up for new elections in 2008. With tight restrictions on political demonstrations it was hoped that the Save Zimbabwe Campaign, running an ostensibly non-political prayer vigil, would be able to demonstrate concern for the country's future in a way that would help the MDC–T. Around 100,000 people were expected to turn out, mainly from poorer 'high density' suburbs; Tsvangirai was due to speak.

But the police, now politicised under commissioner Augustine Chihuri, were ordered to break up the rally. They put up road blocks, fired tear gas and live ammunition. MDC supporters threw stones at them; an activist named Gift Tandare was killed, others were injured. There were detentions, beatings and sixty MDC and civil society activists were arrested. Shockingly, a number of MDC leaders were tortured in prison; Grace Kwinjeh almost lost her ear and subsequently fled to England; Sekai Holland suffered multiple fractures and managed to get to Australia for treatment; worst of all was the assault on the MDC's president. Morgan Tsvangirai had his head repeatedly smashed against a wall in his cell, fracturing his skull; when his release was ordered by the High Court three days later so that he could get medical help, his head and face were terribly bruised. Photographs of the battered opposition leader went around the world, causing outrage.[9]

Well-publicised violence continued for a further week, and serious damage had been done to the regime's image. These were not assaults on white farmers, but on poor black Africans who took a different view from the government, and on their legitimate leaders. Two SADC presidents, Kikwete of Tanzania and Mwanawasa of Zambia, broke ranks to criticise Mugabe, as did the South Korean secretary general of the UN, Ban Ki-moon. Although a SADC summit in Tanzania later in March expressed support for Mugabe, and for ZANU's position on land, it 'mandated HE President Thabo Mbeki [to] continue to facilitate dialogue between the opposition and the Government'. While the MDC complained bitterly that SADC had not denounced the Zimbabwe government, this innocuous statement gave a push to the Mbeki mediation, which was to have big consequences.

Mbeki achieved at least three important results. First, he was responsible for inaugurating 'harmonised' elections in March 2008. In the past there had been separate timings for presidential, parliamentary and local government polls. For a country which was essentially bankrupt, with a record of violence prior to an election of any kind, a combined poll would save money and conceivably reduce physical abuse. Mbeki was probably influenced to bring forward elections by his desire to avoid a Zimbabwe debacle coinciding with the FIFA World Cup in South Africa in

2010. But this change might also make it harder for ZANU, facing obvious unpopularity, to win at all levels.

A second change, the significance of which ZANU failed to spot in the pre-election negotiations, was that results would be posted up at each polling station. With local observers and mobile phones it was possible for the results to be tallied at party offices as they came in, and manipulation by the government-appointed Zimbabwe Election Commission (ZEC) could be exposed. This strategy had had a striking impact in the presidential election in Ghana in December 2000, won for the opposition by John Kufuor, where mobiles were used to report results from local polls to independent radio stations. Zimbabwe did not have in-country independent radio stations like Ghana, although Radio South West Africa and the Voice of America as well as the BBC and the South African Broadcasting Corporation had considerable audiences, but the posting of local results was a move to transparency. In principle, each party could add up these local results, independently of the ZEC, to get parliamentary and presidential outcomes.

Third, Mbeki helped stimulate the emergence of a breakaway ZANU–PF candidate in Simba Makoni, the former minister of finance and secretary general of SADC. Makoni's run for president, even though he only got 8.3 per cent of votes according to the official figures, set the stage for a fairer election, and one that Morgan Tsvangirai could win. Makoni was an interesting figure, who had been in and out of favour with Mugabe, seen as a technocrat rather than a politician. He was only 30 in 1980, with a doctorate in pharmaceutical chemistry from Leicester Polytechnic, when he was made deputy minister of agriculture. He was then made minister of industry and commerce and, although there was only lukewarm regional support for him, was slipped in as secretary general for SADC from 1983 to 1993; there, based in Botswana, he survived a corruption scandal. He was brought back into government as minister of finance from 2000 to 2002, following ZANU–PF's election setback and the economic crisis precipitated by the land invasions.[10] But his devaluation strategy could not stem the decline, and Mugabe fired him.

A ZANU–PF party congress in December 2007 had renominated Mugabe, by then 83, as the party's candidate to be president. It was clear that, like the late President Banda in Malawi, the party had accepted that he would be president for life. He himself could be at risk, from the International Criminal Court or from prosecution after regime change inside Zimbabwe. Many party members, particularly the older and more senior ones, had a great deal to lose – confiscated farms, cronyistic relations with the Reserve Bank of Zimbabwe, and sometimes direct involvement in human rights abuse. The congress put a stop to speculation that a 'reformed ZANU–PF' could emerge in a hurry.

Makoni was squeezed out of a ZANU–PF candidacy in the House of Assembly, allegedly because he had left his nomination for a party primary too late. On 5 February 2008 he announced that he would run as an independent candidate for the presidency. With a retired officer and Ibbo Mandaza, a nationalist intellectual, standing by him, he said,

> I share the agony and anguish of all citizens over the extreme hardships that we all have endured for nearly 10 years now. I also share the widely held view that these hardships are a result of failures of national leadership, and that change at all levels is a prerequisite for change at other levels of national endeavour.

It was a courageous stand, for he was at once expelled from ZANU–PF, denounced by Mugabe as a prostitute and tool of the West, and his life was threatened by Joseph Chinotimba, a leader of the war vets. But although his candidacy gave Arthur Mutambara of MDC–M, who had little chance, an excuse to pull out of the presidential race, and he recruited a motley group of supporters including Edgar Tekere, Fay Chung and Dumiso Dabengwa (who would seek to revive ZAPU after the election), his campaign did not take off. Tsvangirai said he would not work with him. The great bulk of ZANU–PF, with its instruments of state coercion and propaganda, stayed loyal. Although there were rumours that Solomon Mujuru (a key ZANU faction leader) would back him, he remained silent.

With the crackdown at and after the Day of Prayer, and the build-up to harmonised elections in 2008, there had been the usual depressing increase in human rights violations which preceded every election in the twenty-first century. The annual totals collected by the Zimbabwe Human Rights NGO Forum showed increases between 2006 and 2007 as follows: torture – 368 to 586; death, murders and executions – 1 to 3; kidnappings and disappearances – 11 to 19; and unlawful arrests and detentions – 2,917 to 3,352. Although it took care over its statistics, the NGO Forum was initially listing cases where perpetrators might be prosecuted, and then just those which were brought to members' attention. Its totals were therefore underestimates.

To begin with, Tsvangirai and the MDC–T were complaining of bias in the Zimbabwe Election Commission, intimidation of supporters, and the ploys of ZANU–PF which had made earlier elections unfair; these included the lack of polling stations in urban areas which supported the opposition and the inability of Zimbabweans outside the country, estimated at up to 3 million, to vote.[11] But in the seven weeks between Makoni's declaration and the harmonised elections on 29 March, there were fewer complaints and ordinary voters started to believe that they could change the government. Significantly, Jonathan Moyo, former ZANU loyalist, struck a deal with MDC–T to seek election as an independent for his Tsholotsho constituency in Matabeleland.

By 1 April, Robert Mugabe and the ZANU and military high commands realised that they had lost at all levels – for the

presidency, in parliament and in local government. When the
Election Commission concluded its satirically slow release of
the results, on 2 May, it stated that Tsvangirai had 47.9 per cent,
Mugabe 43.2 per cent and Makoni 8.3 per cent.[12] The MDC–T
had swept the towns in the local government elections. In the
House of Assembly the MDC–T had 99 seats, ZANU–PF won
97 and MDC-M had 10; Moyo was elected as an independent
with MDC support. For the first time since independence a large
number of rural electors, outside Matabeleland, had broken ranks
to vote against ZANU–PF. Thanks to his ability to nominate 30
seats, Mugabe still had an overall majority in the lower house.
In the Senate, which MDC–T had not contested before, government and potentially combined opposition had the same numbers
– with 30 for ZANU, 24 for MDC–T and 6 for MDC-M.

The details were embarrassing for the regime. Patrick Chinamasa, the hard-line attorney general, was defeated, as were six
other ministers. The MDC–T had actually got fewer votes than
ZANU in the parliamentary elections but ended up with more
seats because the government piled up majorities in rural Mashonaland, where traditional loyalties and coercion by militias and in
food distribution confirmed its turnout. A number of the MDC
wins were with small majorities.

What would Mugabe and his henchmen do? The MDC, using
figures collected at individual polling stations, claimed at once
that Tsvangirai had won outright, possibly with 57 per cent of
the vote, as was announced by Tendai Biti, MDC–T's bright
young secretary general. MDC supporters started to celebrate.
But they were premature. It now seems that Mugabe offered his
resignation to close colleagues and the JOC once and possibly
twice in the days immediately after the election.[13] He knew that
Tsvangirai was not a vengeful person; there was no disguising
the loss of popularity of a man who saw himself as father of his
nation. But both Grace Mugabe and his immediate family, and

the military-intelligence junta in the JOC, dissuaded him. Both groups were worried that, even if Robert Mugabe might escape into an easy retirement, they would be exposed to loss of power and wealth, and possible retribution.

Winning time, by a slow release of the results, which went uncriticised by Mbeki, the JOC and ZANU insiders hatched a plan to hang on to power by brute force. They would go for a second round in the presidential election, to be held on 29 June, but in the meantime would unleash the youth militias or 'green bombers',[14] the CIO and all their agencies of control. Never had Zimbabwe had such a cruel demonstration of ZANU–PF's determination to hang on to authority at all costs. Militia groups, 'war vets' and other thugs roamed around, creating fear in rural Mashonaland, with rapes and beatings, and attacking the remaining handful of white farmers in the countryside. The main targets were individuals, villages and constituencies which had defected from ZANU–PF. The Zimbabwe Human Rights NGO Forum reported that murders and executions, numbering only 3 in 2007, reached 107 in 2008; there were also 156 kidnappings and disappearances. Most of these crimes took place in April, May and June and the murderers and kidnappers operated with impunity.

The Zimbabwean scholar Brian Raftopoulos has written,

> The violence inflicted by the ruling party on the electorate, as punishment for its loss in the March election and as a warning against the repeat of such a vote, was the worst seen in the country since the Gukurahundi massacres in the mid-1980s.[15]

Unlike the Gukurahundi violence, however, this was widely reported around the world, and significant South Africans, including Jacob Zuma, now president of the ANC, spoke out against the horror. Tsvangirai was prevented from campaigning in the Shona countryside and there was no way that the presidential run-off was going to be free and fair.

The heroic stoicism of those who had suffered appalling brutality and torture was recorded by Peter Godwin, who interviewed survivors who managed to get to The Avenues clinic in Harare. Inevitably, with the collapse of medical services and the departure of doctors and nurses, care and medicine in Zimbabwe were scarce and no longer of the best quality. But the resilience of the injured was amazing. Godwin wrote:

> I wish there was a better word than 'victims' to describe what these people are. It seems so inert, so passive, and weak. And that is not what they are at all. There is dignity to their suffering. Even as they tell me how they have fled, how they have hidden, how they have been humiliated and mocked, there is little self-pity here. Survivors, I suppose, defines them better. Again and again, as I play stenographer to their suffering, I offer to conceal their names or geographical districts to prevent them being identified. But again, and again, they volunteer their names, and make sure I spell them correctly. They are proud of their roles in all of this, at the significance of their sacrifice. And they want it recorded.[16]

The government's campaign of repression put Tsvangirai and the MDC–T in a quandary. He had spent much of April out of Zimbabwe, seeing friends in Europe and elsewhere; while his defenders said that his life was in danger inside the country, his critics thought he was in danger of living up to ZANU–PF's stereotype as a 'pawn of the West'; those with longer memories could recall Joshua Nkomo's trips out of Rhodesia, gathering international support, at times when his followers inside were under attack. Should Tsvangirai boycott the run-off or carry on? Boycotting the Senate election in 2005 had not been a brilliant tactic, giving political space instead to the Mutambara fraction, and was not well understood by African electors.

With his supporters bloodied, Tsvangirai soldiered on until almost the last moment, withdrawing on 22 June, a week before the poll. He said that eighty-six of his people had been murdered, and 200,000 driven away from their homes. Tendai Biti was held in prison on treason charges from 12 to 26 June, temporarily knocking out one of the MDC–T's best brains. The repression had also hit civil society. When Mugabe was sworn in as president on 29 June, having received over 2 million votes in a no-contest, he got scant recognition. President Mwanawasa, the ailing president of Zambia, who was chairing SADC, described the result as an embarrassment; President Khama of Botswana refused to recognise Mugabe as president. At the United Nations, Russia and China vetoed an attempt by the EU and the USA to introduce UN sanctions. But the most striking reaction came in the negative findings of election observers from SADC and the African Union. SADC had been trying to introduce new standards for the holding of elections in the region, and observers pulled no punches in denouncing politically motivated violence by ZANU–PF, the inability of the opposition to hold rallies and 'the regrettable inaction of the law enforcement agencies'.[17]

Mbeki, whose political base in South Africa was weakening fast, spent the period between July and September as the SADC mediator, desperately trying to create his long-sought government of national unity. Secret talks between ZANU–PF and MDC–T began in July. The suspicion between them was deep, and reinforced by the recent atrocities. But the two parties could not ignore the fact that the Zimbabwean economy was reaching a nadir, with shortages of power, water and food, hyperinflation, and a collapse in the health and education systems. Public attitudes in southern Africa had changed, as was symbolised in the refusal of dockers in Mozambique, Durban and Namibia to unload arms destined for Zimbabwe from a Chinese ship. Mugabe and ZANU–PF had exhausted the tolerance so long extended to a fellow liberation movement.

Further, the riots in Kenya earlier in the year, which had followed a disputed election on 27 December 2007, were an awful warning. Mwai Kibaki had lost little time in claiming that he had been re-elected as president, getting himself sworn in, although most informed Kenyans were sure that his opponent, Raila Odinga, had won in reality. Around a thousand people were then killed, and 200,000 were displaced in inter-ethnic violence. The brutality only ended when Kofi Annan, the former UN secretary general, managed to negotiate a government of national unity. Although Tsvangirai was committed to non-violence in Zimbabwe, and the government had put down previous demonstrations by force, its pariah status now exposed it to new risks.

The talks to create an inclusive government in Zimbabwe dragged on, and the grandly named 'global political agreement' of 15 September 2008 was extremely slow in implementation. But it represented a desire by ZANU–PF to retain power, in the face of electoral defeat and international scepticism, while seeking some economic revival and the removal of the individual sanctions and asset freezes which inconvenienced 200 of its own elite. For the exhausted leadership of the MDC–T it meant a share of power – albeit they were not to realise how limited – and a recognition that a Mugabe who was not going to retire voluntarily had to be made a part of the solution. Keenest of all on the agreement was the group round Arthur Mutambara, whose MDC–M had been shown in March to have small electoral weight. Senator David Coltart of MDC–M, who had been a prominent human rights lawyer in Bulawayo and had helped publicise the Matabeleland massacres in 1990s, argued that there was no alternative.[18] Neither the West nor SADC were going to remove Mugabe, he said; the opposition had to make the best deal possible with him.

There was a strong whiff of 'motherhood and apple pie' about the political agreement, known as the GPA. It appeared to lay down all kinds of commitments which flew in the face of what ZANU–PF had actually been doing; some of them would be costly and probably unaffordable for a government which had run out of money; and the strength of the political guarantee represented by SADC – for Mbeki signed the agreement as 'SADC Facilitator' along with the three political leaders – was questionable. Five days after signing the GPA, Mbeki announced he would step down as South African president, after being recalled by the ANC's national executive committee. The GPA was given status as constitutional amendment number 19, and looked forward to the creation of a new constitution before further elections could be held.[19]

Although far from comprehensive or watertight, the GPA, in its 24 articles, sought to cover political issues, economic issues, and issues of violence and human rights. As in Kenya after its disputed election, it created a new structure, of executive president (Robert Mugabe) alongside an executive prime minister (Morgan Tsvangirai). The president would chair the cabinet and the National Security Council, backed up by two ZANU–PF vice presidents, and would formally appoint the prime minister. The prime minister would implement cabinet policy and ensure the relevant legislation; he would be backed by two deputy prime ministers (one from MDC–T, one from MDC–M) and 31 ministers, of whom 15 would be nominated by ZANU–PF, 13 by MDC–T and 3 by MDC–M.

There were two main problems with this scheme, rather different from the time when Canaan Banana was president and Mugabe prime minister. First, it virtually guaranteed friction between two figures with rival authority. A Joint Monitoring and Implementation Committee (JOMIC), supposed to harmonise differences within the inclusive government, became a testy battleground. Second, it was expensive. The 31 ministers became 41, and nearly all were equipped with an official Mercedes; 15 deputy ministers became 20.[20]

As for the economy, which had been in free fall in 2008, 'the parties are committed to working together on a full and comprehensive economic programme to resuscitate Zimbabwe's economy.'[21] Although it was hoping that its MDC partners would rescue the country from hyperinflation and collapse, ZANU–PF stuck to several lines in its creed: it wanted sanctions lifted (including the Zimbabwe Democracy and Economic Recovery Act in the USA, as well as targeted travel bans); and stated that land redistribution since 2000 was irreversible and that the UK had to accept primary responsibility for compensation, although it looked to a comprehensive and non-partisan land audit. In a swipe at the UK government under Blair, it pronounced in article 9.2(c) 'that no outsiders have a right to call or campaign for regime change in Zimbabwe'.

The agreement included several articles covering free political activity, respect for the rule of law, freedoms of association and expression. It called for depoliticisation of state organs, including the National Youth Training Programme – whose 'Green Bombers' had been a crucial tool in ZANU–PF's campaign of intimidation – and that both state institutions and NGOs should avoid bias in the humanitarian relief on which so many Zimbabweans had come to depend. While complaining about foreign radio stations targeting the country, it proposed an 'open media environment' with licences for more papers and private broadcasters, an end to hate speech, and steps to ensure that public media provide balanced coverage to all political parties.

There was an unreality about these human rights and related provisions. Was ZANU–PF really willing to unwind its machinery of coercion and propaganda? In the background there were also two new institutions, which had been talked of in the past: a Human Rights Commission and an Anti-Corruption Commission. Both were still not operational two years after the GPA was signed. There were also two intriguing elements in the GPA: a proposal for a new organ to promote national healing (article 7.1(c)) and a rather cautious proposal to prosecute those accused of political violence in the March and June 2008 elections. Article 18.5(j) stated,

> that while having due regard to the Constitution of Zimbabwe and the principles of the rule of law, the prosecuting authorities will expedite the determination as to whether or not there is sufficient evidence to warrant the prosecution or keeping on remand of all persons accused of politically related offences arising out of or connected with the March and June 2008 elections.

Given that there had been no prosecutions arising from either the Gukurahundi massacres in the 1980s, or the forced removals in Operation Murambatsvina in 2005, it would be an extraordinary turnabout if those responsible for the JOC crackdown in 2008 were to face justice.

Actually converting the GPA into a working, if sometimes dysfunctional, government took almost five months of arduous negotiation over the portfolios, with an enfeebled Thabo Mbeki trying to assist as SADC facilitator, though no longer South African president. When the inclusive government of national unity was formed on 11 February 2009, Zimbabweans could see that the MDC had picked up key social and economic ministries, while ZANU–PF had retained key positions responsible for the military, police, agriculture and mines. MDC–T's most prominent appointment was of Tendai Biti as minister of finance, but it also won health and child welfare, while MDC–M picked up education and industry. But ZANU–PF took foreign affairs (Simbarashe Mumbengegwi), defence (Emmerson Mnangagwa), local government (Ignatius Chombo), justice and legal affairs (Patrick Chinamasa), mines (Obert Mpofu) and both the agricultural and land ministries. Given that ZANU–PF had actually lost the 2008 elections it had retained many of the strategic arms of government and, in spite of perennial and inaccurate stories that he was ailing, the cabinet was still presided over by a wily, intelligent and ruthless octogenarian in Robert Mugabe. The future of the inclusive government was to be reviewed two years after it was set up, in February 2011.

But what was the state of Zimbabwe in 2008, the year in which it sought a new escape from its socio-political crisis? It faced hunger; a collapse in health and education; hyperinflation; personal insecurity for those outside ZANU–PF; and mass emigration. In the middle of the year it was a failed state, by any analysis of a government's minimal provision for its citizens. Millions depended on remittances from family members who had gone abroad, and on humanitarian relief supplied by the World Food Programme, NGOs and others.

Let us consider, first of all, hunger, in what had been a bread-basket for southern Africa. By 2007–8 it was estimated that countries which were billed as enemies of Zimbabwe – European Union nations, the United States and the United Kingdom – were getting basic foodstuffs to between 30 and 50 per cent of the population, via the United Nations and NGOs.[22] The UN's World Food Programme, which had started its assistance in 2002, was reaching 5.4 million people out of a population of between 8 and 9 million in 2008, although there were complaints that the government gave preference to ZANU–PF cardholders.

In a peak month after a poor harvest, February 2009, it was estimated that 70 per cent of the population depended on food aid. The World Food Programme had been feeding over 4.5 million at the beginning of that year, with a coalition of NGOs feeding another million; shortages of donor funding and supplies – for South Africa had become a net food importer in 2007 – meant that the WFP had to cut the core maize ration from 10 kg to 5 kg a month in February.[23] But food aid was insufficient to ward off malnutrition, which became a factor in the increase in perinatal mortality, premature death, the ravages of AIDS, and emigration.[24] The crucial maize output was only 647,000 tonnes in 2008, just over a third of the average for the 1990s.[25] Extended families, often without male breadwinners, went days without conventional food and scavenged for roots and leaves.

The fast-track land seizures and the cronyistic way that the commercial farms were allocated had less impact on the smaller farms; but they too suffered from hyperinflation and a difficulty in getting credit, fertiliser and other inputs. This was partly due to insecurity of title. But the reality was that, while commercial farmers had been getting 12–14 tonnes of maize per hectare, the smallholders were only getting 300 kg per hectare.[26] Many of the new, smaller farmers found it incredibly tough going, sometimes combining agriculture with other work to scrape a living.[27] Nonetheless they were making progress by the end of the decade. By 2008 the 4,000 or so white commercial farmers of 2000 had dwindled to some 300, nearly all of whom were under attack. A significant proportion of the black commercial farmers – over a thousand in 2000 – had also been the subject of invasions or government takeover. An Asian family, including a judge with Zimbabwean citizenship, had its farm taken over in the fashion accorded to whites; a black judge, awarded a white farm, was foolish enough to invite people round to an open day, only to be told that Mrs Mugabe wanted his farm.

Though seemingly hopeless, some white commercial farmers kept up a legal challenge. One, which received wide publicity in the documentary film *Mugabe and the White African* involved an appeal to the SADC Tribunal in Botswana by two white Zimbabwean farmers, Mike Campbell and his son-in-law Ben Freeth. They argued that most of the takeovers were discriminatory and racist, because they were aimed at whites. In the end, though beaten up and having had their homes set on fire, they won their case. At some point in the future this victory may prove important; in the meantime it was pyrrhic, as the Zimbabwean authorities dismissed the ruling as not affecting them – although

Zimbabwe was a SADC signatory – and an attempt was made to freeze the powers of the Tribunal. Nonetheless in 2010 two Gauteng High Courts in Johannesburg, acting to enforce the Tribunal's decision, agreed to attach and auction a Zimbabwe government property in Kenilworth, Cape Town in partial settlement of debts owed to Campbell and two other farmers.[28] Other challenges were mounted, by owners of other nationalities, based on international agreements.

Visitors to Zimbabwe, and outside journalists who smuggled out footage of the countryside, saw people begging by the roadside and formerly fertile land returning to bush. Hungry people, as well as poachers, ransacked the game parks, which had been attractions in the days when the country had a tourism industry. Above all there was enormous waste. Some of the commercial farms had been trashed by 'war vets' and only a handful of occupiers remained, growing for their own subsistence, often by the roadside. Not many of the ZANU–PF elite, who had been given farms in return for their loyalty, were seriously interested in farming.[29]

Mugabe's call in the 1990s for no more than one farm per owner had been supported by some in the white farming community, who would have liked the chance to get a farm. Ironically, near the end of the first decade of the new century, it was the multiple ownership of those in or close to government that was a scandal, and a reason why ZANU–PF prevaricated over the GPA's promised land audit.

A forensic examination by the website ZimOnline in November 2010 demonstrated not only the transfer of commercial farms to a ZANU–PF elite, but the scale of multiple ownership. Mugabe and his wife Grace owned fourteen farms, and each ZANU–PF minister and deputy minister had more than one; vice president Joice Mujuru, her husband and their close relatives had at least twenty-five. All of the party's 56 politburo members, 98 MPs and

35 elected and unelected senators were given former white farms, as were 90 per cent of the nearly 200 officers in the army from the rank of major to lieutenant general. Some 40 per cent of the best land had gone to this elite in large holdings, while between 150,000 and 300,000 ZANU supporters, whom the reform was supposed to benefit, got between 10 and 50 hectares.[30] This was a cronyistic land transfer on a scale matched only by Cecil Rhodes in the 1890s. A Facebook protest campaign, which persuaded Nestlé to stop buying milk from Grace Mugabe's Gushungo dairy estate in 2009, was a token gesture of criticism by disgusted international consumers.

The nadir year of 2008 saw a large-scale collapse of education, particularly of schools in the countryside where some had been taken over as torture bases by ZANU. Teachers who were not paid went home, to the towns or out of Zimbabwe altogether. When the unity government tried to get a grip on the situation in the middle of 2009 it not only found the ministry building in Harare in disrepair, with computers not operational and water shortages, but an absence of some 20,000 teachers country-wide.[31] One of the great achievements of the 1980s, particularly pleasing to Robert Mugabe, a former teacher, was nullified. Children were unable to go to school. The University of Zimbabwe, the premier higher education institution, barely operated in 2008 after several years of decline – its two teaching hospitals were closed; many students had left; geology, veterinary science and surveying departments had closed; and the science department had ceased all experiments in 2007. Services for sewerage and running water – problems all over the city of Harare – had packed up; UNICEF brought in water tanks.

Lack of pay, and the hyperinflation, also crippled the health services. Doctors and nurses left the country. Harare had only two neurosurgeons, an insufficient peer group to discuss the challenge of a complex brain tumour. There was no money for drugs and equipment. Malnutrition and the collapse of the water and sewerage infrastructure led to opportunist illness, diarrhoea, and the continuance of AIDS. Most worrying was a cholera outbreak. Cholera is a disease of infected water and, although people can be inoculated against it, it can be fatal quickly. In 2008, 51 out of 62 health districts had cholera cases; by the first week of January 2009, by which time it was under control, there had been 33,579 cases, with nearly 1,700 deaths.[32] The South African government declared its Vhembe district in Limpopo province a disaster area, because sufferers were streaming over the border for medical care.

Overarching the separate aspects of Zimbabwe's tragedy lay the collapse in the Zimbabwe dollar. Whereas the highest denomination note in 2006 had been Z$20,000, by 2008 it had reached $100 million; altogether there were three ineffectual attempts by Gideon Gono, Reserve Bank governor and key ZANU money man, to knock noughts off the currency. At the same time he kept printing money, and there was a particular splurge in the run-up to the 2008 elections and shortly after. People went around with bricks of notes, lucky to find basics in the shops. Other types of value, including petrol coupons, were tried by individuals. With the exception of some who benefited from cross-border trade, those in the countryside continuously lost out. Country people were always running behind the depreciation, as were pensioners and those with savings in Zimbabwe currency. Barter and queueing became a way of life. But gradually, although frowned on by the authorities, the US dollar and South African rand crept into circulation. In the mid-1990s, when the Mozambican metical was distrusted, the US dollar was for a while the Mozambican currency. Gono accepted the inevitable in January 2009, on the eve of formation of the unity government, and let the Zimbabwe dollar take a rest. But the switch to US dollars – the rand had more purchase in Bulawayo and the south – was not without cost. Many lost money. Elderly people had to keep on working. While banks rushed to bring in dollar notes, the lack of small-denomination American coins fuelled inflation in the shops.

Human rights abuse and the lack of personal security had been a worsening story in the first decade of the twenty-first century. It reached epidemic status in 2008, although interestingly Beatrice Mtetwa, a former president of the Law Society of Zimbabwe, who had never been afraid of taking on the state in the courts, said in March 2010: 'it has never been as bad as it is now.'[33] Through much of the decade the prosecution and courts were biased; the police were operating as a political force and unwilling to investigate claims of abuse brought by civil society and the MDC; the prisons were filthy and prisoners underfed; the 'war vets', youth militia, police, military and CIO were all able to act with impunity. In 2008, statistically the worst year, individuals were assaulted, women raped, cattle and homes burnt. Brutality was licensed in the aftermath of the March election round, in Operation Mavhoterapapi, and was particularly sharp in Shona areas which had had the impertinence to vote for the MDC. The Research and Advocacy Unit reported, for instance, that Moses Bashtiano, a villager in Kavamba, was beaten, made to climb a tree with a rope round his neck, and hanged, and his relatives were made to bury him immediately. It was a major encouragement to human rights defenders when the SADC Tribunal in Windhoek, in December 2010, ruled that nine persons who were victims of organised violence and torture should receive compensation from the Zimbabwe government.[34]

Sadly, the judiciary had become politicised and was almost an arm of the state. Most of the Supreme and High Court judges had accepted taken-over commercial farms for themselves;[35] the Reserve Bank of Zimbabwe had also given each of them a rather smaller prestige inducement, for free – a flat-screen television set, satellite decoder and generator. The fallout from the land invasions at the beginning of the decade had seen direct bullying of the Supreme Court, when it was invaded by some 200 war vets. There had been a series of amendments to the Lancaster House Declaration of Rights, after its ten-year guarantee was up, and the use of the presidential pardon to amnesty those accused of human rights abuse had driven a stake through protection. Specifically, a Clemency Order of 1998 from the president had pardoned all violations arising from the Gukurahundi massacres. Anthony Gubbay, a white chief justice, was forced out of office in 2001; by the new century the optimistic era of Enoch Dumbutshena, chief justice from 1984 to 1990, when his court could declare that whipping a man was unconstitutional and a hangover from the dark ages, seemed ancient history.

The gallant band of civil society activists, who had recorded as many as possible of the human rights abuses, frequently with names and photographs, kept the world and the Zimbabwe diaspora informed of what was going on. The arrival of the Internet, with blogs and online news services, meant that the goings-on in Zimbabwe could not be concealed. Most of the victims were MDC supporters and office-holders, and people involved in civil society. But there was also some evidence that ZANU–PF could devour its own. Over the years there had been a number of suspicious car crashes involving the deaths of party figures such as Chris Ushewokunze, Moven Mahachi and Border Gezi; Eddison Zvogbo survived a serious crash. The poor state of roads and vehicles could explain much, but the idea got about that murder by car crash was one of the instruments of the regime, and that it could be used to settle disputes between political or kleptocratic factions within the ruling party. Zimbabwean society remained caught between modernity and the belief in spirits and prophetic voices.

Hunger, the frustrations of a failing state and ambition forced millions of Zimbabweans to flee the country. Zimbabwe borders four states: Zambia, Namibia (just, at the Caprivi strip), Botswana and South Africa. The boundaries are porous and no one knows exactly how many have left. A careful examination by Jonathan Crush and Daniel Tevera[36] threw doubt on assertions in South Africa that there are 3 million Zimbabweans in the country, a number quoted as a constant by the media between 2003 and 2009. But these authors suggest that whereas 500,000 had crossed legally into South Africa in 2000, the number had more than doubled to 1.25 million by 2008. Further, around 55 per cent of émigré Zimbabweans had moved to South Africa; whereas nearly a third of the Zimbabweans in SADC were in Zambia and Mozambique in 2001, migration to these two had fallen in the first half of the decade; and nearly 30 per cent of the SADC total were in Botswana.

But the migration had already become world-wide, with nearly 20 per cent of Zimbabweans outside the country in western Europe as early as 2001. The UK, a traditional destination outside the African continent, saw a reduction from 51,320 Zimbabweans entering in 2004 to 39,250 in 2007, probably due to tighter restrictions; only some of these would settle in the UK.[37] Contrary to a history of largely male migration, there were roughly as many female as male departures from Zimbabwe, and their experience in South Africa was mixed. While some Zimbabweans found good jobs, others faced xenophobia or low-paid farm work. In May 2008, just as ZANU–PF unleashed its strategy of violence at home, there was a nasty burst of xenophobia in the South African townships, of which Zimbabweans were the main victims. The rainbow nation had an ugly side.

The Methodist Central Church in downtown Johannesburg reckons to have provided short-term care for up to 30,000 Zimbabweans between 2004 and 2010, some of them in a pitiful condition; Paul Verryn, who runs the centre, estimated that fifty buildings in the central district were, in February 2010, being squatted by Zimbabweans.[38] Hungry and vulnerable people, including the blind and mothers with small babies, took part in this exodus. Although a South African immigration Act in 2002 made Zimbabwean immigration easier, the authorities continued to take a hard line on 'illegals'; a deportation holding centre was established at a place called Lindela and migrants, transported home, made repeated efforts to enter South Africa; in 2005 as many as 150,000 were deported.

The best guess was that between a quarter and a third of Zimbabweans had left the country. These were not people likely to vote, without coercion, for Robert Mugabe or ZANU–PF. Although some would campaign for the voting rights of the diaspora, they had, quite literally, voted with their feet. In the meantime their role was vital in sustaining desperate extended families with their remittances. A croupier on a cruise ship working out of Miami, for instance, was sending home a hundred dollars a month. Even those who had got poorly paid jobs as labourers on South African farms were crucial to family survival back home. Would the inclusive government, formed at last from three parties on 11 February 2009, be able to turn round this lengthy, draining socio-political crisis?

The omens for the new government were not good. The JOC, the military–security cabal, boycotted the opening ceremony, apparently because they could not accept Morgan Tsvangirai as prime minister. Roy Bennett, nominated by Tsvangirai as deputy minister of agriculture, was promptly remanded in unpleasant custody in Mutare police station.[39] A successful white farmer before his farm was taken over, he was MDC treasurer and a fluent Shona speaker. Elected MDC MP for his home district of Chimanimani in 2000, he had fled to South Africa after a parliamentary fracas. Invited to join the inclusive government by Tsvangirai, he was instantly caught by a trumped-up treason charge. Mugabe simply would not accept him. He escaped to South Africa, where he lived under protection. It looked as though the grudge matches of the past were carrying forward into the new dispensation.

The life of the unity government, which could be aborted by any of the parties after two years, was punctuated by a series of rows over appointments, by jostling over a new constitution and the timing of another election, and by the continuing distrust between ZANU–PF and the larger MDC faction, MDC–T. The role of the small Mutambara faction – Mutambara was replaced as its leader by Welshman Ncube in January 2011 – seemed to be to suggest that all problems were soluble, and to keep the leaky ship from sinking. Essentially ZANU–PF wanted the MDC to rescue the economy, bring in financial help from Europe and the USA, and remove the sanctions and asset freezes which inconvenienced 200 of its high-ups and friends. It wanted all this without conceding real power. For Tsvangirai and his supporters the intention was different. While doing what it could to reduce kleptocracy and restore the economy and social services, the party hoped to launch a democratic transition. It wanted movement to an effective rights-based constitution and an end to Zimbabwe's culture of violence. Although the full achievement of a new dispensation might not happen until after Mugabe's death, the change of direction had to start now.

The battle over appointments was continuous. The MDC–T wanted to get rid of Gideon Gono, the Reserve Bank governor who was acting as financier to ZANU–PF and who had presided over one of the world's worst cases of hyperinflation. Although Tendai Biti as finance minister tried to get a grip on the nation's finances, and a Reserve Bank amendment bill was passed by parliament in an effort to achieve transparency, Gono was backed by Mugabe and stayed in post. The same was true of Johannes Tomana, the attorney general. There were rows over appointments of ambassadors and provincial governors, with the president taking partisan decisions on a unilateral basis which, according to the GPA, should have been by consensus with the approval of Tsvangirai and Mutambara.

There were periods when it seemed as if both Mugabe and Tsvangirai wanted the deal to work. There were also moments of humanity, as when, after Tsvangirai's wife Susan was killed in a car crash on 6 March 2009 and Morgan was in hospital, Robert and Grace Mugabe visited him and Grace was weeping. Although there were suspicions about this accident, on a notoriously dangerous Harare–Masvingo road, Tsvangirai himself dismissed them.

But for much of the time the picture was one of friction, described by the MDC tactician Eddie Cross as 'street fighting'. In late 2009 the MDC–T partially disengaged from the government for a brief period, and talked of walking out if its demands were not met. For at least a month, in late 2010, Tsvangirai and Mugabe never met in cabinet. Civil society and the trade unions complained that the prime minister seemed to be not only a junior partner but an accomplice in a continuation of ZANU–PF rule. Tsvangirai toured capitals in Europe and North America seeking aid, and the removal of targeted sanctions which had been imposed because of human rights abuse. When he spoke to Zimbabweans in London's Southwark Cathedral in June 2009, telling them it was safe to go home and that they should do so, he was booed.

In fact there were different dimensions to a unity government which had several subterranean aspects; while the JOC still had its apparatus of coercion, many of ZANU–PF's leaders were, like Mugabe himself, old; younger people in the civil service knew well enough that these leaders were not immortal, and that the party was unpopular and unsuccessful. To whom should they give their loyalty? When ought they to jump ship? Did the modest improvements in the country reflect the MDC's contribution or would they, as ZANU–PF argued, be even greater if all international hostility was lifted?

The unity government was billed as a temporary phenomenon, until superseded by a new constitution and new elections. In the meantime it was to be kept on track by SADC and South Africa;[40] it was supposed to revive the country; it was committed to an end to violence, the support of human rights and national healing; and it was expected to resume a more respected position in international affairs. One of the most disappointing outcomes related to the SADC facilitation, now in the hands of President Zuma, who appointed three aides to conduct the 'heavy lifting' of diplomacy – Mac Maharaj, a former South African minister of transport and leading figure in the SACP and ANC during the anti-apartheid struggle; Lindiwe Zulu, an international affairs adviser to Zuma; and Charles Nqakula. While Zuma rationed his visits to Harare, these three were in and out more often, talking to the party leaders.

Much hope for change had been invested in Zuma, who took over from Mbeki as SADC facilitator in 2009. He had criticised Mugabe before becoming president of South Africa. One of his daughters was married to Welshman Ncube, of MDC–M. As a Zulu he had kinship with the Ndebele, who had had such a rough experience with ZANU–PF. His political support base in COSATU and the SACP had been the most critical of ZANU–PF in the ANC-led triple alliance. And of course he was a living embodiment of democracy in a liberation movement. The ANC had recalled and deselected its leader, Thabo Mbeki, even though he was president of the country.

But, whether because the obstacles between the parties in Harare were too great, or Zuma was reluctant to wield a big stick, it seemed to observers that his quiet approach was not much different from his predecessor's. He ignored the kind of economic and interventionist critique of Tony Blair, who on a visit to South Africa as a former prime minister claimed that the republic's gross national product had suffered by 1 per cent as a result of Zimbabwe's implosion, and that it should push for regime change. South Africa slowed down the legitimation of Zimbabwean refugees, when the authorities required them to regularise their papers in 2010, and bureaucrats served them slowly in Pretoria. And Mugabe made mischief at Zuma's expense when Julius Malema, the brash, loud-mouthed leader of the ANC Youth League, visited Harare and hailed ZANU's land occupations and indigenisation strategy for companies. It was not clear how far other SADC leaders, such as President Guebuza of Mozambique, were exerting pressure for fulfilment of the GPA, either via Zuma or directly, and deadlines for progress came and went. Significantly, President Khama of Botswana, who had rejected the 2008 second round election result, made up with Mugabe in the course of 2010. It seemed to be a recognition that power had not shifted away from ZANU with the arrival of a unity government.

By 2010 the main development in Zimbabwe's politics concerned the consultation for a new constitution. Work had started slowly, with ZANU–PF blaming foreigners for being unwilling to fund an outreach programme. When it got going, under the supervision of a parliamentary committee, it was clear that ZANU–PF were keen to push what was known as the Kariba draft – a draft constitution developed earlier, with apparent support from MDC–T. The current constitution had been amended eighteen times by parliaments dominated by ZANU–PF, and could no longer be described as the Lancaster House constitution. But the Kariba draft would retain a strong executive presidency, and for that was criticised by many civil society bodies. In late October the Law Society of Zimbabwe proposed a model constitution which built on experience in Zimbabwe and South Africa. Its main features included an extensive, enforceable Declaration of Rights, the vesting of executive functions in a prime minister rather than a president, and extensive devolution of powers to the provinces, with each province having an elected governor, and its own legislature and police force.[41]

ZANU–PF disrupted a number of the outreach consultations, including in Harare. Initially it was hoped there could be a referendum on a new constitution in June 2011, but the parliamentary committee then deferred it to September; this left Mugabe with the option of calling an election before that under the old rules. In Kenya, of course, the two rivals – President Kibaki and Prime Minister Odinga – had joined forces to win a referendum for a new constitution, which within a year was leading to the prosecution of corrupt ministers.

While military and ZANU–PF leaders continued to proclaim that power would never shift to someone who had no credentials from the liberation struggle, the politics of the unity government continued to be dominated by concern for the Mugabe succession. In ZANU–PF there were pressures for him to be canonised as a 'president for life'. But mortality could not be deferred for ever, and in the course of 2010 he lost through death one of his vice presidents, Joseph Msika, and his sister, Sabina. A significant incident took place at the beginning of September in Chitungwiza, the high-density suburb adjoining the capital. Thugs supporting Solomon Mujuru beat up council employees, claiming that they supported Emmerson Mnangagwa, and overpowered police who tried to rescue the officials. It was a hint that, given traditions of violence and the widespread distribution of weapons, ZANU factions could end up shooting each other in the event of a sudden vacancy in State House.

On the opposition side there was also some evidence of fracturing. Not all of the MDC ministers, some of whom had never had serious jobs before, were on top of their portfolios. There was an issue about the term of Morgan Tsvangirai as his party's president, which under the party constitution should rotate after two five-year stints, and the government press sought to stimulate jealousy with Tendai Biti, the younger finance minister. There were similar issues in MDC–M, where Welshman Ncube successfully challenged Arthur Mutambara for the leadership at the start of 2011. MDC–M councillors in Bulawayo were trickling back to the MDC–T. Slightly to one side of the ZANU–MDC debate were the continuance of Simba Makoni's small third force and an attempt by Dumiso Dabengwa, former ZIPRA intelligence chief, to revive ZAPU.

The one clear benefit of the unity government was the appearance of goods in the shops and an improvement in some social services. The end of hyperinflation and the death of the Zimbabwe dollar were marked when Tsvangirai and Biti arranged to pay all government workers, including soldiers and police, in US dollars – initially $100 a month. Reluctantly, ZANU–PF had permitted the use of the US and South African currency in September 2008, when inflation was said to be running at billions per cent. But it took the arrival of the unity government to provide wages, though hardly enough to live on, in hard currency. Supermarkets began to fill with goods again, but many families without access to remittances still depended on barter and food aid.

Biti, who won the grudging respect of Mugabe,[42] launched a Short-Term Economic Recovery Programme which identified the need for about US$8.5 billion in resources. By October 2010 inflation was down to 3.6 per cent a year, compared with an official statistic of 230 million per cent a year in 2008, when independent observers thought it was running in the billions.[43] But attempts to get substantial external support from Western sources ran up against scepticism about the degree to which the MDC's two wings were really in control of the government, and a reluctance to end targeted sanctions by the EU and USA while there were still questions about human rights and the prospect of fair elections. President Obama in November 2009 branded Mugabe a dictator who clung to power by force.[44] The land audit scheduled by the

GPA had not begun. The sinister Joint Operations Command had not been replaced by a transparent National Security Council of the three government parties. Hence, although Western governments provided humanitarian aid, and coordinated it through weekly meetings of a 'Fishmonger group' in Harare, substantial investment to rescue a shattered economy was slow in coming. The UK, for instance, was providing around £60 million a year in aid in 2009 and 2010.

The decline in health and education services was such that, even with MDC ministers trusted by donor governments, recovery could not be quick. Health, where two-thirds of the budget was provided by donors, had priority; the cholera outbreak was brought under control. But power cuts and water shortages crippled hospitals; Harare's central hospital was still without running water, reliant on water trucks, in early 2010. Ordinary services, including rubbish collection and road maintenance, were still erratic. By the middle of 2010 most of the schools which had been closed had reopened, and exams were sat and marked on time; David Coltart, the minister of education, said that whereas in November 2009 only 1,500 of the 20,000 absent teachers had returned to work, by the July 2010 the number was 15,000.[45] Whereas schools were open for only an average of 26 days in 2008, they were open for nearly 180 days two years later. An international programme to provide textbooks, and a planning process for the ministry, gave hope for a gradual improvement. But many parents had difficulty in paying the US$100–300 a term, which was the cost of a primary school place.

An honest appraisal of the economy would suggest that it was bumping along the bottom, although a small increase in gross domestic product was reported for 2010.[46] A North American who visited Harare earlier in the year said that he had only seen one tower crane – his test of commercial activity for any capital – as he flew in. The FIFA World Cup in South Africa produced few tourism benefits for its neighbour, although significant numbers of international visitors were returning to see the natural wonders of Victoria Falls. Tackling the large number of 'ghost workers' on ministry payrolls had hardly begun.[47] While Biti appeared to be in command of the economy, and the Reserve Bank of Gideon Gono had lost control of the currency and 75 per cent of its staff, Mugabe still had power to disrupt. He revived a bill for 51 per cent indigenisation of any firm, which had been passed prior to the 2008 elections when ZANU–PF had a parliamentary majority but never implemented.[48] Tsvangirai denied that it was valid. But the threat was enough to discourage even South African firms from investing new money in Zimbabwe, and at the ZANU–PF conference in December 2010 Mugabe threatened UK and US firms with total expropriation if their countries continued to support sanctions against him. Although commodity prices were helpful, uncertainty was bad for business, and early in 2011 youths attacked a number of foreign-owned shops in Harare.

If ZANU–PF had lost the power to print money, it had gained something more precious – an income from diamonds. The murky world of human rights abuse, Chinese assistance and the Zimbabwe military came together in the story of the Chiadzwa diamond fields in Marange district, south-west of Mutare and not far from the Mozambique border. Cecil Rhodes would have relished the irony that 'his' country was at last found to have one of the richest diamond deposits in the world. Although a British company, African Consolidated Resources, had bought the reserves in February 2006, it was not able to gain effective control. At one point it was thought that as many as 15,000 people were working as freelance miners, in primitive conditions, with gems smuggled out through Mozambique.

But in October 2008, as the Zimbabwe government searched for new income in a collapsed economy, it sent in the army to clear the area; some 400 people may have died, and extraction, under army control, began again, with new human rights abuses including the exploitation of women and child labour. The Chinese built an airfield, and helped to fly out the product. However, as a result of scandals in Sierra Leone and elsewhere, and an unremitting non-governmental campaign, a Kimberley certification process has been introduced. With widespread international support, this aims to prevent so-called 'blood diamonds' from entering the legitimate trade. The ZANU–PF mines minister, Obert Mpofu, succeeded in getting the Kimberley process to give temporary and then permanent permission for Zimbabwe sales, and members of the inclusive government claimed that it was now in control. In August 2010, the first month for Kimberley sales, there was an income to the treasury of US$30 million. But many thought that senior officers and ZANU–PF were still helping themselves to more, and there was a revival in cholera among freelance miners who were panning just outside the army-controlled area. Approval for diamond exports from Chiadzwa, without more effective protection for the workers and controls on smuggling, seemed to show up the weakness of the Kimberley process.

What was the situation for human rights and freedom of expression under the unity government? It had not improved as much as might have been expected if the GPA had been honoured in full. There were some high-profile setbacks. Manfred Nowak, United Nations special rapporteur on torture, was detained and turned back in October 2009 when he came to investigate torture and intimidation in rural areas. Jestina Mukoko, director of the Zimbabwe Peace Project, who was kidnapped by secret police in December 2008, was tortured and not released on bail until March 2009; a ludicrous charge that she had been recruiting persons to train as insurgents and saboteurs was not killed by the Supreme Court until September 2009. When the Human Rights NGO Forum launched a campaign with posters, calling on Zimbabwe to sign the UN Convention against Torture, the authorities tore them down.

Initially, after the formation of the unity government, there was a drop in reported incidents of human rights abuse. But incidents continued, sometimes linked to the constitutional consultations, and there were rumours that ZANU–PF's bases for intimidation were being readied for action before new elections. An independent analyis of the constitutional outreach operation in the Harare district, seriously disturbed by ZANU–PF in September 2010, found that in the following month participants had been coached, diversity of views was prevented, and the operation was being so managed by ZANU–PF that it could not be said to produce unbiased results.[49] Both South Africa and the UK, where Zimbabwean migration had become a sensitive issue, had an interest in promoting the idea that the country was now safe again, and in the UK the new coalition government announced in late 2010 that, after virtually eight years of amnesty, it would deport failed asylum-seekers again.

The GPA's commitment to freedom of expression made no difference to the hard-line ZANU–PF propaganda of the state media, now once again assisted by Jonathan Moyo, who had rejoined the party. However, international journalists from the BBC and other organisations were able to report freely; *The Zimbabwean*, an independent anti-government publication brought in three times a week from South Africa, was available on the streets; new papers were given licences, including *Newsday*, the first to appear, and the *Daily News*, which had been finally closed in 2003 after bombings and arrests. But the government was not making it easy. It bought all the newsprint from the only Zimbabwean factory in Mutare, forcing other publishers to import paper expensively from South Africa. *Newsday*'s print run was restricted to 25,000 a day for this reason. Important as the press is, the broadcasting media are of at least equal significance. Although hate speech and bias were not removed from the state broadcasters, other sources were available to many Zimbabweans. In 2008 a large number of people in rural areas were given free short-wave radios. Radio SW Africa and Voice of America's Studio Seven have substantial audiences; ZBC is reckoned to reach only 70 per cent of the population; and, all round the boundary, Zimbabweans can listen to and watch their neighbours' output. But the government has used Chinese help to try and jam stations it deems hostile, such as Radio SW Africa; and in November 2010 a spokesman said that there would be no licences for new radio or television stations, contrary to the GPA commitment.

A rather utopian feature of the GPA was the establishment of an organ of national healing, jointly led by prominent members of each party – John Nkomo of ZANU–PF, Sekai Holland of MDC–T, and Gibson Sibanda, a leading trade unionist who joined MDC–M and who died in the course of 2010. The aim was to end the violence that had been endemic in Zimbabwean society for decades, and promote a civil and democratic spirit. Sekai Holland argues that at least a million people have been severely traumatised by violence since the 1970s; they have suffered directly, witnessed violence, or perpetrated it. She sees the breaking of cycles of violence as crucial to her country's future, and points out that, throughout the history of the land now known as Zimbabwe, those who were victors by conquest became victims in their turn.

The organ of national healing is operating differently from either the Truth and Reconciliation Commission of South Africa or the legalist approach stressing justice and punishment. It aims to provide therapeutic help for those most severely damaged, and to develop strategies for youth, ex-soldiers, women and other categories. It is looking to promote a more plural understanding of Zimbabwean history, to move away from the sharp distinction between 'patriots' and 'sell-outs' which has been central to government discourse in the ZANU–PF era. Its critics argue that it has too little funding to be more than cosmetic, that it has been slow to tackle the ZANU–PF security ministries, that it avoids hard questions of impunity, or speaking out. Mrs Holland has claimed that its approach is one that is appropriate to African societies, and that there was a marked fall in reported violence in August 2009 after party leaders launched the process on 26–28 July 2009.[50] Interestingly, in late 2010, Vice President Joice Mujuru called on ZANU–PF to abandon violence.

However, the organ of national healing had only a limited influence, particularly over the security services and partisan youths. In early 2011, shortly after a declaration against violence by the principals of the GPA, the Zimbabwe Human Rights NGO Forum reported violent clashes between ZANU–PF and MDC youths in Harare, Bindura, Gutu, Bikita and Chitungwiza.[51] Talk in ZANU–PF of early elections, on top of the constitutional debate, had stimulated the party's traditional resort to intimidation; but it was also clear that MDC youths were now more ready to defend themselves.

Was this a transitional government for a country on the way to greater democracy? Or was it a gimmick to disguise the continuing control of ZANU–PF? The world was changing, and in ways that gave Zimbabwe different salience on the international scene. China's importance in Africa, with regular meetings for African leaders in Beijing, was becoming more pronounced, even though countries like Angola and Mozambique sought to put an end to the use of Chinese labour to build factories and infrastructure. ZANU–PF's friendship with China, going back to the days of Maoism, was a continuing reality. Zimbabwe residents were struck by the increasing number of Chinese they saw, from petty traders to major businessmen. In 2008 China signed a US$42 million loan to support Zimbabwe's farm mechanisation, and the following year Zimbabwe secured credit lines of US$950 million to support infrastructure projects and to buy Chinese goods.[52] In early 2011, Tapiwa Mashakada, minister of economic planning and economic promotion, told Reuters that China was ready to invest up to US$10 billion in Zimbabwe, in mining, agriculture, infrastructure and information technology; this large if not quite credible sum could substantially rebuild the economy.[53]

The rise of emerging powers outside China was also significant. President Lula of Brazil, who was pursuing a vigorous South–South agenda, authorised a match in Harare between Brazil and the Zimbabwe football team in the run-up to the FIFA World Cup in South Africa.

The IMF might get back into Zimbabwe and there were allegations that Western banks were getting around sanctions.[54] But, given Mugabe's demonisation of Tony Blair and the Labour Party, cordially reciprocated, the arrival of a new government in the UK was of special importance. Prior to the May 2010 election, Mugabe said that he hoped the Conservatives would win. In fact David Cameron, the Conservative leader forced to make a coalition with the Liberal Democrats, had indicated that he wanted to lead his party away from its old foreign policy obsessions, including with Zimbabwe. The coalition acquired new priorities. The bankruptcy of Labour's liberal interventionism, which had led to the corrosion of torture in Iraq, recognition of an unopposed president in Afghanistan whose legitimacy was no better than Mugabe's, and unaffordable military adventures, was laid bare. The coalition was more interested in trade, and in aligning its development aid with UK security. The UK, where Gono's resort to printing money had been laughed at, was doing something similar by 'quantitative easing' of the money supply to recover from a deep recession. In the changed scenario, British diplomacy, an important influence on the EU and Western donors, might lean more to helping Zimbabwe's economy to recover than to helping to perfect its democracy. Nonetheless, ZANU-PF was not going to make reconciliation easy. The UK high commissioner walked out of a Harare conference when the indigenisation minister, Saviour Kasukuwere, said he would 'buy British last'. Mugabe, gearing up at his party's December 2010 conference for a possible 2011 election, hurled traditional insults at the British.

The abiding question, as Zimbabwe completed thirty years of independence, was whether South Africa on behalf of SADC had the will or capacity to break the ZANU/MDC logjam. President Zuma had called for a roadmap that included a new constitution, a referendum, a clean electoral register and properly managed elections. Although many in business and the public could see the advantage of postponing elections, to defer violence and prolong a hesitant recovery, it was obvious that Mugabe was tempted to short-circuit the process by calling for a poll as soon as he could. While Mbeki had persuaded Mugabe to bring forward 2010 elections to 2008, it was not clear whether Zuma would be equally successful in postponing those that could take place after two years of the inclusive government, in 2011.

Attitudes were changing in Africa, where the West African states of ECOWAS, the AU and the UN all objected when the outgoing president of Ivory Coast, Laurent Gbagbo, claimed to have won an election in which Alessane Dramane Ouattara had verifiably captured 54.1 per cent of the vote. Morgan Tsvangirai denounced the possibility of an inclusive government of these two, on the Kenyan and Zimbabwean pattern. ECOWAS threatened to invade Ivory Coast, to ensure that the will of the electors was respected, and a successful rebellion removed Gbagbo.

More dramatic, of course, were events in North Africa. A popular uprising in Tunisia saw the departure of President Ben Ali, a long-serving dictator, on 14 January 2011. The spirit of democratic revolt then spread throughout the Arab world, leading to a huge popular and youthful mobilisation against Hosni Mubarak in Egypt, a key member of the African Union. Mubarak had become president in 1981, less than a year after Robert Mugabe became prime minister of Zimbabwe, and Mubarak was 82 when he too was forced from power. Autocracies in Libya, Yemen and Bahrain were challenged.

And, ominously for human rights abusers in Zimbabwe, the International Criminal Court decided to prosecute six leading Kenyans – including the minister of finance Uhuru Kenyatta – for their part in the political violence of 2008. While fixing election results to the benefit of an incumbent government might be getting harder, the need to hang on to power, for those wanting to avoid justice, might be greater.

EIGHT

HOW DID IT GO WRONG?

Speaking at leisure in a Harare garden, a retired Zimbabwe diplomat mused on whether Robert Mugabe was a good leader who had turned bad, or whether he was a bad man all along. Relaxing in London over lunch a British school friend once seriously suggested that a successful sniper who could pick off Mugabe with a bullet would have saved his country much agony. That there was and is a Mugabe factor in the catastrophe of modern Zimbabwe is undeniable, but as an explanation for what has gone wrong it is not only simplistic and inadequate, but misleading. Metaphorically, there is blood on many hands. Indeed the sudden death of the president, which could unleash a firefight among ZANU–PF factions, is one of the great fears of those who wish for the country's recovery. Before turning to consider the Mugabe factor, therefore, it is worth analysing other elements of explanation.

The geography and history of southern Africa are givens that are sometimes overlooked. While Cecil Rhodes led white invaders northwards from Cape Colony, the black liberation movements from the 1960s onwards were pushing southwards, with South Africa the last, greatest goal. Had South Africa been liberated from apartheid first, before independence turned Salisbury into Harare, the history of Rhodesia/Zimbabwe might have been quite different. Further, the role of Europeans in this part of Africa began seriously in South Africa in the seventeenth century, but did not impinge on what is now Zimbabwe until the late nine-teenth century. White occupation was recent. Stan Mudenge told Chief Anyaoku that, sixteen years after the Second World War the US and UK were justifying the restitution of Jewish property in Germany and western Europe, but would not accept the restitu-tion of lands to Africans which had been grabbed by the Smith regime as recently as 1969.[1]

Two key issues in the explanation of Zimbabwe's tragedy have to be the nature of the liberation movement that is ZANU–PF, and the nature of UK colonialism in this part of Africa. ZANU–PF is not unique among southern African liberation movements in retaining its first leader as president into the twenty-first century; Jose Eduardo dos Santos, MPLA president of Angola since 1979, has geared up for an election in 2011 which could see him in power until 2022. All these liberation movements also tend to share the belief that history stopped when they won power,[2] and a suspicion of Western governments that had opposed or obstructed them during their time of struggle. Nonetheless ZANU–PF is dif-ferent from FRELIMO in Mozambique, where Armando Guebuza took over as president from Joaquim Chissano in 2005, and from Namibia, where SWAPO's Sam Nujoma was succeeded in the presidency by Hifikepunye Pohamba in 2005. Nujoma, a strong supporter of Mugabe and ZANU's land programme, had actually been president of SWAPO from its inception in 1960 until 2007, and had three terms of office as president of his country from its independence in 1990. His 'father of the nation' status was stronger, and less contested, than Mugabe's.

Hence, although Angola, Namibia, Zimbabwe and Mozam-bique shared ruling parties with a Marxist heritage – with an apparatus of central committees and top-down direction – two of these countries saw rotation at the top. Quite soon, in all of them, the generation which had surfaced during the liberation wars would be passing on. In Zimbabwe the ageing Mugabe was like a cork holding down fissiparous tendencies in the bottle beneath. Further, although there were complaints from rivals about the fairness of elections, electoral processes were helping to renovate the ruling parties in Mozambique and Namibia.

The most significant comparison, which showed up the autocracy and increasing strangeness of ZANU–PF, was with South Africa's ANC. The ANC was a very old and experienced political formation; like the Indian National Congress party and the British Labour Party its roots lay in the early years of the twentieth century.[3] Although categorised as a liberation movement, which had an armed wing in the late twentieth century, it had had a long if frustrating life as a peaceful campaigning body for equal rights. Its Zulu leader, Chief Albert Luthuli, who had actually been born in Southern Rhodesia, had received a Nobel Peace Prize in 1960. Its Freedom Charter of 1955, created with allies after widespread consultation, was specifically multiracial. Although it too had been influenced by Marxism – and the participation of white and Indian communists had helped keep it multiracial – it was democratic and consensual in spirit. The evolution of the ANC after South Africa's first multiracial election in 1994 was different from ZANU–PF's after 1980. Mandela only served one term as president. President Mbeki was recalled by the party, losing party leadership and presidency. A strong South African constitution, enforced by an independent judiciary, protected pluralism, the distribution of power, and both civil and political rights and, with more difficulty given poverty and unemployment, socio-economic rights.

As in other liberation movements, there had always been a streak of ruthlessness in ZANU–PF. This came on top of a history of violence in African politics in Rhodesia, partly born of frustration, division and the manipulation of white police and intelligence services. Opponents in the townships, labelled as 'sell-outs', could be attacked physically or see their homes burnt down. The violence unleashed by the Badza/Nhari rebellion in ZANLA in the 1970s was one of the peaks of conspiracy and killing inside ZANU–PF's armed wing. The ruthlessness and violence were justified on the grounds of necessity: liberation was the goal, and the Rhodesian regime was equally harsh, not only on its armed opponents but on the rights of supposed fellow citizens. By the early years of the twenty-first century there was little sign that ZANU–PF, now closely integrated with senior military who had done well out of the Congo war, had outgrown its traditions of coercion. ZANU–PF had become militarised, and officers were given places in parastatals and the civil service. The possibility that the top Zimbabwe military could be politically neutral, in the way that the Egyptian military claimed to be in February 2011, was unthinkable.

While Leninist principles of party control still influenced ZANU–PF into the twenty-first century, along with its deliberate confusion of state with party, the influence of economic Marxism seemed to have waned. Although party leaders blamed ESAP for loss of popularity in the 1990s, and there were attempts to use price controls to restrict the growing inflation after 2000, the truth was that ZANU–PF was embracing capitalism with an indigenist twist. In this it followed the example of China, rather than North Korea. North Korea inspired the architecture for Heroes Acre, the monumental graveyard outside Harare in which ZANU leaders, including Robert Mugabe's sister Sabina, were buried.[4] But its idiosyncratic dynastic communism was too exotic.

ZANU–PF's friendship with China took on a new quality after Maoist economics were abandoned in Beijing and China's economic growth and interest in African raw materials exploded.

Mugabe's 'Look East' policy, a rejection of decadent Western policy as he saw it, was slow to win traction, because of the chaos in Zimbabwe's economy. But it came to include arms supplies, involvement in the Chiudzwa diamonds, and other joint ventures. China's potential veto in the UN Security Council meant that Western critiques of Zimbabwe's human rights record were stalled.[5] The Mugabe family and others could ignore Western sanctions on shopping expeditions in Hong Kong, where Robert and Grace's daughter Bona was a student. Above all, China taught the Zimbabwe government that an iron fist paid. China had recovered from the economic disaster of the 'Great Leap Forward' in the 1960s, just as it had weathered Western disapproval of the crackdown in Tiananmen Square in 1989. Who was to say that, in twenty years' time, Western prime ministers and businessmen might not be trooping into Harare, avoiding awkward questions but greedy for commerce, just as they did in Beijing?

Two other aspects of ZANU–PF that helped explain its partisan nature lay in its Shona capture, especially by the Zezuru clan to which Mugabe belonged, and its exclusivist sense of history. Even in 1980, the first election prior to independence, it was obvious that voting was following ethnic lines. With the passage of time, and the cruelties of the Gukurahundi, Shona dominance became clearer still. 'Others', whether whites, Ndebele or those with ancestors from neighbouring countries, were shamelessly demonised in hate speech, and actively discriminated against. ZANU–PF became a racist organisation. And ZANU–PF had its own view of history, tirelessly promoted in party rallies and by state media. Only this party had heroically led effective resistance to the Smith regime; Joshua Nkomo would have sold out. Only this party was returning stolen land to Africans, and preventing Zimbabwe from being 'recaptured' by neo-colonialism. This was a justification for the 51 per cent indigenisation of companies, which just happened to benefit an elite close to ZANU–PF.

As with the Soviet Communist Party, it was difficult for outsiders to know what was really going on inside ZANU–PF; outsiders had been wrongfooted when Khrushchev fairly soon succeeded Stalin in the 1950s, and Gorbachev succeeded a gerontocracy in the 1980s. But it was clear that the nature and evolution of ZANU–PF had much to answer for in the tragedy of Zimbabwe in the first decade of the twenty-first century. Mugabe was not a personal dictator removed from the context of his party and its military allies; indeed after he lost the 2008 election he was arguably a front man for the JOC.

But the British also had much to answer for, in explaining the tragedy. Some of course would argue that the conquest, promoted by Rhodes with his pioneer column near the end of the nineteenth century, was the start of lasting problems. But in the imperialist spirit of the times it is also arguable that if Rhodes had not got there other European conquerors would have, and that in any case the situation of Ndebele and Shona under Lobengula and the Ndebele kingship was hardly a happy one. Nonetheless it is a fact that twentieth-century decolonisation in Africa was much less complicated in countries like Malawi or Tanganyika, where there were few white settlers, even if post-colonial experience in several African countries was disappointing. White occupation in Rhodesia smashed and subordinated pre-existing African society, and did not permit the 'indirect rule' which was a feature of the British Empire in Nigeria, India and elsewhere.

Rhodes and his British South Africa Company were freebooters, ignoring the imperial government whenever possible. Although Liberal governments and oppositions in London might speak up for the rights of Bulgars and Irish in Europe, dispossession of and cruelty and discrimination against Africans in central Africa were an issue for only a handful of missionaries. The land allocations and structuring of the company's colony were designed to underpin white immigration, and on lines that owed much to law and practice in Cape Colony and thereafter the Union of South Africa.

It has been said that the British Empire was acquired in a fit of absence of mind. Certainly there was an absence of London control over much that happened in Southern Rhodesia, and this was given formal recognition after the 1922 referendum in Southern Rhodesia, won by Coghlan and the advocates of 're-sponsible government'. It is intriguing to imagine what would have happened if the South African party had won, and Rhodesia had become a fifth province in the Union; it is quite possible that the Afrikaner-backed National Party would have had difficulty in ever winning a majority in a South African election.

For nearly sixty years after the referendum, however, the United Kingdom had international responsibility for, but not enough authority over, what was going on in Southern Rhodesia and its successor state. This became politically difficult as pressure for African rights and decolonisation developed after the Second World War. Confusion over the relative status of the Westminster parliament and the Salisbury government was not dissimilar to the confusion between Stormont and Westminster as the civil rights movement grew in Northern Ireland at the end of the 1960s. But whereas the Conservative government of Edward Heath imposed direct rule from Westminster on Northern Ireland in 1973, it would not have dreamt of doing the same in Rhodesia following the Pearce Commission report on African attitudes the previous year.

In the 1920s the UK government was pleased enough to let the white settlers run Southern Rhodesia, on a basis that seemed to cost it nothing. The assumptions at the time were racist and that the British Empire was immortal. Southern Rhodesia had quasi-dominion status in the interwar era, and it did not seem one of the Empire's most valuable dependencies. But the white settlers, stressing their loyalty to the Crown, were nevertheless digging in as an autonomous society with their own elected government. Progress for the expanding black population was not a priority. In retrospect the autonomy consolidated by the whites, protected against Colonial Office concern for subject peoples by their different status, proved disastrous.

The next error of British policy occurred at the creation of the Central African Federation. As was seen earlier, there were mixed motives among the protagonists. Liberal Conservatives in the UK were hoping to establish a friendly Commonwealth state in central Africa, with more equal racial values than the apartheid state in South Africa. But most Southern Rhodesians were not terribly progressive, and were chiefly hoping to strengthen their economy by closer coordination with the Copperbelt, and to benefit in a bigger state; they recognised that white demography would be diluted, and saw little advantage in the addition of Nyasaland. The concept of 'racial partnership', not carefully defined, looked different in London and Salisbury.

London was warned early on that the Federation scheme lacked African support in Northern Rhodesia and Nyasaland. It tried to build in some guarantees for the populations of those two territories, but was unwilling to challenge the self-governing whites of Southern Rhodesia. Prior to the independence of Ghana, and slow to see that the independence of South Asia must inevitably be followed by independence for the African colonies, the UK government was more concerned with the Cold War, and its own country's post-war recovery. The Federation was an unstable, three-legged piece of political furniture, resting chiefly on optimism. As African opposition grew, and the UK suffered humiliation at Suez in 1956, it began to fall apart. While there was an exit route for Nyasaland to become Malawi, and for Northern Rhodesia to become Zambia, the politicians and officials in London did not have an effective plan that would square the white rulers of Southern Rhodesia with the ambitions

of Africans who lived there. Further, Africans had few votes in
Southern Rhodesia and none at all in Britain, where there was a
vocal pro-Rhodesian lobby in the ruling Conservative Party. It
was too easy for London to disregard them.

In the long story of Rhodesia becoming Zimbabwe, from the
1880s to the first decade of the twenty-first century, UDI in 1965
must rank as the greatest misfortune. It led to war, casual violence
and abuse, bitter and undying hatred. It was a unique event in
British decolonisation, only matched by the attempts of white
pieds noirs in Algeria to take over there, snuffed out after General
de Gaulle came to power in France in 1958. By 1962 de Gaulle
had recognised Algerian independence, and around a million
pieds noirs were on their way to France. If the Rhodesian Front
and the African nationalists had been able to agree terms that
pre-empted UDI, the evolution of Zimbabwe would have been
much less bloody, even though apartheid South Africa would
have sought to destabilise it.

The UK, as theoretically the colonial power, was able to grant
independence to Rhodesia. But to a large extent the white rulers
had it already. Both the Conservative government under Douglas-
Home and the Labour government under Wilson, which came
into office in 1964, were keen for a deal that implied a gradual
transfer of authority from the whites to the blacks – something
that some had assumed must happen anyway if 'partnership'
was to be meaningful. But this was anathema to Ian Smith's
Rhodesian Front. Smith and his colleagues were running a police
state, disparaging their black fellow citizens. They lacked the
political imagination to negotiate, had overthrown Garfield Todd
and Edgar Whitehead when they had shown an interest in doing
so, and took comfort in the apparently armour-plated strength of
apartheid South Africa.

Why did Harold Wilson not take physical control in Salisbury,
using the UK's residual powers under legislation, and military

force? Some of the explanations, relating to the weakness of his government in 1965 and attitudes in the Conservative opposition and media, were discussed earlier. But two others, concerning the generally pacific nature of Wilson, and racism in British society at the time, also mattered.

Difficult as it is to imagine, for those who have seen a more recent Labour government under Tony Blair embarking on wars from Afghanistan to Sierra Leone, via Iraq and ex-Yugoslavia, the Labour governments from 1964–70 were committed to peace, even in the midst of the Cold War. Wilson resisted strong pressure from President Johnson to join the USA in Vietnam, even though Australia, Britain's Commonwealth ally, sent troops there. Labour had a strong faction in favour of unilateral nuclear disarmament, and withdrew UK forces east of Suez. Wilson himself belonged to a Labour generation which had fought and survived the Second World War, and was philosophically unsympathetic to military action. The only war he declared was a 'War on Want', against poverty.[6]

But Wilson and the Labour leadership were also well aware of undercurrents of racism in British society, not least in the urban working class which was the bedrock of the party's support.[7] Three years after UDI the Conservative politician Enoch Powell made a speech in the Midlands in which he foresaw 'rivers of blood' if black immigration from former colonies – which he himself had stimulated when minister of health – was allowed to flow unchecked into the UK. Working-class supporters of Powell marched, and his following was thought to have been a factor in the Conservative victory in 1970, and in Wilson's return to office in 1974 after Powell surprisingly endorsed Labour. Hence for Wilson, a supreme electoral calculator, Ian Smith's appeals to white 'kith and kin' could not be ignored.

But the failure of the UK to act in 1965 looked hypocritical to Rhodesia's Africans. For in January 1964 British troops had

helped the newly independent East African governments of Tanganyika, Kenya and Uganda to put down army mutinies. In Dar
es Salaam, then the capital of Tanganyika, mutineers captured
the airport and arrested the British high commissioner. Within a
week, British commandos based in Aden, where the UK had its
Middle Eastern headquarters, had put down the revolt in Dar. If
the British could restore legitimate authority in East Africa, why
not in Rhodesia?

UDI, unchallenged by any UK military response, was a disaster. But there were further mistakes in British policy thereafter. Looking back, from Zimbabwe's collapse at the start of
the twenty-first century, it would seem that the Lancaster House
negotiations, the Matabeleland massacres of the 1980s, and the
long-running saga of the white-owned land could all have been
handled differently. While it is easy to use hindsight for criticism,
it is also a fact that there were always some at the time who
foresaw trouble ahead.

At Lancaster House it was Shridath Ramphal and Chief
Anyaoku, not formally part of the talks, who could see that Lord
Carrington was playing a dangerous game in seeking to sidestep
the issue of land ownership. Carrington was pressing hard to
get an agreed constitution to last for a decade, with property
rights and apparent human rights protections for the white community. He did not want to waste time on disagreements over
the complex land issue. But he probably also hoped that, after
the war ended and Zimbabwe reached recognised independence,
peaceful processes would permit land transfers in a more tranquil
atmosphere. Foreign and Commonwealth Office advice was that
Bishop Muzorewa or Joshua Nkomo were likely to win the election; radical change was thought unlikely.

The UK also stored up trouble in treating the Rhodesian
whites as a bloc, with their own MPs and protections. That was
how the Rhodesian Front presented them, and the UK had to

do a deal with Muzorewa and Smith in a 'Zimbabwe–Rhodesia' where the Front had the military power. But, by writing the whites into the constitution on the basis of race, Carrington was inviting African politicians to see them as whites first and Zimbabwe citizens second. That approach could lead to racism in reverse. Significantly, when South African parties negotiated with each other in the run-up to the 1994 election, rights and protections were agreed on a non-racial basis.

The racially skewed approach of the UK, and the priority the government gave to developments in South Africa, also helped explain its official silence over the Gukurahundi in Matabeleland. As described in Chapter 3, the UK government in London and its High Commission in Harare kept their heads down. They wanted Zimbabwe 'to succeed'. They did not wish to risk a loss of influence with the Mugabe government by public protests. Although a similar assault on whites would have led to outrage – and the torture of Air Vice Marshal Hugh Slattery in 1982 did lead to complaint – the officially concealed deaths and suffering of the Ndebele were overlooked. Yet some of the facts were known, for both the *Sunday Times* and the *Observer*, two quality Sundays in the UK, published accounts of the repression.[8]

By the 1990s, time was up on the ten-year moratorium on the Lancaster House constitution, and its willing-buyer, willing-seller approach to land transfers. When a British initiative could have made a difference, after 1990, UK policy was not proactive. By the second half of the decade, with a new Labour government in London, the priorities were different and it was unwilling to recognise any historic responsibility to Africans, or to compensate rich white farmers. There was an ideological deadlock between ZANU–PF's land claims and a Department for International Development which was suspicious of cronyism, focused on the poorest, and too ready to tell a recently independent state how to manage its affairs. The UK, with diminishing influence in

Zimbabwe as land invasions and economic setbacks got under way, seemed constantly on the back foot, responding with shock and megaphone diplomacy as the situation spiralled out of control. UK support for the donors' 'Washington Consensus' in developing countries, with its emphasis on privatisation and cost recovery in social services, had contributed to the economic decline.

How far did the white community, following independence in 1980, bear responsibility for the events which led to collapse in the first decade of the twenty-first century? One account of the toughening stance of Mugabe towards the whites in the 1980s has it that he felt they had rejected his efforts at reconciliation, obdurately sticking to Ian Smith and the former Rhodesian Front political leadership. Certainly some members of the white community acted as though they could continue with the privileged lifestyle and attitudes of the former regime, without fully understanding the huge political change that had come with independence, and their good fortune in emerging economically unscathed from a vicious civil war. A visitor to Harare in 1982 was struck by the sense of confidence and wealth in members of the white community, and their social and spatial separation from black compatriots.[9] White farmers, in buying and selling their properties, were too complacent in supposing that the 'no government interest' certificates meant what they seemed. Photographed handing cheques to the MDC, at the start of the new century, it was easy for ZANU–PF to paint them as counter-revolutionaries.

But whites had some grounds for caution, if not suspicion of the new government, particularly when Joshua Nkomo left it, and former ZIPRA guerrillas began to melt away from the unified army. The arrest and torture of Air Vice Marshal Slattery in 1982, and the arrest of a white MP, Wally Stuttaford, suggested a spirit of vengeance in ZANU. Robert Mugabe as prime minister was already being nicknamed 'Comrade Bob' by whites, without affection. His acquisition of an executive presidency, and termination of the white seats in parliament following the unity accord with ZAPU, indicated that the Lancaster House guarantees could no longer be relied on. If white support for the new order after 1980 was half-hearted, and the farming community had its head in the sand over continuing inequities of ownership, there were nonetheless real reasons for their concern.

How about the political opposition, and those in civil society, the churches and human rights? Were there things they could have done differently which might have averted Zimbabwe's decline? In the 1980s and 1990s the Catholic Church and human rights bodies tried to promote the rule of law, and sought justice after the Matabeleland massacres and lesser human rights violations. The Catholic Church in particular had credibility, because it had spoken out against the excesses of the Smith regime. But for a long time, after independence, the Zimbabwe government was being given the benefit of the doubt; this was why many found it hard to believe that Mugabe himself had authorised the Gukurahundi. The country was unstable. Apartheid South Africa was sponsoring a civil war in Mozambique, and threatening to do the same in Zimbabwe. Voices speaking up for a human rights culture, as the respected Judge Enoch Dumbutshena did in the 1980s, were not changing the zeitgeist.

However, by the 1990s, following the Commonwealth conference in 1991 and the revolution in South Africa in 1994, attitudes in Zimbabwe towards human rights began to alter. A study of 189 students in five secondary schools in the Harare region, in 1995–97, demonstrated a real interest in human rights, supported by parents, even though a compulsory Education for Living course had low priority. Head teachers and subject heads thought that human rights were so important that teaching should start in primary schools. Interestingly, at a time when state media were not as aggressive as they became, 93.5 per cent of the Zimbabwean sample said they learnt about human rights from radio and television, and 91.2 per cent from the press – responses much higher than from parallel samples in Botswana, India and Northern Ireland.[10] Nonetheless the human rights concern, more powerful in urban areas and among middle-class professionals, had less impact in rural areas.

Human rights organisations, along with civil society bodies concerned about the lack of transparency and corruption in government, joined forces with the ZTUC to launch a campaign to reform the Lancaster House constitution. This constitution, though conventionally described as being that of Lancaster House, had been amended many times by parliaments controlled by ZANU–PF. The draft constitution which was defeated in the referendum of 2000, by which time the MDC had come into existence, would have put a limit to Mugabe's presidency of two more terms of five years, and would have authorised land takeovers without compensation.

Arguably the campaign against the draft constitution got side-tracked by personal attacks on Mugabe. Although the turnout was low, the referendum on the constitution became a referendum on everything to do with the government, and especially its president. But political experience of effective opposition in Zimbabwe was modest, because oppositions had been regularly marginalised and crushed over twenty years; this had happened in the past to ZAPU, to ZUM and to the Forum group. Ignoring the liberation movement's self-appointed right to permanent rule, there was no coherent opposition strategy, after victory in the referendum, beyond the hope that the MDC would win a subsequent election and be permitted to take office.

'Change' was indeed part of the MDC's title, and its mantra. But it contained a wide coalition, with quite varied views on priorities, especially on the economy. Its supporters in the labour movement were not attracted to the free-market economics which had lain behind ESAP in the 1990s, and which were pushing privatisation in neighbouring Zambia. Its supporters in the white farming community were involved in a marriage of convenience with labour, which could encourage Tsvangirai into risky friendship with the largely white Democratic Alliance, the opposition to the ANC in South Africa, when the ZCTU had a historic connection to COSATU, the ANC's partner.

Central to the MDC was of course the brave and popular figure of Morgan Tsvangirai, frequently subject to assassination attempts, badly beaten in 2007, and who lost his wife Susan, killed in a car crash in March 2009. But how wise was Tsvangirai, in the difficult situation he faced, where Mugabe made it clear that he would not surrender at the ballot box the power he claimed to have won through the barrel of a gun? Was Tsvangirai naive? Much of the outside assistance Tsvangirai obtained, such as the ill-concealed desire for regime change from Tony Blair and others in the Western community, was almost worthless. His support on the streets was of declining value, as the economy itself declined, so that by 2008 a strike call was virtually ignored by the lucky few who had a paying job.

As early as 2000, Arthur Mutambara set out a critique of the vagueness of a 'change' which allowed ZANU–PF uncontested rights over the war veterans and the land issue. He wrote:

> They [MDC] should pay special attention to the issue of the
> quality of political change, that is, the content and substance of
> change. It is not enough to ride on a wave of popular discontent
> and engage in reactive anti-Mugabe politics. It is insufficient
> to react to Mugabe's positions on land, war veterans and the
> economy....ZANU–PF owns neither the liberation war legacy nor
> the war veterans.[11]

Although there were splits in the war veterans' movement, not all supporting ZANU–PF, one critique of Tsvangirai's leadership was that he had not tried hard enough to recruit those nationalists who had become disillusioned with the ruling party. Margaret

Dongo, for instance, would have been prepared to join the MDC, and she believed Eddison Zvogbo and Edgar Tekere would have done also.[12]

The change from a movement, as the MDC was in 1999–2000, to a political party as it developed in the early years of a new century faced many difficulties. There were frictions between workers and intellectuals, and a kitchen cabinet around Tsvangirai met opposition; the management of funds from supporters abroad was a source of suspicion. In all of this the MDC leadership, and especially its members in rural areas, faced not just demonisation but physical risk. Nonetheless the break-up of the unified MDC, with the Mutambara faction competing in Senate elections while MDC–T boycotted them, was a serious setback. It led to much bad publicity about the internal practices of the MDC, and allegedly dictatorial actions by Tsvangirai.[13] It was always going to be hard for the MDC to replace ZANU–PF in government. A divided MDC had much less chance.

If fission in the MDC was perhaps the biggest error that could be ascribed to Tsvangirai – he was also criticised for changing his mind too often – participation in the GPA and unity government was not. However this government might end, Tsvangirai and Mutambara were right to give it a try, because there was nowhere else to go. ZANU–PF had not recognised its presidential defeat in the 2008 elections, and SADC was not going to remove Mugabe. A portion of power and respect was given to an MDC which had had almost none before from ZANU–PF. An attempt became possible to turn round the decayed economy; negotiations on a new constitution and civil liberties could start; health and social services, and even the damaged agricultural sector, could be offered new hope. As part of the government, the MDC factions could press SADC to ensure that the next elections would be managed more fairly. President Zuma's roadmap, with a new constitution, followed by a referendum and cleaned-up electoral processes, offered genuine hope. Continued unilateralism by Mugabe, and the lurking, continuing power of the JOC military cabal, were perhaps inevitable.

Perceived as a junior partner in the unity government, Tsvangirai had an uphill struggle, particularly as the Mutambara faction seemed more willing to appease and excuse ZANU–PF. In public, both SADC and the South African facilitators took the view that the government was making progress, and that differences between the parties were minor. But deadlines for the removal of disagreements between the parties came and went. Tsvangirai's MDC conducted a partial withdrawal from the government in November 2009 and Mugabe would not give ground over his unilateral appointment of the attorney general, Tomana, and of the Reserve Bank governor, Gono; nor would he tolerate Tsvangirai's appointment of Bennett as deputy minister for agriculture. In October 2010 Tsvangirai said that his party would not recognise Mugabe's appointment also of five judges, six ambassadors, ten provincial governors and members of the Police Service Commission. Although these appointments were supposed in the GPA to be the product of consensus between president and prime minister, it was clear that President Mugabe was acting as if his executive authority was untrammelled. Whether Tsvangirai could have used his weak hand more skilfully, as prime minister, was a moot point. Certainly the MDC believed that Zuma's roadmap would lead to a post-Mugabe era and the longed-for transition to democracy; in the meantime it hoped to gain credit from the start of economic recovery.

The role of civil society, at a period when Zimbabwe was in freefall, is not easy to assess. The act of witness, the demand for an end to impunity, the sheer stamina of a small number of dedicated persons – these were totally admirable. But was there more this gallant and variegated band could have done? Many were disappointed that the arrival of the unity government had not resulted in more progress in the areas of democracy, human rights and media freedom. But a dependence on elections, as the key avenue for change, had been baulked by the reality that it is possible to manipulate elections, and to intimidate voters into giving the answer a ruling party demands. The ZTUC, which had regular briefings with MDC members of the government, felt that the MDC was slipping away from its roots in organised labour.[14]

There was also a continuing conflict between demands for justice and the need for pacification, if not reconciliation, inside Zimbabwe. At an international level there had been enormous progress for human rights and accountability in the last twenty years, driven by Western and non-governmental pressure, and concern at appalling crimes in the former Yugoslavia, Rwanda and elsewhere. Key events had been the setting up of an international criminal tribunal for former Yugoslavia in 1993, an international criminal tribunal for Rwanda in 1994, and the establishment of an International Criminal Court in July 2002; in 2003 the Special Court for Sierra Leone issued its first indictments for crimes committed in the civil war. By the second half of the first decade of the new century the United Nations had accepted a 'responsibility to protect', which could allow for international intervention where a state had failed in its duty to prevent genocide, war crimes, ethnic cleansing and crimes against humanity.

It did not need a great deal of imagination to see that Mugabe and his key supporters, as well as the former ruler of Ethiopia, whom they were sheltering in Harare, could be caught by these new international processes. There were rumours that Mugabe himself in the late 1990s had considered retirement, but been dissuaded by the thought that the Gukurahundi could be used to prosecute him. Where did the embattled human rights community in Zimbabwe stand on such issues? Inevitably there were divisions between those who wanted justice and those who wanted the country to move on to a more peaceful era, even if it meant tolerating Mugabe's crimes. By late 2008 it was clear that opposition politicians, from Tsvangirai to Coltart, had decided that a deal with Mugabe was more important than his prosecution.

From ZANU–PF's perspective the independence of many of the civil society groups was tarnished by their involvement in the National Constitutional Assembly, which had supported the MDC at its birth; maybe these groups did not do enough to be seen as apolitical. Foreign funding was also a point of attack; Stan Mudenge, as foreign minister, complained to Chief Anyaoku, as Commonwealth secretary general, that the Westminster Foundation in the UK and the Heritage Foundation in the USA were funding the opposition in an unacceptable way. Anyaoku said he should make a statement to the Commonwealth Ministerial Action Group – the body of foreign ministers which later suspended Zimbabwe – which he did. Robin Cook for the UK was silent. Lloyd Axworthy, for Canada, said he was surprised.[15] As the first decade of the twenty-first century went on there were signs that Western aid for advocacy groups inside Zimbabwe began to dry up, even though currency collapse made it more vital.

The churches and traditional religion formed an important part of Zimbabwean civil society, and in eastern Europe the robust attitude of the Catholic Church had been a factor in the downfall of communism. Mugabe himself was, at least nominally, a Roman Catholic and his excellent Jesuit education had helped his rise in life.[16] At Easter 2007 the Catholics published a pastoral letter titled 'God Hears the Cry of the Oppressed' which criticised repression. The government trapped Archbishop Pius Ncube, one of its strongest Catholic critics, in a sex sting. It also acted to deflect criticism from the Anglican Church, by sponsoring a pro-ZANU breakaway in the Harare diocese. In South Africa the churches had helped in the overthrow of apartheid, with personalities like Archbishop Tutu providing moral leadership when political leaders were imprisoned. There was nothing quite like this in Zimbabwe.

Traditional religion, with spirit mediums providing continuity for clan identity, had been significant in assisting ZANLA during the second *chimurenga*, as it had in the risings against British rule in the first. Spirit mediums could raise fear, among the CIO and militia torturers and murderers who went unpunished in the countryside. They were individuals, and did not declare war on ZANU–PF as a group. But Peter Godwin recounted how an important spirit medium for the Ndau people, Makopa, sent a bottle of 'sacred snuff' to Roy Bennett when he was in prison, and greeted him at his release.[17]

How far was South Africa to blame in the long-drawn-out agony of Zimbabwe? It was easy for those living further away to criticise this powerful neighbour, yet the European Union had not covered itself with glory during the bloody break-up of Yugoslavia. Rhodesia had so nearly been a South African province, and the withdrawal of Pretoria's backing for the Rhodesia of UDI had been a key factor which led to independence in 1980 via Lusaka and Lancaster House. Many in the West assumed that Mugabe would be a pushover for Presidents Mbeki and Zuma. Undoubtedly, if Nelson Mandela had still been South African president when Mugabe stole two elections in 2008, with accompanying violence, South Africa would have reacted more sharply.

But by 2008 the Mbeki/Zuma strategy, which became one of creating a government of national unity, was not irresponsible. Given the collapse of Zimbabwe, and the weaknesses the South Africans saw on both sides of the country's polarised landscape, it seemed essential to try and bind up the wounds in a formula which had been reasonably successful in South Africa after 1994. It was before 2008 that the South African government should have been much more frank with the Mugabe regime; the way in which South African election observers claimed that his election wins in 2002 and 2005 were free and fair, when they plainly were not, damaged the credibility of President Mbeki as a good neighbour and friendly mediator. Mbeki appeared to be putting his membership of the club of liberation leaders above a proper concern from south of the Limpopo. Realities in Zimbabwe made nonsense of the African renaissance and NEPAD. After the GPA was declared in 2008 the South African negotiators should have worked much harder to make the agreement stick, even though they faced resistance, principally from ZANU–PF.

In theory SADC was overseeing the South African mediation, and, in an even remoter and more shadowy way, so was the African Union. But although the formalities were observed, so that Zuma had to report to the SADC security organ in Maputo when this was chaired by President Guebuza, SADC was not a powerful player. The MDC regularly appealed to it, and Mugabe spoke as a member. Yet it was South Africa that counted, if it so chose. As the Zimbabwe economy teetered on the edge of recovery, with government officials getting US$200 a month by late 2010, twice the pay at the start of the unity government, questions were beginning to be asked about the future of the country's currency. Would Zimbabwe seek to revive the defunct Zimbabwe dollar, or would it join the South African rand zone? South African investment could be crucial to a full economic recovery, but to permit a rand takeover was an insult to sovereignty. The South African mediators in Harare do not seem to have used the economic leverage they had.

Further away, but intrinsic to the history of Rhodesia and Zimbabwe, lay the Commonwealth. Following withdrawal from this grouping by the Zimbabwe government in 2003, the Commonwealth, whose 'healing touch' had been lauded by Jawaharlal Nehru, was formally out of the picture. There was no coordinated assistance for Zimbabweans in exile, as had happened for black Rhodesians after UDI, although so many had migrated to

Commonwealth countries. But some London-based Commonwealth activists were keen that Zimbabweans not be forgotten
and in 2007 the Royal Commonwealth Society organised a public
meeting in the wings of the Kampala summit, addressed by Morgan
Tsvangirai. By November 2009, at the Port of Spain summit, President Zuma was responsible for a communiqué paragraph which
welcomed the GPA, hoped that it would be implemented 'faith-
fully and effectively', and 'looked forward to the conditions being
created for the return of Zimbabwe to the Commonwealth'.[18]

In London a Zimbabwe committee was formed, consisting of
members of Commonwealth non-governmental bodies, which used
funding from the inter-governmental Commonwealth Foundation
to provide small-scale support for professionals and educational
planning in Zimbabwe. Soon after Zimbabwe's departure the
Foundation, which is tasked to assist civil society, had been
banned from helping Zimbabwean bodies. But attitudes had
changed, particularly after the unity government was formed. In
2010 Secretary General Sharma had amicable conversations with
Mugabe at international meetings. The Commonwealth of 2010
was less assertive and well financed than it had been in 1979–80,
but it was still possible to imagine that it could be a vehicle for
supporting transition in Zimbabwe; in late 2010 a number of
Zimbabweans, from across the public arena, began to call for a
re-engagement with the Commonwealth.

The response of those in the international community who
have given primacy to the creation of a worthwhile democracy
in Zimbabwe has not always been well conceived. The United
States, the European Union, the UK and the international financial institutions have failed to coordinate their sanctions and to
assess their consequences. Sanctions-busting by the Chinese and
the ZANU–PF patronage system, using front companies similar
to those used by the Rhodesians after UDI, have found big gaps
in measures designed to promote change. Only Denmark, which

broke diplomatic relations in 2002 in protest at the consequences of the land invasions, has gone that far.

The idea that sanctions are limited to some 200 persons in the ZANU–PF elite does not do justice to wider impacts, or explain the ferocity of government propaganda for their removal. A 2010 report from IDASA explained that 'Zimbabwe has been most affected by restrictions imposed by International Financial Institutions (IFIs) and from a marked decrease in Official Development Aid (ODA) entering the country.'[19] Travel bans and asset freezes against ZANU–PF persons who had come to dominate the business community actually limited the chances of economic recovery. After 1990, with leadership from the Commonwealth Secretariat, countries which had introduced sanctions against apartheid South Africa followed a calibrated policy for their removal. As progress was negotiated towards multiracial democracy, so sanctions were lifted. For Zimbabwe, after the inclusive government was formed in 2009, the Western countries were slow to implement anything similar.

Two other broad factors, which help to explain the ongoing crisis of Zimbabwe, lie in failed economic policies and a culture of violence. For many developing countries the 1980s were a lost decade, when commodity prices were in decline, and the neoliberal policies of donors damaged education and social services. For Zimbabwe the effects were greater in the following decade, exacerbated by the costs of war in the Congo and payments to war veterans. The ESAP structural adjustment policy did not work, but nor did price control or state intervention in the market. The end of the 'Front Line', which had protected Zimbabwean industries from South African competition, added to pressure on an economy that looked stronger than it was. Economic mismanagement, and some arbitrary decisions by government, set the scene for the developing hyperinflation of the first decade of the new century.[20]

Looked at purely in economic terms, the land invasions which started on a large scale in 2000 had a huge impact. This went far beyond the collapse in food production and exports. With the destruction of so many commercial farms came the destruction of all the supporting activities to which they were linked – insurance, fertilisers, machinery and so on. Property had been a store of value, a collateral against which banks had been able to secure loans. In the uncertainty of ownership created by chaotic occupations it became difficult for anyone to borrow money, especially with escalating inflation. Ownership of firms and housing came into question – a question that arose again in 2009 when ZANU–PF resuscitated its indigenisation laws. A sickly economy took a wider hit.

For ZANU–PF's folly, in launching such a disorderly expropriation in 2000, had other consequences. It suggested people could get something for nothing, encouraged low-level as well as high-level corruption, and the idea that might is right in the countryside. For much of Zimbabwe was and still is a rural society, and the expulsion of farm workers after the takeover of the commercial farms had knock-on social effects, including damage to children's schooling and to health services.

The land occupations were also unnecessary, in achieving the changes that ZANU–PF purported to want. If Mugabe had stuck to his stated aim of 'one farm for one farmer' he could have broken up the large white-owned estates at a stroke, and with limited political risk. UNDP and other funds were available for small-scale settlement, and with back-up for new small farmers they could have got the support in seeds, fertiliser and advice which was woefully lacking after 2000. Management of the 'certificates of no government interest' to support changes of ownership, plus bank support for the growing class of black commercial farmers, could have transformed rural ownership quite soon, without loss of production.

The culture of violence, which Sekai Holland said had left a million Zimbabweans tortured or traumatised, also had a capacity for reproducing itself. If peace is habit-forming, so is its opposite. There had been hidden violence in white control of the African population, well before UDI, and disagreements among the nationalists were often not pacific. After the growth of the civil war in the 1970s there was an almost continuous appeal to violence, including the Gukurahundi and involvement in the Mozambican civil war in the 1980s, repression of strikes and the Congo war in the 1990s, and the third *chimurenga* and Operation Murambatsvina in the first decade of the twenty-first century. One reason why the MDC factions thought it worth joining ZANU–PF in the unity government was to try and break the cycle of violence; one reason why they feared new elections and a constitutional referendum was that, given the attitudes in the JOC and ZANU–PF, there could be another spike in intimidation, beatings and death. Only a genuine transfer of power and a lengthy period of socio-economic recovery could hold out the promise of a lasting reduction in violence; and changes in the police, military and national youth service would be prerequisites also.

And then, of course, in any explanation of Zimbabwe's decline, there is the character and leadership of Robert Mugabe to consider. While it is a mistake to suppose that everything that went wrong in his country can be laid at his feet, it is equally clear that by the 1990s he was running an unsuccessful and increasingly corrupt government, following hard on his ruthlessness in putting down 'super-ZAPU' in the 1980s. In the first decade of the twenty-first century, as an octogenarian, he presided over disaster. The two other states which emerged from the Federation of Rhodesia and Nyasaland, Malawi and Zambia, had overthrown their fathers of the nation: Hastings Banda, 'president for life', saw his one-party state dismantled in a referendum in 1993, and he was defeated in 1994 in presidential elections; Kenneth Kaunda abandoned the one-party state and permitted multiparty elections in 1991, in which his United National Independence Party was defeated. Mugabe, however, has not permitted electoral defeat to remove either himself or ZANU-PF.

Mugabe's character was formed by the devotion of his mother, Bona, his family experience after his father deserted, the quality of his Jesuit education, and his own early hard work and study. For much of his life he has been a loner. His period in prison and in the run-up to his election as prime minister in 1980 at the age of 56, had been one of dedication to nationalism and Marxism. He sought power for ideals he shared with his wife Sally and his ZANU comrades. He felt surrounded by conspiracies, and that the British, Ian Smith and fellow Africans were aiming to trick him. He had grounds for his suspicions.

But in the 1980s, as prime minister and then executive president, aspects of his leadership that would bring trouble became more obvious. Three elements were entwined: a willingness to resort to force, a lack of skill in building coalitions, and an absence of a sense of pluralism and human rights. These defects came together in the dangerous failure to build genuine reconciliation in a divided society, exemplified in the repression of Gukurahundi, so soon after independence.

In the final phase of the civil war, and the 1980 election, Mugabe believed that it was the military effort of ZANLA which had won power. Although votes had enabled him to form a government, it was the armed struggle for liberation which had delivered the votes. The role of the military and of force became an underlying factor in his successive governments, and the use of state violence was a factor in the country's decline in the twenty-first century.

But the ultimate reliance on force was linked to his preference for the one-party state, and his practical failure to build coalitions.

Whether with ZAPU after the unity accord in the 1980s, or with the MDC from 2008, Mugabe was unable to work with other politicians on anything but a basis of his superiority and their subordination. Jesuit and Marxist attitudes to authority linked to his own evolving personality, and the increasing hero-worship of his supporters. This was also a reason why he was not good at planning his own succession, playing divide-and-rule among the ZANU–PF factions. Although Mugabe maintained the form of elections in Zimbabwe, he was not keen that they should produce a result other than his victory, and that of his party.

Given these attitudes he had little sympathy with pluralism, civil society and human rights. Both Jesuits and Leninists have been criticised for a belief that the ends justify the means, and from Gukurahundi onwards Mugabe has shown ruthlessness towards those he supposes to be opponents. But in riding roughshod over enemies he has also squashed the opportunity for new approaches and renewal, which are assets in a plural democracy. His leadership has literally impoverished his country, stimulating cultures of intimidation, and of entitlement to assets without personal effort. It has encouraged those who think differently to leave, rather than aid the country's reconstruction.

As seen earlier, the 1990s were the period in which Mugabe's own leadership deteriorated markedly: his personal life changed with his second marriage, his ideology became confused, he failed to understand the war veterans or to resolve the land issue peacefully. He became isolated from the public, driving around in long convoys. He and Grace commandeered planes from Air Zimbabwe when they felt like it, and she won an unloved title as 'First Shopper'. They tolerated increased corruption, and the ZANU–PF elite began to behave like a kleptocracy. Ideologically the move to ESAP, and the uncertain moves away from a one-party state, suggested a leadership that was losing its earlier bearings, without reinventing itself in social democracy.

The anger of the war veterans came near to unhinging the government, led to the diversionary takeover of the commercial farms, and to a war of words with the UK government. For Mugabe, and a leadership that was well aware of its debts to ZANLA, this was an extraordinary failure. How was it that he did not see that so many of the veterans were suffering in post-independence Zimbabwe? They were people who were rooted in the peasantry; if land was important to them, as it certainly was to some, he could have shown more interest in the resettlement programmes, which petered out in the late 1980s. Following the peace treaty that ended the civil war in Mozambique, which Mugabe promoted, a more effective programme for veterans had been introduced there.

The Congo war was in part an attempt to consolidate support among Zimbabwe's military leadership, which made money out of it, as well as to strengthen the country's political standing in the region. But this concern for senior officers was in contrast to the lack of rapport with the humbler veterans earlier. Then Mugabe, taken aback, authorised wanton payments of Z$50,000 to each of them, which helped wreck the currency and began to bankrupt the economy.

Mugabe's own complicated attitude to the British played into his mishandling of the land issue and the erstwhile colonial power. There were aspects of the UK he admired. He had already collected three London University degrees by the time he moved from Northern Rhodesia to Ghana in 1958. Even in old age he dressed like a British gentleman, and his affection for the British royal family was embarrassingly shown in April 2005 when he shook hands with Prince Charles, who had represented the Queen at Zimbabwe's independence, at Pope John Paul II's funeral in Rome. By that stage he was widely anathematised as a man with blood on his hands, who had been manipulating food aid against the MDC in the most recent election.

But Mugabe was also deeply suspicious of the British government, believing it had backed out of compensation after Lancaster House, and that Blair's Labour snubbed him in 1997 and insulted him thereafter. His fury boiled over in the land invasions after his defeat in the constitutional referendum of 2000, in which he was lashing out simultaneously at the British, the whites, the MDC and the farm workers. In his frustration he was condemning his country to economic decline and dependence on food aid, and many fellow citizens to premature death or exile. But it was as with Mao's disastrous 'Great Leap Forward' in China: ideology, in this case black land ownership and an appeal to national sovereignty, joined with the need to retain power, to trump mundane concerns for the economy and citizens' well-being. Did he realise what he was setting in train? Would he have cared if he did?

It is not known whether Mugabe had always envisaged himself becoming a president-for-life, although he never willingly foresaw ZANU–PF being replaced as a government by elections. Much of its behaviour, and his own, may be explained simply by the desire to hang on to power at all costs. But as he lived on in the twenty-first century, well-preserved with a careful diet, yoga and no smoking or alcohol, he became more important to his party. It had become incapable of producing an agreed successor while he survived. He was central to its version of patriotic history. The thousands of portraits in offices around the country reminded all Zimbabweans of their leader. The extravagant birthday parties and the praise-singing of the official media provided a cloak of adulation, even as the life of most Zimbabweans was harsh, often on the edge of the cash economy. The MDC had a portion of power, in the economic and social ministries. The secretive JOC and ZANU–PF had much of the hard power and means of coercion. But the symbolic position of the octogenarian Robert Mugabe, dominant for thirty years, continued to cast a long shadow.

Yet, how important is the Mugabe factor in explaining the disaster that befell his country? It is necessary, but insufficient. There is little doubt that if either Mandela or Kaunda had been the first leader of an independent Zimbabwe its future would have been different. Indeed, if apartheid had collapsed and the Mozambican civil war had ended when Zimbabwe won independence, the whole of southern Africa might have had a more peaceful transition. But, as argued here, the nature of Mugabe's own character and leadership has to be seen alongside issues of party, race, land, the economy and regional and international politics. Zimbabwe's history, back to the great land grab by Cecil Rhodes and before, had involved brutal struggles. The ideology of 'civilisation' espoused by Rhodes and Ian Smith was as partial as the 'patriotic history' which buoyed up Mugabe and ZANU–PF.

On many dimensions of importance to its citizens, Zimbabwe had become a failed state by the second half of 2008. The collapse in life expectancy, the shrinkage of the economy, the emigration, and the decline in basic services – these were accompanied by politicisation of army and police, and unacceptable abuse of citizens. But some have argued that, in an African context, the Zimbabwe situation was not that terrible – compared, for instance, with the huge loss of life in the Democratic Republic of the Congo where it is said that in six years 3.8 million people died, or the fraud in Nigerian elections, strongly criticised by a Commonwealth observer group in 2007.[21] State failure in Zimbabwe, however, has to be viewed against the optimistic expectations and achievements of the 1980s. The situation in the new century was very bad, when it could have been much better.

In a discussion of how the new state went into decline it is tempting to speculate on how it might recover. Is this a matter of political leadership, and a new consensus between advocates of national sovereignty and advocates of democracy? Could a turnaround happen quite quickly? Could the food shortage be met within a year, as Justice for Agriculture, the pressure group for commercial farmers, has claimed, if only competent, well-resourced farmers were again allowed to work the land?[22] Could a few well-chosen prosecutions end a culture of corruption?

Analysis based on a long view would suggest that, with the best will in the world, which is almost certainly missing, genuine progress for Zimbabwe will take many years of effort. The neighbouring countries of South Africa and Mozambique have struggled economically to see growth rates translated into well-being for their poorer communities. Both have suffered from serious issues of corruption. Twenty years after the fall of the Berlin Wall, in spite of tremendous expense by one of the world's richest nations, disparities between the former West and East of Germany remain.

Even with mobile phones and the excitement of Africa's Twitter generation, political and social recovery will take time. Thanks to the existence of the MDC, and its persistence, Zimbabwe has the most viable party political system in southern Africa. Thanks too to the work of civil society, Zimbabwe has a rich and varied polity, which a freer media could help to flourish. Recovery of schools and the health service will turn on recruitment and the attitudes of staff, as much as the necessary physical investment. Providing paid employment, in a society and region where this has been an ongoing problem, will require new approaches – small-scale lending and training as much as capital investment.

Attitudinal change can be the hardest, requiring generations. It can also be gradual, as the political evolution of the Soviet Union into the authoritarian political system of modern Russia has shown. Failure and hardship can be the best teachers, however, and Zimbabweans have suffered greatly over the past decade. External defeat, as in Argentina in the 1980s, can accelerate political and social change, but the ZANU–PF regime has sensibly avoided a war it could lose; the Congo adventure was not of that kind.

But what perhaps all Zimbabweans have realised is that their situation cannot be rescued by outsiders – neither by South Africa nor by SADC, nor by the MDC's admirers in the West, nor by ZANU–PF's friends in China and North Korea. Outsiders may assist or damage, but it is Zimbabweans who will have to go on living with each other and who must take the lead in rebuilding what was described at independence as 'Africa's jewel'. Given the polarisation before and since the unity government was formed, this is not an easy lesson to digest. But what went wrong in Zimbabwe was also the product of decades when prominent Zimbabweans (and Rhodesians) did not see their fellow citizens as equal members of their society. To make their country go right, they must work hard, share, exchange and avoid the monopolisation of power, and learn a meaningful respect.

NOTES

PROLOGUE

1. Following the Treaty of Versailles, the British Empire was given several League of Nations mandates; it also had informal control of countries such as Iraq, Transjordan and Egypt; it was at its maximum extent.
2. It was founded in 1891; as *The Rhodesia Herald* it fought the censorship of the Smith regime after 1965; today, as *The Herald*, it is the voice of Mugabe's ZANU-PF.
3. This information comes from the 22 February 1924 weekly edition of *The Rhodesia Herald*, kept at the British Library, Colindale.
4. Reports from *The Times* of London.

ONE

1. Another was Ibn Saud, 1876–1953, who conquered most of the Arabian peninsula in the first decades of the twentieth century. His desert kingdom was renamed Saudi Arabia in 1932, and he lived to see it transformed by oil wealth.
2. Harold Macmillan, British prime minister, told the South African parliament in Cape Town on 3 February 1960 that decolonisation was spreading through Africa, and implied that a system based on white control was becoming untenable. Ghana had become independent in March 1957.
3. An early will of Rhodes had envisaged that his legacy should fund a secret society which would spread the British Empire throughout the world; this ambition inspired Sir Evelyn Wrench, founder of the Royal Over-Seas League and the English-Speaking Union, though he saw no need for secrecy; he wanted to recruit a million members for the League (initially a Club) as soon as possible.
4. An excellent short account of pre-colonial Zimbabwe appears in a chapter by

Gerald Chikhozo Mazarire, 'Reflections on Pre-colonial Zimbabwe, c.1850–1880s', in Brian Raftopoulos and Alois Mlambo, eds, *Becoming Zimbabwe*, Weaver, Harare, 2009, pp. 1–38.

5.   Ibid, p. 23. Mutinhima escaped, and went to the Mai yaVaHera hills in Buhera.

6.   Charles Rudd estimated 60, Frank Thompson 200 (Antony Thomas, *Rhodes: Race for Africa*, London Bridge, Lake Havasu City, 1997, p. 184).

7.   Rudd was nearly ten years older than Rhodes, and also a Cape MP. They were almost equal partners in the De Beers diamond business until 1886, after which Rhodes played a junior role in their Gold Fields company while Rudd was a junior in the Chartered Company. The relationship broke down after the Jameson Raid, of which Rudd disapproved (see John Cormac Seekings, *Rudd: The Search for a Cape Merchant*, Klipdrift Books, Klipdrift, 2009).

8.   Quoted by Brian Roberts, *Cecil Rhodes: Flawed Colossus*, Hamish Hamilton, London, p. 99.

9.   Thomas, *Rhodes*, p. 196.

10. Thomas Pakenham, *The Scramble for Africa*, Abacus, London, 1991, p. 373.

11. Rhodes advised Jameson to read chapter 14, verse 31 of Luke's gospel, which states: 'What king going to make war against another king, sitteth not down first and consulteth whether he be able with ten thousand to meet him that cometh against him with twenty thousand.' Jameson replied that, although outnumbered, he could attack Lobengula with confidence in victory. This exchange illustrates a strain of Victorian Christianity in the conquest of Rhodesia, which may be compared with attitudes among Spanish Conquistadors in the Americas (Thomas, *Rhodes*, p. 249).

12. The House of Commons in London was informed 'on fairly reliable information' on 19 February 1894 that Lobengula had died a month earlier of fever or smallpox; there have also been suggestions that he died from dysentery or poison.

13. Pakenham, *The Scramble for Africa*, p. 494.

14. Ngwabi Bhebe and Terence Ranger, eds, *The Historical Dimensions of Democracy and Human Rights in Zimbabwe*, vol. 1, University of Zimbabwe Publications, Harare, 2001, pp. xxiv–v.

15. Ian Phimister (*An Economic and Social History of Zimbabwe, 1890–1948*, Longman, London, 1988, p. 16) estimated that between 100,000 and 200,000 cattle had been stolen from the Ndebele in the thirty months to March 1896, leaving them with only 74,000.

16. An archive belonging to Baden-Powell's commander, Frederick Carrington, contradicted B-P's account that Uwini had fired on his men; B-P was cleared by an inquiry (see *Sunday Times*, London, 6 December 2009).

17. H.C. Thomson, *Rhodesia and its Government*, Smith, Elder, London, 1898, pp. 142–3, quoted by Apollon Davidson, *Cecil Rhodes and His Times*, Progress Publishers, Moscow, 1984.

18. Quoted by Bhebe and Ranger, *The Historical Dimensions*, p. xxv.

19. By 2009 over 7,000 students, from the United States, Commonwealth countries and Germany, had benefited from this bequest. Following South Africa's first democratic election in 2004 some of this money was used to set up the Mandela

Rhodes Foundation, with South African purposes.

20. Quoted by T.O. Ranger, *Revolt in Southern Rhodesia, 1896–7*, Heinemann, London, 1967, p. 104.
21. Quoted in ibid., p. 3.

TWO

1. This brief description is based on Robert Blake, *A History of Rhodesia*, Methuen, London, 1977, pp. 149–51.
2. Phimister, *An Economic and Social History of Zimbabwe*, pp. 27–8.
3. Blake, *A History of Rhodesia*, p. 197.
4. Ibid., p. 178.
5. Phimister, *An Economic and Social History of Zimbabwe*, pp. 118–19.
6. Ibid., p. 85. The proportion dropped from around 71 per cent to around 34 per cent, and Rhodesian Africans were replaced by Mozambicans and Nyasas. There was an anti-farmer mentality which saw it as beneath the dignity of Rhodesian Africans to work for the whites; this pattern of imported labour persisted up to the farm invasions of Zanu–PF from 2000 on.
7. Information from Sir Brian Donnelly.
8. The British South Africa Company, which had hung on to mineral rights in Northern Rhodesia, benefited enormously from the copper discoveries, although other firms developed them.
9. This manipulation of apparent egalitarianism for racial advantage is reminiscent of a story of Huey Long, populist but racist governor of the state of Louisiana in the same era. It is said that a group of black nurses, frustrated at their lack of promotion, approached Long with a request for help. He said, 'I'll help you, but you won't like the way I do it.' He subsequently told white nurses that the particular speciality or level sought by the black nurses was 'nigger work', and white nurses should let them do it.
10. See Phimister, *An Economic and Social History of Zimbabwe*, p. 150; Nyamanda and his nephews Albert and Rhodes were advised by the African National Congress in South Africa, but their petition to King George V was rejected out of hand.
11. Figures from Blake, *A History of Rhodesia*, p. 221.
12. Phimister (*An Economic and Social History of Zimbabwe*, p. 185) argues that white farmers were paid up to five times the price per bag of maize available to black farmers, under complicated quota systems in the Maize Control Acts of 1931 and 1934.
13. Ibid., p. 177; all agricultural exports were worth less than 20 per cent of the total of primary exports in 1938, and gold had provided over half of the revenue from 1932 onwards.
14. This account relies on an excellent history of the Samkange family by T.O. Ranger, *Are We Not Also Men? – The Samkange Family and African Politics in Zimbabwe, 1920–64*, Baobab, Harare, 1995.
15. Information from Cameron Duodu, Ghanaian journalist, who is writing about Major Seth Anthony, a Ghanaian officer who went to Sandhurst.
16. Phimister, *An Economic and Social History of Zimbabwe*, p. 261.

17. There were of course many white members of the South African Communist Party, often of East European Jewish origin.

18. Phimister, *An Economic and Social History of Zimbabwe*, pp. 263-4.

19. Quoted in ibid., p. 264.

20. See Shula Marks's chapter on 'Southern Africa', in *Oxford History of the British Empire*, Volume 4: *The Twentieth Century*, ed. William Roger Louis and Judith Brown, Oxford University Press, Oxford, 1999, p. 555.

21. In the 1960s he wrote a poignant article for the *Guardian* newspaper, then opposed to his politics, which recalled the joys of listening to classical music on wind-up 78 rpm records in the African bush.

22. Significantly, the official Colonial Office policy of African paramountcy was dropped in 1948, to be replaced by the woollier concept of 'racial partnership' (Clyde Sanger, *Central African Emergency*, Heinemann, London, p. 47).

23. As late as 1960 it was estimated that, with a black-white ratio of 330:1, there were fewer whites in Nyasaland than Yugoslavs in Britain.

24. Labour had given the idea of federation some cautious support when James Griffiths was colonial secretary, in 1950-51, but on condition that African rights were protected (see Sanger, *Central African Emergency*, pp. 40-42); when Clement Attlee, by then leader of the Opposition, visited Northern Rhodesia, he was unimpressed by African arguments against federation (evidence supplied to a witness seminar at the Institute of Commonwealth Studies, London, 14 December 2009, attended by Simon Zukas and Peter Fraenkel, who had been sceptics in Northern Rhodesia about the proposed federation); although most Labour MPs opposed federation in votes on the Bill, Patrick Gordon-Walker and a handful of others abstained.

25. Joshua Nkomo, then president of the Southern Rhodesia African National Congress, commented acidly, 'When evening comes, the rider goes into his comfortable house, while the horse is sent to stay in the stables.' Quoted by E.M. Sibanda, *The Zimbabwe African People's Union, 1961-87*, Africa World Press, Trenton NJ, 2005, p. 44.

26. See chapter on 'The Anatomy of an Unequal Society' by Coenraad Brand, in Colin Stoneman, ed., *Zimbabwe's Inheritance*, Macmillan, London, 1981, p. 39.

27. Quoted by Blake, *A History of Rhodesia*, p. 312.

28. Christian missions from the Church of Scotland had played a key role in evangelising Nyasaland. As late as 2007 the political connection was demonstrated when Jack McConnell, until then Scotland's first minister under the devolution settlement in the United Kingdom, was appointed British high commissioner to Malawi (formerly Nyasaland).

29. Robert Blake estimated that only 4 per cent of adult Africans would be qualified to vote in electoral districts, producing 15 seats; it was estimated that members for the 50 constituency seats would be elected by Europeans (*A History of Rhodesia*, p. 333).

30. Sibanda, *The Zimbabwe African People's Union*, pp. 54-5.

31. A report in 1960, by a cross-party group chaired by Jack Quinton, recommended opening up all land, in towns, the countryside and the protected native reserves, for purchase irrespective of racial group.

32. Sir Roy Welensky had toyed with the idea of a unilateral independence for the Federation; Whitehead also aimed for independence for Southern Rhodesia, but recognised that he would have to demonstrate that Africans would benefit if the British government was to agree.

33. Harold Macmillan, *At the End of the Day: 1961–1963*, Macmillan, London, 1973, p. 327, quoted in Blake, *A History of Rhodesia*, p. 348.

34. For a ZANU version of the split, see Nathan Shamuyarira, *Crisis in Rhodesia*, Andre Deutsch, London, 1965, pp. 173–93.

35. The commissioner of police, in his annual report, stated: 'In 1963 there was almost a state of civil war between supporters of rival nationalist parties in the African townships' (quoted in ibid, p. 173).

36. Blessing-Miles Tendi, *Making History in Mugabe's Zimbabwe*, Peter Lang, Bern, 2010, p. 55. ZAPU was supported by Eastern Bloc countries.

37. Judith Todd, *Rhodesia*, McGibbon & Kee, London, p. 130.

THREE

1. A comparison of the two autobiographies, *Bitter Harvest* by Ian Smith (Blake Publishing, London, 2001) and *The Labour Government 1964–70* by Harold Wilson (Penguin, Harmondsworth, 1971) depicts a mirror image of distrust.

2. Wilson also insisted that they be given a proper meal.

3. It is salutary to compare this message from the churches with the criticism of the Blair Labour government, from similar sources, as it prepared to launch an invasion of Iraq in 2003.

4. See Alex May, ed., *The Commonwealth and International Affairs: The Round Table Centennial Selection*, Routledge, London, 2010, pp. 120–23.

5. Derek Ingram, leading commentator on the Commonwealth in the late twentieth century, has always believed that the British could have put down the rebellion with minimal casualties.

6. Guy Arnold, director of the Africa Bureau in London during the UDI period, argues that the RAF squadron was not designed to threaten Rhodesia, or reassure Zambia, but to prevent attacks on Rhodesia.

7. The UN imposed an oil embargo in April 1966 and comprehensive sanctions in May 1968. The United Kingdom had imposed trade sanctions, and expelled Rhodesia from the sterling area and Commonwealth preferences, almost immediately after UDI.

8. Bechuanaland, a British colony adjoining Rhodesia, became independent as Botswana in September 1966.

9. See Fay Chung, *Re-living the Second Chimurenga*, Weaver Press, Harare, 2007, p. 78. In August 1967 James Chikerema for ZAPU and Oliver Tambo for the ANC announced a military alliance between the two organisations.

10. Fay Chung also mentions a pioneering ZANLA attack in Chipinge, led by William Ndangana, as early as 1965 (ibid., p. 90).

11. Rhodesian estimates cited by David Martin and Phyllis Johnson in *The Struggle for Zimbabwe*, Faber & Faber, London, 1981, p. 145.

12. Interview with Wilfred Mhanda, 9 February 2010, and his commentary on Chung, *Re-living the Second Chimurenga*.

13. See Heidi Holland, *Dinner with Mugabe*, Penguin, London, 2008, pp. 27–8. One may compare the impact on Mugabe of his son's death with the effect on Nelson Mandela of the death of his eldest son, Thembi, when Mandela was in jail, in July 1969. Thembi, by then the father of two, was killed in a car crash and Mandela was not allowed to attend the funeral; he had not been permitted to attend his mother's funeral the year before. Though heartbroken by these events, Mandela emerged from prison determined to conciliate the Afrikaners and South African whites.

14. Sabina died in 2010, after years of ill health. Robert Mugabe used a speech at her burial in Heroes Acre, Harare, to tell his Western enemies that they could go to hell, and that Zimbabwe would never be recolonised.

15. The full story was recounted by the *Independent on Sunday*, 6 April 2008, which had accessed documents under the UK's Freedom of Information Act; it suggested that Sally Mugabe had a breakdown after her son's death.

16. See Peter Stiff, *The Silent War: South African Recce Operations 1969–1994*, Galago, Alberton, 1999, p. 274. The murder was carried out by 'Taffy', a former British SAS man, in charge of a CIO team.

17. See Chung, *Re-living the Second Chimurenga*, pp. 90–92, for the view that they were ideologically driven Marxists; this is strongly challenged by Wilfred Mhanda, a guerrilla commander at the time who helped put down the rising from Tanzania.

18. Albie Sachs, later Justice of South Africa's Constitutional Court, was invited to Lusaka in the mid-1970s by Oliver Tambo, president of the ANC, to help draw up a code for the protection of its prisoners (lecture at the Institute of Commonwealth Studies, London, 1 March 2010).

19. 'If the truth be told, however, by the end of April 1975 the guerrilla war inside Rhodesia had virtually ended. All the rear operational bases in Zambia and Mozambique had been closed by the host governments; and all the fighters disarmed and rounded up so as to enforce the Lusaka Accord of 7 December 1974.' Statement by Wilfred Mhanda in commentary on Fay Chung, *Re-living the Second Chimurenga*, courtesy Weaver Press.

20. See chapter on the war in Rhodesia, 1965–80 by J. Mtsi, M. Nyakudya and T. Barnes in Brian Raftopoulos and Alois Mlambo, eds, *Becoming Zimbabwe*, Weaver Press, Harare, 2009; Ian Smith (*Bitter Harvest*, pp. 175–82) claimed that he had arranged to meet nationalists at Victoria Falls, led by Bishop Muzorewa, on the basis of no preconditions on either side, but Muzorewa had opened with a demand for one man, one vote, and the release of imprisoned guerrillas and activists.

21. The history here is strongly contested among themselves by participants such as Chung and Mhanda (whose *nom de guerre* was Dzinashe Machingura).

22. Interview with Wilfred Mhanda, 9 February 2010; Mhanda alleges that he crossed with the connivance of Rhodesian authorities.

23. See Martin and Johnson, *The Struggle for Zimbabwe*, pp. 209–11.

24. Smith, *Bitter Harvest*, p. 223.

25. 'Rhodesia – Proposals for a Settlement', White Paper of September 1977, Command 6919.

26. Smith (*Bitter Harvest*, p. 223) wrote of the 'communist-inspired Common-

wealth', which was plainly nonsense.

27. See Raftopoulos and Mlambo, *Becoming Zimbabwe*, pp. 132–3.

28. Ibid., p. 138.

29. This sermon is quoted by Lauren St John, *Rainbow's End*, Hamish Hamilton, London, 2007, p. 123.

30. Chung, *Re-living the Second Chimurenga*, p. 144.

31. Information from Derek Ingram, British journalist, who by chance was at Chimoio shortly after the raid; his presence allowed Joshua Nkomo to claim erroneously that the British had known about the raid in advance. The role of black soldiers in the Rhodesian forces was not insignificant, and their motivations were mixed.

32. There is a River Pungwe in what is now Mozambique.

33. See Raftopoulos and Mlambo, *Becoming Zimbabwe*, p. 149.

34. Colleagues in the Foreign and Commonwealth Office, London, were aware that Robin Renwick, head of the Rhodesia department, and subsequently a key aide to Lord Carrington at Lancaster House and ambassador to South Africa, would have resigned if the Thatcher government had recognised the internal settlement.

35. See chapter on Ramphal and Southern Africa by Patsy Robertson, in Richard Bourne, ed., *Shridath Ramphal: The Commonwealth and the World*, Hansib, Hertford, 2008, p. 51.

36. It was during her visit to Cape Town Cathedral, as the then Princess Elizabeth, that she made a public vow to support the Commonwealth throughout her life. Professor Philip Murphy, director of the Institute of Commonwealth Studies, London, and an expert on the headship of the Commonwealth, has unearthed evidence that the Queen might have visited Southern Rhodesia during a potential Africa tour in the early 1960s which never took place.

37. Interview with Sir Shridath Ramphal, 10 August 2010.

38. An unpublished thesis by Matthew Neuhaus, Australian ambassador in Harare since 2011, who has been Australian high commissioner to Nigeria and director of the Political Affairs Division, Commonwealth Secretariat, argued in the 1980s that the leak may have been designed to prevent the British backtracking on the agreement.

39. FCO 36/2444, 'Rhodesia: Report of Constitutional Conference', National Archives.

40. Lord Carrington's memoir, *Reflect on Things Past* (Collins, London, 1988), makes almost no mention of Ramphal's role; he regarded the Commonwealth secretary general as an obstacle, and was reluctant to acknowledge a Commonwealth share in Lancaster House.

41. Interview, Chief Emeka Anyaoku, 6 September 2010.

42. See interview with Shridath Ramphal, in G. Moyo and M. Ashurst, *The Day after Mugabe*, Africa Research Institute, London, 2007, pp. 158–63.

43. See Robert Renwick, *Unconventional Diplomacy in Southern Africa*, Macmillan, London, p. 43.

44. Ibid, p. 51.

45. A British journalist, Patrick Keatley, reported that Carrington had written ABM – 'Anyone But Mugabe' – on a note pad at one stage; interestingly, Ian Smith's

memoirs suggest that he too established a good relationship with Tongogara.

46. A handful of officials, drafting the short radio broadcast in which Soames announced that he was resuming British authority as governor over 'Southern
Rhodesia', saw him go to his wife – then in the bath – in search of a ringing
conclusion. 'For a war-weary country, the prize is great', he announced. As
Mary Churchill, she had visited Berlin with her father in July 1945, inspecting
the ruined Chancellery and Hitler's bunker.

47. It is said that at one point during the Lancaster House talks President Nyerere
had reassured Mugabe that 'the British did not know how to rig an election'.

48. *The Zimbabwean*, 19 August 2010.

49. See Chung, *Re-living the Second Chimurenga*, p. 248. Maoist guerrilla theory
of 'the fish in the water' meant that ZANLA troops had been trained to melt
into and indoctrinate the non-combatant peasantry.

50. Information from Robert Jackson, July 2010.

FOUR

1. See S. Onslow, 'Zimbabwe at Independence', in R. Holland, S. Williams and
T. Barringer, eds, *The Iconography of Independence*, Routledge, Abingdon,
2010, pp. 88–97.

2. Interview, Chief Anyaoku, 6 September 2010.

3. This speech is available, for example, at http://blogs.timeslive.co.za.

4. Quoted by Onslow, 'Zimbabwe at Independence', p. 95.

5. Figures for deaths and injuries are unreliable; the *Guardian* cited 27,000 deaths
on 17 April 2010, in an article about the thirtieth anniversary of independence,
but others, including the Catholic Commission for Justice and Peace, have suggested 30,000. The concerns of the war-disabled were a political issue which
continued for more than the first decade of independence. Many rural Africans
had been displaced by the Rhodesian authorities to live in 'protected villages',
to cut them off from guerrillas.

6. According to Peter Stiff, *The Silent War: South African Recce Operations
1969–1994* (Galago, Alberton, pp. 314–15), the ANC launched a three-year
politico-military strategy in 1979–81, with Vietnamese advice. This aimed to
raise the quality of opposition to the apartheid state inside South Africa.

7. See Fay Chung, *Re-living the Second Chimurenga*, Weaver Press, Harare, 2007,
p. 248.

8. Information from Professor Reg Austin.

9. See Catholic Commission for Justice and Peace and Legal Resources Foundation, *Gukhurahundi in Zimbabwe: A Report on the Disturbances in Matabeleland and the Midlands, 1980–88*, Hurst, London, 2007, , p. 53.

10. Chung, *Re-living the Second Chimurenga*, p. 180.

11. South Africa's Truth and Reconciliation Commission unveiled some of the truth
about 'Operation Drama', which involved training ex-Rhodesian military and
black Zimbabweans in Venda, and then infiltrating them into Zimbabwe.

12. *Gukhurahundi in Zimbabwe*, p. 48.

13. Ibid., p. 71 suggests that this may have been a covert South African
operation.

14. In the United Kingdom the two broadsheet Sunday papers, the *Sunday Times* and the *Observer*, both published reports about the massacres.
15. *Gukhurahundi in Zimbabwe*, p. 94.
16. Interview with Denis Norman, 9 June 2010.
17. Information from Richard Ralph, Head of Chancery, UK High Commission in Harare, 1983–85.
18. Some white officers approved of the approach of the Fifth Brigade. Lt Col. Lionel Dyke, who commanded the paratroops in 1983–84 said, 'The fact is that when 5 Brigade went in, they did brutally deal with the problem. If you were a dissident sympathiser, you died. And it brought peace very, very quickly' (*Gukhurahundi in Zimbabwe*, p. 93). Sabotage of the Zimbabwe Air Force planes, organised by South African agents, was followed by torture of senior white officers, including Air Vice-Marshal Hugh Slattery and Wing-Commander Peter Briscoe, on whose behalf the British government made informal protests.
19. *Gukhurahundi in Zimbabwe*, p. 117.
20. One consequence was that he dismissed Denis Norman, his white agriculture minister, though Norman returned to the government later.
21. Statistics quoted by Fay Chung in *Re-living the Second Chimurenga*, p. 279. Chung was director of education planning from September 1980, and subsequently minister of education.
22. Information from Peter Freeman, First Secretary (Development), British High Commission, Harare, 1980–83.
23. See, for instance, a chapter by James Muzondidya in Brian Raftopoulos and Alois Mlambo, eds, *Becoming Zimbabwe*, Weaver Press, Harare, 2009, pp. 184–8.
24. Information from Carl Wright, then director of the Commonwealth Trade Union Council.
25. I am grateful to Professor Robin Cohen for pointing this out.
26. Estimate from John Worswick, Justice in Agriculture, Harare.
27. Quoted in the Africa All-Party Parliamentary Group report, *Land in Zimbabwe: Past Mistakes, Future Prospects*, December 2009, House of Commons, London, p. 19.
28. These numbers, sourced from DFID as UK contributions from 1980 on, are quoted in ibid., p. 28. These statistics have been contested.
29. See D.R.Norman, *The Success of Peasant Agriculture in Zimbabwe, 1980–1985*, FARM, Oxford, 1986, p. 15.
30. Information from Peter Freeman, a former DFID official, some published in *The Zimbabwean*, 25–31 October 2007.
31. These were the findings of the long-term monitoring by the Zimbabwe Rural Households Dynamics Study led by Bill Kinsey, and quoted in I. Scoones, N. Marongwe, B. Mavedzenge, F. Murimbarimba, J. Mahenehene and C. Sukume, *Zimbabwe's Land Reform: Myths and Realities*, Weaver Press, Harare, and James Currey, Woodbridge, 2010, pp. 18–19. The study argued that it took time for the farmers to benefit from their new land.
32. Interview with Chief Anyaoku, 6 September 2010.
33. Statistics quoted by James Muzondidya, 'From Buoyancy to Crisis', in

Raftopoulos and Mlambo, eds, *Becoming Zimbabwe*, p. 169.

34. See Brian Raftopoulos and Lloyd Sachikonye, *Striking Back*, Weaver Press, Harare, p. 4.

35. Article by Clyde Sanger for *Diplomat* magazine, January 2010, quoting Geoffrey Nyarota's *Against the Grain*, who added that editorship was arguably the most endangered occupation in Zimbabwe.

36. At a thank-you dinner in Downing Street for officials who had worked on Rhodesia/Zimbabwe Mrs Thatcher spent three minutes in a tribute to Cecil Rhodes; her perceived triumph in the Falklands War was more to her taste than Zimbabwe's independence.

37. Comment from Wilfred Mhanda.

38. Interview with Sir Shridath Ramphal, 10 August 2010.

39. The author, then deputy director of the Commonwealth Institute, Kensington, was one of those consulted before the prize was awarded, and recommended Mugabe.

FIVE

1. See Martin Meredith, *Mugabe*, Public Affairs, Oxford, 2002, pp. 98–101.

2. Dumbutshena, who had a long history in nationalist politics, had called for the promotion of a 'culture of human rights' as chief justice. In 1995 he was part of an influential Commonwealth Human Rights Initiative mission to Nigeria, then ruled by a dictatorship; its report, *Nigeria – Stolen by Generals*, helped persuade the Commonwealth summit in New Zealand to suspend the Nigerian regime.

3. Estimate given to the author by a diplomatic observer, Harare, February 2010.

4. Quoted by Stephen Chan, *Citizen of Africa*, Academica Press, Bethesda, 2006, p. 128. See also Chan's *Robert Mugabe: A Life of Power and Violence*, I.B. Tauris, London, 2003.

5. Sally Mugabe died in 1992 aged 60; her mother lived until 2009, when she was 101. There are rumours in Harare that Sally Mugabe's kidney problems were not accidental.

6. John Major said of the Commonwealth, 'We must use it or lose it.'

7. In 1995 it was estimated that a quarter of companies listed on the Zimbabwe Stock Exchange had no black directors, and most only had one or two.

8. See Raftopoulos and Mlambo, eds, *Becoming Zimbabwe*, p. 188.

9. See Raftopoulos and Sachikonye, *Striking Back*, pp. 156–7.

10. See T.F. Kondo, Advocacy Coordinator, ZCTU, *The 'Workers' Driven' and 'Peoples-centred' Development Process for Zimbabwe*, ZCTU, Harare, 2000, pp. 4–5.

11. See Africa All-Party Parliamentary Group report, *Land in Zimbabwe: Past Mistakes, Future Prospects*, December 2009, House of Commons, London, p. 34.

12. Interview, Japhet Moyo, 2 February 2010.

13. See Joseph Hanlon, 'It Is Possible to Just Give Money', *Development and Change* 35(2), 2004, pp. 375–83; also F. Christie and S. Barnes, *Report of the*

Reintegration of Demobilised Soldiers in Mozambique, 1992–1996, United Nations Development Programme, Maputo, 2001.

14. See Mark Rule Papers, Rhodes House library, Oxford.

15. These were Nigeria, Sierra Leone and the Gambia.

16. See Catholic Commission for Justice and Peace and Legal Resources Foundation, *Gukhurahundi in Zimbabwe: A Report on the Disturbances in Matabeleland and the Midlands, 1980–88*, Hurst, London, 2007, p. xx. There have also been suggestions that one or two outrages blamed on the MNR may actually have been committed by Zimbabwe's Fifth Brigade.

17. Ibid., p. xv.

18. Estimate supplied to the author by Eddie Cross, MDC economic spokesman.

19. Using documents released under the UK's Freedom of Information Act, the *Independent* has reported (30 August 2010) that the Foreign and Commonwealth Office twice urged Blair to meet Mugabe, one to one, prior to the Commonwealth Heads' meeting in Edinburgh. In one memo, dated 11 June 1997, the FCO argued: 'This may be a useful opportunity for an exchange of views in advance of CHOGM. After South Africa, Zimbabwe is the most important country in Southern Africa to us both commercially and politically. Despite domestic criticism arriving from recent financial scandals, and his failure so far to respond to renewed serious allegations by Zimbabwean NGOs of his involvement in atrocities in Matabeleland in the early 1980s, Mr Mugabe remains a senior African and Commonwealth figure with whom there would be advantage in establishing early close relations. We recommend that the Prime Minister sees him if his programme permits.' Several sources confirm that Blair's failure to meet Mugabe was taken as a snub.

20. Clare Short tried to arrange a sandwich lunch in Edinburgh with the Zimbabwe delegation but was frustrated by the Foreign and Commonwealth Office, which, she thought, was still put out by the creation of the DFID.

21. Quoted by Heidi Holland, *Dinner with Mugabe*, Penguin, London, p. 95.

22. At least one of her officials, Peter Freeman, thought the Irish reference might actually trigger more understanding in Harare.

23. It is unclear exactly how much was unspent. The APPG report (p. 32) states that £3 million was left; an official speaking to the author on terms of anonymity suggested that it could have been as much as £14 million.

24. Information given to the author by the late Joan Lestor, when she was shadow spokesperson on overseas aid. Blair showed consistent interest in poverty issues, particularly in Africa, where his father had worked in Sierra Leone, and for which he sponsored an Africa Commission which reported to the G8 meeting of world leaders in 2005.

25. Peter Longworth was UK high commissioner in Harare from 1998 to 2001.

26. See chapter by N. Marongwe, 'Farm Occupations and Occupiers', in A. Hammar, B. Raftopoulos and S. Jensen, eds, *Zimbabwe's Unfinished Business*, Weaver Press, Harare, 2003, p. 162.

27. See J. Alexander, '"Squatters", Veterans and the State', in ibid., p. 97.

28. Interview, John Worswick, Justice for Agriculture, 8 February 2010.

29. Mark Rule Notes, 12 December 1998–1 January 1999, Rhodes House library.

30. One US dollar was worth Z$18.5 on 9 January 1998; it was worth Z$37.5 on 31 December 1998 and Z$43.2 on 15 January 1999.
31. I. Scoones, N. Marongwe, B. Mavedzenge, F. Murimbarimba, J. Mahenehene and C. Sukume, *Zimbabwe's Land Reform: Myths and Realities*, Weaver Press, Harare, and James Currey, Woodbridge, 2010, p. 18.
32. Interview, Peter Hain, 6 October 2009.
33. The arrest of these journalists coincided with another African human rights conference in Harare, organised by the Commonwealth Human Rights Initiative (CHRI) and funded by the Ford Foundation. Margaret Reynolds, a former Australian minister and Maja Daruwala, director of the CHRI, led a protest deputation to Harare central police station.
34. See Mark Gevisser, *A Legacy of Liberation: Thabo Mbeki and the Future of the South African Dream*, Palgrave Macmillan, New York, 2009, p. 266.
35. See Peter Godwin, *The Fear: The Last Days of Robert Mugabe*, Picador, London, 2010 p. 33, quoting Human Rights Watch. Large numbers of Ethiopians died in famines also.
36. Report on human rights in 1999 by the Zimbabwe Human Rights NGO Forum, in conjunction with the Amani Trust, Harare, March 2000.
37. Chief Anyaoku referred to the CMAG initiative at Durban in an address on the modern Commonwealth to a joint centenary event of the Round Table journal and the Royal Over-Seas League, London, 5 July 2010. He had also given details at a seminar on the Harare Declaration at the Institute of Commonwealth Studies in 2009.

SIX

1. Intellectual debate surrounds the 'failed state' category. Here it is assumed that a state in which there is proven economic collapse, life expectancy falls from around 60 years to around 34 in a decade, an estimated quarter to a third of the population emigrates, a majority depend on food aid, and human rights are violated on a substantial scale, is a state that has failed its citizens.
2. See Martin Meredith, *Mugabe*, Public Affairs, Oxford, pp. 140–41.
3. See Raftopoulos and Mlambo, eds, *Becoming Zimbabwe*, p. 207.
4. Ironically, although this constitution was voted down in 2000, Mugabe could continue in office for an indeterminate period under Lancaster House provisions, and in 2010 was exceeding the ten years proposed.
5. Quoted by Meredith, *Mugabe*, pp. 164–5.
6. See Mark Rule Notes, 12–25 February 2000, Rhodes House library.
7. Philip Barclay, *Zimbabwe: Years of Hope and Despair,* Bloomsbury, London, 2010, p. 150.
8. The Zimbabwe Human Rights Forum reported in 2010 that, according to human rights groups and the Commercial Farmers Union, at least seven farmers were killed in violence between 2000 and 2010.
9. It is difficult to be sure of these estimates. The 200,000 total was quoted by UNDP, but in 2009 the Commercial Farmers Union reported that more than 250,000 farm workers had lost their livelihoods. Justice for Agriculture (JAG)

and the General Agricultural and Plantation Workers Union of Zimbabwe (GAPWUZ) argued that, altogether, 1.3 million farm workers and their families were affected by the violence.

10. See CIIR report, *Land, Power and Poverty: Farm Workers and the Crisis in Zimbabwe*, London, 2000.

11. Zimbabwe Human Rights NGO Forum, *Land Reform and Property Rights in Zimbabwe*, Harare, 2010, p. 10.

12. See Africa All-Party Parliamentary Group report, *Land in Zimbabwe: Past Mistakes, Future Prospects*, December 2009, House of Commons, London, Table p. 36.

13. A new book, *Mao's Great Famine,* by Frank Dikotter (Bloomsbury, London, 2010) gives chilling details of this man-made Chinese famine.

14. According to I. Scoones et al. (*Zimbabwe's Land Reform: Myths and Realities*, Weaver Press, Harare, and James Currey, Woodbridge, 2010, p. 6), the A1 plots averaged 40 hectares, while the A2 farms ranged in size from 71 to 600 hectares.

15. Miles-Blessing Tendi, *Making History in Mugabe's Zimbabwe*, Peter Lang, Bern, 2010, p. 220.

16. Mugabe had become so addicted to taking degrees in prison that he flew to Geneva to take a London University external degree after he had become prime minister.

17. See Meredith, *Mugabe*, pp. 180–89.

18. Interview with the author, 15 December 2009.

19. In fact life expectancy dropped from around 60 years to around 34, although AIDS was not the only explanation; a Harare cab driver told the author in February 2010 that, at 55, he was 'an old man', which was actuarially correct in Zimbabwe.

20. See CIIR report, *Land, Power and Poverty*, p. 25.

21. Mark Rule Notes, 21 April to 4 May 2001.

22. Interview with Eddie Cross, 4/2/2010.

23. A Wikileaks file from the US embassy in Harare, quoted in the *Observer*, 19 December 2010, claimed that Kofi Annan had been the intermediary for a deal under which Mugabe would make a graceful exit, with a safe haven and financial package; he had rejected it after consulting his wife.

24. Quoted by Stephen Chan, *Citizen of Africa*, p. 57.

25. Statistics from the Zimbabwe Human Rights NGO Forum; these were cases reported to member bodies, and possibly not comprehensive; nearly all cases of political violence were committed by ZANU-PF or state agencies.

26. Quoted by Chan, *Citizen of Africa*, p. 32.

27. See CIIR, *Land, Power and Poverty*, p. 43.

28. There were various unproven rumours about the Mbeki–Mugabe relationship, which hinted that the Zimbabwean might have some hold over the South African; one was that Govan Mbeki, Thabo's father, had helped pay for Mugabe's studies at Fort Hare University; another was that Mugabe had saved Mbeki's life in a firefight during the liberation struggle. Such rumours were used to explain Mbeki's seeming partiality towards Mugabe.

29. While Clare Short was a dominant figure in the Labour cabinet, the importance

of aid policy for British High Commissions in Africa preceded her and the Labour government; high commissioners had been answerable to Lady (Lynda) Chalker, who was simultaneously overseas aid minister and Africa minister in the Foreign and Commonwealth Office, in John Major's Conservative government.

30. P.J. Patterson's personal relations with Mbeki, which had been good, did not recover from Mbeki's denunciation of the statement agreed by the Commonwealth mediation group in Abuja. Those with long memories recalled that Margaret Thatcher, at a Kuala Lumpur Commonwealth summit in 1989, had disowned an agreement made by her then foreign secretary, John Major.

31. Zimbabwe's 'First Family' commandeered Air Zimbabwe planes for shopping expeditions, sometimes overloading them with purchases.

32. See Chris Alden, *China in Africa*, Zed Books, London, 2007, p. 65.

33. See Brian Raftopoulos, 'The Crisis in Zimbabwe, 1998–2008', in Raftopoulos and Mlambo, eds, *Becoming Zimbabwe*, p. 219.

34. In a February 2010 interview with a ZANU–PF supporter awarded a commercial farm, specialising in tobacco and cattle, the author was informed that these outputs had been maintained. However, the new owner had taken advice from his predecessor, and also paid him compensation for barns, tractors and improvements, though not for the land itself. He was also actively involved in the farm's management, even though he had other business interests.

35. See Africa All-Party Parliamentary Group report, *Land in Zimbabwe: Past Mistakes, Future Prospects*, December 2009, House of Commons, London, p. 36.

36. Mark Rule, Notes on the Economy, 22 December 2005–13 January 2006, Rhodes House library.

37. The Zimbabwe Human Rights NGO Forum, for instance, publishes collations of reports from member organisations, sometimes on a daily basis.

38. *The Effects of Fighting Repression with Love*, report by Women of Zimbabwe Arise, March 2008, www.wozazimbabwe.org.

39. *The Zimbabwean* published a series of interviews with Green Bombers in August 2010.

40. Jonathan Crush and Daniel Tevera eds, *Zimbabwe's Exodus*, South African Migration Programme and IDRC, Kingston, 2010, p. 382.

41. Interview, Paul Verryn, 12 February 2010.

42. Crush and Tevera, *Zimbabwe's Exodus*, p. 3.

43. See Zimbabwe Human Rights NGO Forum website: www.hrforumzim.com.

44. Interview with Sekai Holland, 10 February 2010, who said her vote was not counted. She blamed the split on a clash of male egos, and thought the MDC had been in danger of following the unconstitutional approach of ZANU, when Ndabaningi Sithole was removed from its leadership.

45. See Moyo's website archive at: prof-jonathan-moyo.com.

46. Maurice Vambe, ed., *The Hidden Dimensions of Operation Murambatsvina*, Weaver Press, Harare, 2008, p. 19.

47. Moyo website.Moyo had also been critical of ZANU–PF in the early 1990s.

48. Information from Eddie Cross.

SEVEN

1. See David Moore chapter 'Coercion, Consent, Context', in Maurice Vambe, ed., *The Hidden Dimensions of Operation Murambatsvina in Zimbabwe*, Weaver Press, Harare, 2008, p. 34. The Tibaijuka report (see below) estimated that 18 per cent of the Zimbabwe population had been affected by the programme.

2. See Tendai Chari, 'Worlds Apart: Representations of Operation Murambatsvina in Two Zimbabwean Weeklies', in ibid., to see how pro- and anti-government journalists covered the event.

3. See United Nations, *Zimbabwe: Report of the Fact-Finding Mission to Zimbabwe*, New York, July 2005.

4. Two years later he joined the MDC-T.

5. The JOC did not advertise much, but in 2010 it was thought to consist of: Happyton Bonyongwe, Central Intelligence Organisation; Constantine Chiwenga, Zimbabwe Defence Force commander; Philip Sibanda, army commander; Perence Shiri, air force commander; Paradzai Zimondi, responsible for prisons; and Augustine Chihuri, police commissioner.

6. Mark Rule, Notes on the Economy, 1–14 July 2006. Rule apologised to his circulation list that he had got behind in his commentaries due to repeated power failures and his own illness. He was to die prematurely.

7. See an excellent analysis of Mbeki's stance on Zimbabwe by Merle Lipton, 'Understanding South Africa's Foreign Policy: The Perplexing Case of Zimbabwe', *South African Journal of International Affairs* 16(3), December 2009.

8. Quoted by Lipton, ibid.

9. See Philip Barclay, *Zimbabwe: Years of Hope and Despair*, Bloomsbury, London, 2010, pp. 11–13.

10. Bernard Chidzero and Denis Norman helped Makoni to get the SADC post; in 2000, when he was minister of finance, the author witnessed an uncomfortable Makoni speaking at a seminar at the South African Institute of International Affairs, Braamfontein, under the watchful eye of ZANU and intelligence 'heavies'.

11. Barclay estimated that as many as 50 per cent of adult Zimbabweans were either not on the electoral roll or unable to get to the area where they were registered to vote (*Zimbabwe*, p. 51).

12. Many developing countries now have highly efficient election counts. In Brazil, in October 2010, a population of some 200 million saw results within twenty-four hours which covered presidential, gubernatorial and Senate elections.

13. Mugabe never made a public offer to resign, but reliable sources have informed the author that he broached his departure to intimates.

14. A significant number of these youths were given civil service posts and incomes. *Sunday Times*, 13 February 2011.

15. See Raftopoulos, 'The Crisis in Zimbabwe, 1998–2008', p. 229.

16. Godwin, *The Fear*, p. 133.

17. Barclay, *Zimbabwe*, p. 157.

18. Coltart, an elder of the Presbyterian Church who was made minister of education under the global political agreement, has argued this case publicly on

several occasions. He has stated that, for the sake of building peace in Zimbabwe and restoring its institutions, a purist human rights line is not tenable.

19. The Global Political Agreement was published in three languages, English, Shona and Ndebele, by the Ministry of Constitutional and Parliamentary Affairs, Harare.

20. Senator David Coltart, minister of education, refused to take one; Tendai Biti, minister of finance, said the cars had been bought before the inclusive government had been formed and would have had to be written off if unused.

21. Article 3.1(a) of the GPA.

22. Interview, senior DFID official, London, 7 July 2010.

23. WFP statistics quoted by Chris McGreal, *Guardian*, 29 January 2009.

24. By February 2009 the Zimbabwe Red Cross was feeding about 260,000 people suffering from AIDS, or AIDS orphans, *Guardian*, 13 February 2009.

25. Africa All-Party Parliamentary Group report, *Land in Zimbabwe: Past Mistakes, Future Prospects*, December 2009, House of Commons, London, p. 36.

26. The smallholder output is quoted for 2009 in Greg Mills, *Why Africa is Poor*, Penguin, Johannesburg, p. 145.

27. See Ian Scoones, Nelson Marongwe, Blasio Mavedzenge, Felix Murimbarimba, Jacob Mahenehene and Chrispen Sukume, *Zimbabwe's Land Reform: Myths and Realities*, Weaver Press, Harare, 2010; the authors found a middle group of smaller farmers in Masvingo province who had succeeded with hard graft, and without external help.

28. The case was reported by AfriForum and the Zimbabwe Human Rights NGO Forum and followed decisions by the North Gauteng High Court in March and the South Gauteng High Court in November.

29. There were exceptions; Wilson Manase, a prominent businessman and lawyer, told the author that the output of his cattle and tobacco farm was similar to that of his white predecessor, whom he had compensated for the value of barns and equipment, though not of course for the land itself.

30. Report by ZimOnline, 30 November 2010, www.zimonline.co.za.

31. Remarks by Senator David Coltart, minister of education, in Cambridge in November 2009.

32. UN News Centre report, 7 December 2009.

33. *The Times*, 4 March 2010, quoted in *A Place in the Sun: Zimbabwe*, report of a 2010 mission by the Commonwealth Lawyers Association and others.

34. Gondo and 8 others v. Government of Zimbabwe, case number SADC (T) 05/2008.

35. ZimOnline stated that eight judges had taken over farms, with the chief justice, Godfrey Chidyausiku, acquiring 895 hectares at Concession (www.zimonline.co.za).

36. See their chapter 'Exiting Zimbabwe' in *Zimbabwe's Exodus*, SAMP, Cape Town and IDRC, Ottawa, 2010.

37. Statistics quoted by Crush and Tevera, ibid.

38. Interview, Paul Verryn, 12 February 2010. The author witnessed a raid by the Red Ants security firm on the Chambers building, squatted by vulnerable Zimbabweans, close to Ellis Park rugby ground. It was a pitiful sight, with

mattresses thrown onto the street, and blind people and nursing mothers given small food handouts by Médecins sans Frontières.

39. Peter Godwin visited him in jail, and also reported how he was venerated by local Zimbabweans (*The Fear*, p. 240).

40. The African Union was also, in theory, a guarantor of the GPA.

41. See constitution-watch@veritas.co.zw.

42. Mugabe, who rarely wasted time visiting parliament, sat in to hear Biti deliver his 2010 budget.

43. *The Times* of South Africa online, 15 November 2010.

44. Tendi, *Making History in Mugabe's Zimbabwe*, p. 267.

45. Senator Coltart addressed a London conference on education, supported by Commonwealth bodies, on 22 November 2010. In December he explained to the author that the new teachers who joined did not have the experience and skills, especially in science, maths and English language teaching, of those who had left.

46. A business conference at the Zimbabwe Embassy, London, was told on 3 February 2011 that GDP has grown by over 4 per cent in 2010, and was forecast to grow by 9 per cent in 2011. In a speech in Harare on 15 February 2011, Morgan Tsvangirai forecast a growth of 8.1 per cent in 2011.

47. An Ernst and Young (India) skills and payroll audit of ministries found 75,273 'ghost workers', either not present or actually dead, in a complement of 188,019, according to the *Sunday Times*, 13 February 2011.

48. Other developing countries, notably India, had had rules requiring overseas investors to partner with local investors, but in the twenty-first century these rules were tending to relax.

49. The process was being monitored by a civil society coalition called ZZZI-COMP, comprising the Zimbabwe Peace Project, the Zimbabwe Electoral Support Network and Zimbabwe Lawyers for Human Rights; their findings were reported by the Zimbabwe Human Rights NGO Forum, 12 November 2010.

50. Interview, Sekai Holland, 10 February 2010.

51. Zimbabwe Human Rights NGO Forum statement, 10 February 2011.

52. Report by IDASA, *Restrictive Measures and Zimbabwe*, Institute for Democracy in Africa, Cape Town, 2010, p. 15.

53. Reuters report, 31 January 2011. Chinese investors in ZISCO, the privatised steel parastatal, had got 53 per cent of the equity, although the government claimed to restrict foreign investors to 49 per cent under the indigenisation law.

54. *Africa Confidential* reported, on 5 November 2010 that the UK's Standard Chartered bank was alleged to be routeing loans to Zimbabwe via local banks. Vitaliy Kramarenko led an IMF team in Harare at the end of October 2010 which acknowledged that there had been economic growth, but said that the state had to satisfy further conditions before significant aid could be provided; these included the elimination of ghost workers in the civil service, providing security of land tenure, clarifying the indigenisation law, and dealing with governance concerns in the diamond fields.

EIGHT

1. Interview, Chief Emeka Anyaoku, 6 September 2010.
2. The reported view of Kamalesh Sharma, Commonwealth secretary general from 2008, following his first visit to a SADC summit.
3. The Indian National Congress was formed in 1885; the Labour Representation Committee, which became the Labour Party, in 1900; and the African National Congress in 1912.
4. It was a continuing grievance to other Zimbabweans that Heroes Acre was treated as an exclusive cemetery for ZANU–PF, and that other heroes of the independence struggle were denied burial there.
5. China and Russia vetoed a UN resolution on sanctions after the run-off presidential poll in 2008.
6. Wilson's use of the term 'War on Want' became the title of a well-known activist UK NGO concerned for world development.
7. A Labour canvasser in north London in the 1964 election, of impeccable liberal principles, told the author that when she met white racists on the doorstep who were threatening to vote Conservatives she just asked, 'But who let them in?'
8. Peter Godwin reported for the *Sunday Times* and Donald Trelford for the *Observer*.
9. The author visited Zimbabwe in 1982, researching a potential television news-feature series for Channel Four in the UK.
10. See R. Bourne, J. Gundara, A. Dev, N. Ratsoma, M. Rukanda, A. Smith and U. Birthistle, *School-based Understanding of Human Rights in Four Countries: A Commonwealth Study*, Education Research 22, Department for International Development, London, 1997.
11. Article in *Financial Gazette*, 6–12 April 2000, quoted by Miles-Blessing Tendi, *Making History in Mugabe's Zimbabwe*, p. 215.
12. Ibid., p. 217.
13. See ibid., pp. 209–14, for a frank discussion of MDC's problems.
14. Interview, Japhet Moyo, first assistant secretary general, ZTUC, 3 February 2010.
15. Interview, Chief Emeka Anyaoku, 6 September 2010. During the Cold War the Indian government, concerned to prevent the West and the East funding proxies in India, passed a foreign exchange regulation Act which meant that foreign money for Indian NGOs needed government clearance.
16. Mugabe's spiritual adviser and chaplain, Father Fidelis Mukonori, was introduced to torture victims in 2008 by Peter Godwin (*The Fear*, pp. 97–8).
17. Ibid., pp. 303–4.
18. Paragraph 21, Commonwealth Heads of Government Communiqué, 27–29 November 2009.
19. IDASA, *Restrictive Measures and Zimbabwe*, p. 3.
20. President Mugabe, fed up with mismanagement in the state carrier Air Zimbabwe announced on television that he was appointing a law professor as chairman; it was the first that Professor Reg Austin, watching the programme, had heard of it.
21. See Tendi, *Making History in Mugabe's Zimbabwe*, p. 229, for International

Rescue Committee report that, between August 1998 and April 2004, a thousand people died every day in Democratic Republic of Congo. The Commonwealth Observer Group report on the 2007 Nigerian elections cited estimates that 200 people had died in election-related violence, and stated that there was often no secrecy in the ballot. However, Dr Kayode Fayemi, founder of the Centre for Democracy and Development (NGO), was installed as governor of Ekiti state in October 2010 after a court battle against fraud which lasted three and a half years.

22. Interview with John Worswick, Justice for Agriculture, 8 February 2010. He suggested that 65 per cent of commercial farmers whose land had been taken over would return if they had the chance.

BIBLIOGRAPHY

Alden, Chris. *China in Africa*. London: Zed Books, 2007.

Alexander, Jocelyn. *The Unsettled Land*. Oxford: James Currey, 2006.

Barclay, Philip. *Zimbabwe: Years of Hope and Despair*. London: Bloomsbury, 2010.

Blake, Robert. *A History of Rhodesia*. London: Eyre Methuen, 1977.

Bourne, Richard. *Shridath Ramphal: The Commonwealth and the World*. Hertford: Hansib, 2008.

Carrington, Peter. *Reflect on Things Past: The Memoirs of Lord Carrington*. London: HarperCollins, 1988.

Catholic Commission for Justice and Peace. *Gukhurahundi in Zimbabwe*. London: Hurst, 2007 (1997).

Chan, Stephen. *Robert Mugabe: A Life of Power and Violence*. London: I.B.Tauris, 2003.

Chan, Stephen. *Citizen of Africa: Conversations with Morgan Tsvangirai*. Bethesda: Academica Press, 2006.

Chan, Stephen, and Ranka Primorac, eds, *Round Table* 99(411), special issue: *The Space of Many Voices: Zimbabwe Since the Unity Government*, December 2010.

Chung, Fay. *Re-living the Second Chimurenga*. Harare: Weaver Press, 2007.

Cloete, Stuart. *African Portraits. A Biography of Paul Kruger, Cecil Rhodes and Lobengula*. Bethesda: Simon, 2001.

Cosgrave, Patrick. *Carrington: A Life and a Policy*. London: J.M. Dent, 1985.

Crush, Jonathan, and Daniel Tevera, eds. *Zimbabwe's Exodus*. Cape Town: Southern African Migration Programme, 2010.

Darnolf, Staffan, and Liisa Laakso. *Twenty Years of Independence in Zimbabwe*. Basingstoke: Palgrave Macmillan, 2003.

Gevisser, Mark. *A Legacy of Liberation: Thabo Mbeki and the Future of the South African Dream*. Basingstoke: Palgrave Macmillan, 2009.

Godwin, Peter. *The Fear: The Last Days of Robert Mugabe*. London: Picador, 2010.

Hain, Peter. *Mandela: The Story of a Universal Hero*. London: Spruce, 2010.

Hammar, Amanda, Brian Raftopoulos and Stig Jensen. *Zimbabwe's Unfinished Business*. Harare: Weaver Press, 2003.

Hanlon, Joseph, Armando Barrientosa and David Hulme. *Just Give Money to the Poor*. West Hartford CT: Kumarian, 2010.

Holland, Heidi. *Dinner with Mugabe*. London: Penguin, 2008.

Holland, Robert, Susan Williams and Terry Barringer, eds. *The Iconography of Independence*. Abingdon: Routledge, 2010.

Jacobs, Sean, and Richard Calland. *Thabo Mbeki's World*. Pietermaritzburg: University of Natal Press, 2002.

Marlowe, John. *Cecil Rhodes: The Anatomy of Empire*. London, 1972.

Martin, David and Phyllis Johnson. *The Struggle for Zimbabwe*. London: Faber & Faber, 1981.

Masunungure, E.V. (ed). *Defying the Winds of Change*. Harare: Weaver, 2009.

Matsyszak, Derek. *Law, Politics and Zimbabwe's 'Unity' Government*. Harare: Konrad Adenauer Stiftung, 2010.

Mayall, James (ed.). *The Contemporary Commonwealth: An Assessment, 1965–2009*. London: Routledge, 2010.

Meredith, Martin. *Mugabe*. Oxford: Public Affairs, 2002.

Millin, Sarah Gertrude. *Cecil Rhodes*. Bethesda: Simon, 2001.

Mills, Greg. *Why Africa is Poor*. Johannesburg: Penguin (South Africa), 2010.

Moyo, Gugulethu, and Mark Ashurst (eds). *The Day after Mugabe*. London: Africa Research Institute, 2007.

Norman, D.R. *The Success of Peasant Agriculture in Zimbabwe, 1980–1985*. Oxford: Food and Agricultural Research Mission, Occasional Paper 1, 1986.

Nyangoni, Christopher, and Gideon Nyandoro (eds). *Zimbabwe Independence Movements: Select Documents*. London: Rex Collings, 1979.

Oxford History of the British Empire, Volume 4: *The Twentieth Century*. Ed. William Roger Louis and Judith Brown. Oxford: Oxford University Press, 1999.

Pakenham, Thomas. *The Scramble for Africa*. London: Abacus, 1991.

Phimister, Ian. *An Economic and Social History of Zimbabwe, 1890–1948*. London: Longman, 1988.

Radziwill, Princess. *Cecil Rhodes: Man and Empire Maker*. Gloucester: Dodo, 2007 (1918).

Raftopoulos, Brian, and Alois Mlambo (eds). *Becoming Zimbabwe*. Harare: Weaver Press, 2009.

Raftopoulos, Brian. and Lloyd Sachikonye (eds). *Striking Back*. Harare: Weaver Press, 2001.

Ranger, T.O. *Revolt in Southern Rhodesia, 1896–7*. London: Heinemann, 1967.

Ranger, T.O. *Are We Not Also Men? The Samkange Family and African Politics in Zimbabwe*. Harare: Baobab, 1995.

Ranger, Terence (ed.). *The Historical Dimensions of Democracy and Human Rights in Zimbabwe*. Harare: University of Zimbabwe, 2004.

Renwick, Robert. *Unconventional Diplomacy in Southern Africa*. London: Macmillan, 1997.

Roberts, Brian. *Cecil Rhodes: Flawed Colossus*. London: Hamish Hamilton, 1987.

Sanger, Clyde. *Central African Emergency*. London: Heinemann, 1960.

Scarnecchia, Timothy. *The Urban Roots of Democracy and Political Violence in Zimbabwe*. Rochester NY: University of Rochester Press, 2008.

Scoones, Ian, Nelson Marongwe, Blasio Mavedzenge, Felix Murimbarimba, Jabob Mahenehene and Chrispin Sukume. *Zimbabwe's Land Reform: Myths and Realities*. Harare: Weaver Press, and Woodbridge: James Currey, 2010.

Shamuyarira, Nathan. *Crisis in Rhodesia*. London: Andre Deutsch, 1965.

Sibanda. Eliakim M. *The Zimbabwe African People's Union, 1961–87*. Trenton NJ: Africa World Press, 2005.

Smith, Ian. *Bitter Harvest: The Great Betrayal*. London: Blake, 2001.

Staunton, Irene (ed.). *Damage: The Personal Costs of Political Change in Zimbabwe*. Harare: Weaver Press, 2009.

Stiff, Peter. *The Silent War: South African Recce Operations 1969–1994*. Alberton: Galago, 1999.

Stoneman, Colin (ed.). *Zimbabwe's Inheritance*. London: Macmillan, 1981.

Tendi, Blessing-Miles. *Making History in Mugabe's Zimbabwe*. Bern: Peter Lang, 2010.

Thomas, Antony. *Rhodes: Race for Africa*. Lake Havasu City: London Bridge, 1997.

Todd, Judith. *Rhodesia*. London: McGibbon & Kee, 1966.

Vambe, Maurice (ed.). *The Hidden Dimensions of Operation Murambatsvina in Zimbabwe*. Harare: Weaver Press, 2008.

Wilson, Harold. *The Labour Government 1964–70*. Harmondsworth: Penguin, 1974.

INDEX